Why Can't We Get It Right?

Professional Development in Our Schools

Marsha Speck
Caroll Knipe

CORWIN PRESS, INC.
A Sage Publications Company
Thousand Oaks, California

For information:

Corwin Press, Inc.
A Sage Publications Company
2455 Teller Road
Thousand Oaks, California 91320
E-mail: order@corwinpress.com

Sage Publications Ltd.
6 Bonhill Street
London EC2A 4PU
United Kingdom

Sage Publications India Pvt. Ltd.
M-32 Market
Greater Kailash I
New Delhi 110 048 India

Printed in the United States of America

Library of Congress Cataloging-in-Publication Data

Speck, Marsha.
    Why can't we get it right? Professional development in our schools /
by Marsha Speck and Caroll Knipe.
        p. cm.
    Includes bibliographical references and indexes.
    ISBN 0-7619-7592-6 (c.: acid-free paper) — ISBN 0-7619-7593-4 (p.: alk.
paper)
    1. Teachers—In-service training. 2. Teachers—Training of.
I. Title: Professional development in our schools. II. Knipe, Carol.
III. Title.
    LB1731 .S683 2000
    370'.71'55—dc   00-011144

This book is printed on acid-free paper.

    02   03   04   05   06   07   7   6   5   4   3   2

Production Editor:	Diane Foster
Editorial Assistant:	Candice Crosetti
Typesetter/Designer:	Lynn Miyata
Indexer:	Teri Greenberg

Contents

3 Creating the Culture for a Learning Community   57

7 Designing Your Own Model   143

8 Tools for Implementing a Professional Development Design   170

9 Evaluating Professional Development   191

CORWIN
PRESS

The Corwin Press logo—a raven striding across an open book—represents the happy union of courage and learning. We are a professional-level publisher of books and journals for K–12 educators, and we are committed to creating and providing resources that embody these qualities. Corwin's motto is "Success for All Learners."

Foreword

This is indeed a daring and pioneering book. Seldom have I seen or read such a thorough, comprehensive, and theoretically sound text on professional development. Most such attempts approach the work by examining, critiquing, and creating new dimensions of practice, but this text has set forth a resource book on professional development replete with history and current practice while advancing multiple new perspectives. The "daring" portion is linking professional development tightly to improving student achievement. Unraveling "the little black box" between student achievement and professional development has challenged educators for decades. Speck and Knipe have mapped a journey through the black box with deliberate and forceful approaches.

This journey begins with an analysis of professional development that challenges current practice and travels the landscape of classrooms, schools, districts, and the broader profession. Each chapter unfolds into a broader theater of learning for students and adults. The journey map has signposts, enlarged insets, legends, and examples. Professional development is beyond training, beyond workshops, beyond uniformity—framing opportunities to learn as our primary work in educational communities.

Speck and Knipe recognize that human learning is basically the same for all of us. Educators construct meaning and knowledge together in collaborative settings. Children do so as well. This process of evoking what has been experienced and perceived, challenging those notions with new ideas, and making sense of the encountered dissonance is what we know as "learning." Schools and communities must recognize and perpetuate this congruence of understanding so that student and adult learning can be designed upon similar principles and premises. To do otherwise is to deny both our knowledge and our humanness. Such collaboration is a central theme of this text. The energy that drives both communities and development is engaged learning among and within individuals.

Learning also occurs within a context, a set of structures, and a planned space. This text provides the design and scaffolding for that space by creating images, plan outlines, and evaluation processes. Linkages to student standards and assessment are strong throughout and provide learning structures, content, and suggested pedagogy. Standards are an ever-present international reality. Standards-driven professional development, such as we encounter in this text, acknowledges this preeminence while situating it within a broader context of learning communities and whole-school change.

I have found the comprehensive nature of this work particularly powerful. Graphics consistently gather together meanings and display them in understandable, usable ways. Scenarios and case studies frame key issues and ground them in the dailiness of our work. Each chapter poses essential questions that lead the reader through the complexities of professional development. And at the end of each chapter, Web resources remind us of the technological world we inhabit and the rich resources this world can provide.

Professional development designs can unleash our imaginations and sustain our energies if they are mindful of how we learn together in community and our primary focus. The authors never lose sight of the destination of professional development: an unwavering focus on student and adult learning. I challenge teachers, parents, principals, superintendents, district office personnel, board members, and professors to add this book to your professional library, to use it as a text, and to share it with others. As educators and members of the public school community, we must choose this path if we are to resolve, once and for all, the conundrum of sustainability.

—Linda Lambert
Professor Emeritus, Educational Leadership
California State University, Hayward

Preface

How great is the intent of the U.S. citizenry for schools to consistently educate all students to demonstrate proficiency of national standards? How great is the will of the public to employ teachers who are well educated and well prepared to teach every day? How intense is the desire to sustain classroom learning environments that are resource rich and technologically current? We ask these questions because although as a nation we are so advanced that we have constructed an Internet allowing us to send and receive messages as well as access information from around the world in seconds, still we struggle to educate our youth. Why?

This book is not about excuses or blame, cover-ups or exposures, sleight of hand or show and tell. It is about aligning a nation's vision and resources to focus on student learning and educator competence. It is also about losing patience with isolationists in education, with technologically illiterate professionals, and with educators who have stopped learning. It is about teachers', administrators', and, yes, parents' too having continuous learning needs accelerated by life's changes and the impact of those changes on children. It is about dismay at boards of education that waste resources, causing financial disasters in districts where the only consequence is that members will not run for elected offices again.

It is time for all members of the school community to say what they believe in. Is it in a future that will be framed by our current high school students? If that thought is scary, then maybe legislators need to refocus on public school students and their teachers.

As educators acquire more knowledge about current research and practices to improve student learning; as they practice new strategies, achieve mastery, and teach others; and as they invest more time in consulting with colleagues about the best way to teach each child, they continuously build their capacity as professionals in their classrooms and schools. If they care enough about kids to make teaching a life's work, they will learn, grow, and become increasingly competent. That is what this book is about, the continuous preparation of professionals for a life's work of teaching and learning.

One assumption underlying this text is that we have not done the best job we can of educating all children or of preparing all teachers to educate all children. A second assumption is that when all students can demonstrate proficiency on established standards, we will have attained quality education. A third assumption is that education is lagging behind its business counterparts in its use of technology and other necessary learning resources throughout the system. A fourth assumption is that pathways leading from a teacher's professional development to increased student achievement are possible.

People of like values will change the world. That is, believing in public education, like-minded citizens will persuade legislators to align the vision of public education with the resources for continuous teacher preparedness. As a result, they will change the depth and the breadth of student learning.

Professional development is the process of achieving professional competence through learning, to improve student success. Our goal, therefore, is to deepen our collective understanding about how we can create professional development opportunities and practices in a design that enables teachers to educate all students well. We will learn to view professional development from new perspectives. We, for example, no longer define *professional growth* as a record of when teachers and administrators were trained by outside experts. The focus has changed from what others do to educators to what educators do with inside and outside experiences to increase their capacity to help students achieve. To accomplish the goal, professional learning will permeate the system, resulting in higher academic results for students. Professional learning includes, for example, teachers' examining student work; writing curriculum; determining goals; aligning classroom, site, and district assessments to the standards; and coaching others as they embed standards and assessments in the daily work of students.

With these assumptions, beliefs, values, and goals, we invite you to our text. The scenarios that begin each chapter are intended to ground the reader in the reality of the work. Essential questions will provoke deeper thought about each topic to guarantee the sustainability of the work. To assure readers that professionals have evaluated the concepts over time, we have included the research. The body of the chapters will provide information and challenge current practices. The final section of each chapter, "On the Web," encourages the use of technology for continuous growth.

It is important for readers to select the most meaningful and relevant chapters to read, digest, reflect upon, discuss with colleagues, and incorporate into their collective actions for one purpose, *to improve student achievement.* Because the meaning of adventure includes spirit and excitement, we welcome our readers to the adventure of exploring *Why Can't We Get It Right? Professional Development in Our Schools.*

Acknowledgments

The role of professional development in helping schools, individuals, and districts to continue to learn and evolve is both challenging and vital. We approach our work with passion and commitment to improving schools in order to make a difference in teaching, learning, and student achievement.

Quality professional development is complex and diverse. We have been inspired and informed by those who have kept a clear focus on student achievement through their thoughts and actions in classrooms, schools, and districts. We wish to acknowledge their daily efforts to develop the skills, strategies, and attitudes essential to improving schools.

For expanding the role of professional development in learning and leading in the public schools, we thank the pioneers of our field, Roland Barth, Linda Darling-Hammond, Linda Lambert, Ann Lieberman, Lynne Miller, Judith Warren-Little, Dennis Sparks, and Stephanie Hirsh. Because of them, we have been able to formulate, clarify, and reflect on our vision of professional development as a pathway to improved student achievement.

We wish to thank individuals who read our drafts and offered important critiques to improve the clarity, meaning, and reality of our work. Words are insufficient as appreciation for the review efforts and personal support of Barbara Hansen, Northwest Regional Lab; Michael Kass, Joint Ventures Silicon Valley; Linda Lambert, Professor Emeritus, California State University, Hayward; Jim Negri, Assistant Superintendent of Educational Services, Pleasanton Unified School District; Betty Pacheco, Superintendent Emeritus, Fremont Union High School District; Joan Roberts, Monterey County Office of Education; Maureen Saunders, Executive Director, California School Leadership Academy, Los Angeles; Pat Stelwagon, Interim Superintendent, Berryessa Union School District; and Deborah Walker, Jefferson County Professional Schools Gheens Academy in Kentucky.

We owe a special thanks to Linda Lambert, Professor Emeritus of Educational Leadership, California State University, Hayward, for taking time from her busy schedule and her own writing to review the draft and write the foreword to this book. We especially appreciate her insights and thoughtful criticism as well as her dedication to the profession.

We thank Marty Krovetz, Professor of Educational Leadership, San Jose State University, who helped to launch our work and collaboration through the school and university partnership, University School Support for Educational Reform, where we developed *The Essential Questions and Practices in Professional Development* (1997). Marty, colleague and friend, our work together inspires us and causes us always to reflect on why we do what we do.

To Sue Fettchenhauer, California School Leadership Academy colleague and Leadership Options, Inc. partner, friend, and career educator who never wavered in her support of these important efforts, we offer a special thanks for sending us all the books, articles, critical reviews, Web site locations, and e-mails that helped to inform our work.

Thank you to Alice Foster and Catherine Kantor, our editors at Corwin Press, for your faith and encouragement to tackle a book on professional development with direct pathways to student achievement. Thank you also to Diane Foster, production editor, and to Rachel Hile Bassett, a fine copyeditor. Corwin Press has provided the means to share our work, and we are appreciative.

We are also appreciative of the personal and professional enrichment provided us by the following organizations. We acknowledge the Association of California School Administrators for its leadership in education, the California School Leadership Academy for its intensive work with professional development and school restructuring, the California Staff Development Council for its commitment to improving professional development opportunities, and the San Jose State University of California for providing us with opportunities to make a difference in the lives of students.

We are indebted to and wish to thank our families for the countless hours our work took and the encouragement they provided throughout the process. These wonderful individuals stood by us through it all and kept our work and life in perspective. Without their love, understanding, and support, this book would not be possible. We give sincere thanks to Sue Webber for being a realist and for seeing us through the early stages of critique and proofing, in addition to the entire endless process. Grateful appreciation goes to Marsha's sister, Linda Ramsey, for providing wonderful hospitality after a difficult day of writing. Special thanks go to Caroll's husband, Fritz, for his sense of humor and thoughtful insights; to son Randy Price, for listening and troubleshooting; to daughter Pam Winaker, for being our conscience about the realities of life as a teacher in the public schools; and to son Gene Knipe, for his patient assistance with graphics and computers.

Finally, we need to acknowledge our own unique and delightful collaborative work. Our thoughts, actions, and reflections on what matters most about professional development have been enriched, challenged, and supported by our work together. May we continue our passionate work together as learners and friends.

The contributions of the following reviewers are gratefully acknowledged:

Carol Boyd, Instructor
Eastern Instructional Support Center
King of Prussia, PA 19406

Paul Burden, Professor
Kansas State University
Manhattan, KS 66506

Gini Doolittle
Assistant Professor, Educational Leadership Department
Rowan University
Glassboro, NJ 08028-1701

Antonia Lewandowski
Curriculum Coordinator
Pinnellas County Schools
Largo, FL 33779-2942

Marty Louthan, Instructor
Central Middle School
Bartlesville, OK 74003

Rose Weiss, Instructor
Cambridge Academy
Pembroke Pines, FL 33029

About the Authors

Marsha Speck, Ed.D., is a leader in school reform, educational leadership, and professional development issues. Her professional interests include building leadership capacity among teachers, administrators, and the community to improve schooling and achievement for all students and developing school-university partnerships that model these practices. She is currently Professor of Educational Leadership and Development at San Jose State University. Marsha is the director of the Urban High School Leadership Program, an innovative leadership development program linked as a partnership with regional school districts for teacher leaders and administrators to rethink the American high school and how it meets the needs of students and the community. She has diverse experiences as a teacher, high school principal, assistant superintendent of instruction, and professor, where she has worked collaboratively on school change efforts. She believes in a continued partnership linkage between the university and the school community, which is exemplified in her work. Creating school learning communities has been a central focus of her work with schools. She has published widely, including *The Essential Questions and Practices in Professional Development* and has authored two books, *The Principalship: Building a Learning Community* (Prentice Hall) and *The Handbook for Implementing Year-Round Education in the High School* (National Association for Year-Round Education). Recently, San Jose State University recognized her as a Teacher Scholar 1996-1997 in recognition of her contributions toward promoting the scholarship of teaching, especially in education leadership. She received a B.A. from the University of California, Davis; an M.A. from California State University, Stanislaus; and an Ed.D. from the University of the Pacific.

Traveling, tennis, and reading are a few of Marsha's passions when she is not working on leadership issues. She can be reached at San Jose State University, One Washington Square, San Jose, CA 95192-0072 or via e-mail at MSLVTENNIS@AOL.COM.

Caroll Knipe, M.A., recognized leader and educational planner, is committed to change for student success through building the skills of teachers, parents, administrators, and boards of education. Veteran teacher; site administrator; director of personnel, communications, and curriculum; leadership consultant; published author; university adjunct staff; academy director; speaker; coach; and strategic positioner, she is currently executive director of the consulting firm Leadership Options, Inc.

For 14 years as executive director of the California School Leadership Academy in the Silicon Valley, Caroll facilitated premier leadership development programs recognized nationally and internationally. As president of the 15,000-member Association of California School Administrators (ACSA), she helped to set the state's educational direction. Her presentations include nationwide television seminars by Apple Computers; instructional television series, with roles as moderator and panelist; radio talk shows in Washington, D.C., Los Angeles, and San Francisco; and facilitation at conferences for ACSA, the Association for Supervision and Curriculum Development, California and National Staff Development Councils, and the California School Board Association. Recognized extensively for outstanding leadership by state and national associations, she holds a bachelor's degree from Lock Haven State University in Pennsylvania and a master's degree from Western Washington State University. Having served on state committees in California and nationally with the American Association of School Administrators, she recently joined a state task force charged with determining the professional development framework for future legislative regulations involving education.

At home in California's Santa Cruz Mountains with husband Fritz and two giant dogs, Caroll enjoys leadership facilitation, consulting, writing, teaching, traveling, and keeping up with five grandchildren. She can be reached via e-mail at OPTIONSCK@AOL.COM.

We dedicate this book to our families,
who have supported our work and writing by
encouraging us to pursue our passion of improving education
through quality professional development:

To Marsha's parents, James and Patricia Gurney,
who valued education and made sacrifices.

To Caroll's husband, Fritz,
an educator of excellence for 35 years;
to our children Randy, Pam, Gene, and Heidi,
who give meaning to our lives; and to our exceptional grandchildren,
Carly, Ryan, Matthew, Michael, and Wesley,
our personal reasons for continuing the quest
for high-quality public education.

We also dedicate this book to principals and teachers
who are redesigning their schools to improve achievement for all students.
These professionals have dared to make a difference in teaching
and learning for themselves, their colleagues, and their students.

Introduction

Essential Questions About Professional Development

Three teachers discussed their day as they walked to the parking lot after school. Their conversation turned to other topics.

Josie: *I just heard a report from the Education Trust in Washington, D.C. I don't want to believe what Kati Haycock said. Did you know that out of every one hundred Hispanic kindergarten children, only sixty-one will graduate from high school, and only ten will get bachelor's degrees? She gave statistics for the other groups, but this one reached right into my heart.*

Kim: *I heard that. High schools really have a problem, don't they? I mean, obviously they aren't preparing kids for college.*

Jeff: *Do you really think it's their problem?*

Kim: *I see what you mean. OK, so it's an elementary problem, too. By meeting the standards, all elementary students must be prepared for middle school, and all middle students must be prepared for high school. What an enormous challenge!*

The three were silent as they walked.

1

Josie:	*Isn't anyone going to say the "H" word?*
Jeff:	*What's that?*
Josie:	*How? How do we get our kids to standards? It's not fair to them if we don't know how to do it. Right now our statistics look like those from the Education Trust. Our kids just aren't making it.*
Kim:	*The "H" word response is "PD." How we help kids in new ways is professional development.*
Jeff:	*Right! And I was elected to the PD design team. Now I know why. I've been really vocal about how teachers need more current information on teaching and learning. We need professional development that supports our needs. Some of the old ways just aren't realistic for working with today's kids.*
Josie:	*Go for it, Jeff! And I'll be your alternate. I really care about this!*

The colleagues left the parking lot, but Josie continued to mull over the discussion as she drove to her appointment. Taking charge of their own professional learning felt good. But how would they do it? What questions should they be asking to challenge their practices? She sighed. "We'll have to do the research, look at our own current practices, and decide what's working and not working for students," she said aloud. "That's a starting place." Something great was going to happen for kids; she just knew it.

Pause for a moment to reflect on this essential question.

ESSENTIAL QUESTION

To provide the best teaching and learning opportunities for the achievement of all students, what are the essential questions that must be asked about professional development practices?

Prior reform efforts have not been buttressed by the ongoing professional development needed to prepare teachers to teach in the complex ways that learner-centered practice demands.

—Darling-Hammond, 1997b, p. xv

Introduction

Comprehensive professional development for educators has generally been a neglected or shallow component of school reform efforts for the past 20 years. To increase student achievement and help all students succeed, educators must be well prepared. They must also engage in continuous learning to meet the demands of a changing and diverse student population in a rapidly evolving world. At the core of what schools and districts should be about is recognition of the need for continuous professional growth. No longer can school reform efforts tolerate professional development that is shallow and that never really gets to the heart of providing in-depth experiences for new learning. If reform efforts are to take place, we cannot afford to let quality professional development get lost in the shuffle of shifting reform priorities and the countless time demands that affect the daily lives of teachers, school leaders, and district leaders. Thus, a clear focus on professional development is key to building the capacity of educators to make true school reform happen and to sustain it over time. Research has shown that improving educators' (teachers' and leaders') knowledge and skills is a prerequisite to raising student performance.

Our goal in this book is to deepen our collective understanding about how we can create professional development opportunities and practices in a design that enables teachers to educate all students well. To sustain focused efforts, a well-designed professional development program will nourish the growth of educators and foster a learner-centered environment. If we are to dramatically improve schools and schooling, we must insist on professional development designs and practices that make a difference in teacher learning and student success. The professional learning, therefore, will permeate the system, resulting in higher academic results for students. When district offices, parents, communities, county and state departments of education, educators' associations, and state and federal legislators recognize and support these designs and practices and when all of these groups align their goals with student achievement, the key elements will be in place for responding to the question in the title: "Why can't we get it right?"

In framing the book, we challenge readers with real-life scenarios and essential questions regarding professional development to focus the discussion for each chapter and to cause readers to reflect on their current professional development practices.

Professional development opportunities and practices must provide both the challenge and the support for educators to grow, change, and reflect on their practices. Creating such opportunities requires commitment, understanding, planning, resources, time, and evaluation. This book will provide the reader with knowledge, insights, tools, and designs to assist in creating new professional development opportunities that serve the learning-centered school and improve student achievement.

Educational leaders and teachers must design programs to support professional growth along a continuum of each educator's experience in order to be learner centered and learning centered. The failure by most schools and districts to recognize the importance and need for continuous, aligned, needs-based professional development condemns school reform efforts to ultimate failure. Virtually every effort to improve education since the publication of *A Nation at Risk* (National Commission on Excellence in Education, 1983) has centered on overcoming deficits in student knowledge or dealing with reshaping the structure and organization of schooling. School reform efforts—ranging from increased course content and rigor to establishing charter schools, from testing schools for accountability to lowering class size, and from changing schedules to creating schools within schools—all have largely left the classroom untouched (Sparks & Hirsh, 1999). Thus teachers, despite reformers' efforts, generally continue to teach as they have in the past. No wonder we have seen little or no increase in student results. Research and proven practice demonstrate that expanding teacher knowledge and improving teaching skills are essential to raising student achievement (Darling-Hammond, 1997b). In the redefinition of teacher and student needs, we have created a new meaning of professional development.

What Is Professional Development?

Professional development is a lifelong collaborative learning process that nourishes the growth of educators both as individuals and as team members to improve their skills and abilities. It is the authors' premise that in the public schools, the focus of professional development must be to improve student learning. As fostered in a learner-centered environment, professional development is embedded in the daily work of educators; offers choices and levels of learning; builds on collaborative, shared knowledge; employs effective teaching and assessment strategies; expands teacher knowledge of learning and development; and informs teachers' daily work. It is sustained and intensive, with opportunities for practice, collaborative application through problem solving and action research, mastery, coaching, and leadership. Professional development includes an evaluation of progress as it builds teacher and leadership capacity and as it affects student learning.

The lack of professional development, as well as its misuse by educators, explains the chronic failure of school reform. New professional development models exist that will help propel school reform efforts when used systematically over time. The knowledge, skills, attitudes, behaviors, and practices of teaching are only minimally challenged by current practice. In addition, districts do not provide consistent support and leadership for improving teaching practice. If this is the dilemma, what essential questions should educators ask that would cause them to rethink their current professional development practices?

Essential Questions for Professional Development

Essential questions challenge educators' thoughts about professional development practices and help us transform schools into vibrant learning centers for both students and educators (Table 1.1). The questions help shift the focus from what is to what could be. They engage educators in a reflective process that generates new ideas and designs. They help teachers and administrators in schools continue their growth and challenge their current practices in professional development. Through the examination of professional development practices, educators will better understand what it takes to bring about change and reforms in education that can be sustained to support all students and their success. We challenge the reader to think deeply and reflect on the Essential Questions for Professional Development (Table 1.1), which provide a focus for each chapter in this book.

A Global View of Successful Professional Development

Educators need to explore successful professional development for its simplicity of concept and its complexity of implementation. The visual representation in the Global View of Successful Professional Development

---

TABLE 1.1   Essential Questions for Professional Development

♦ To provide the best teaching and learning opportunities for the achievement of all students, what are the essential questions that must be asked about professional development practices? (Chapter 1)

♦ How will schools design and deliver professional development opportunities based on enabling all students to meet the standards? (Chapter 2)

♦ How will a school design professional development opportunities and policies that are based on student achievement while shaping the school culture and the learning community to sustain the efforts? (Chapter 3)

♦ How will a school design professional development opportunities that are based on meeting teacher work concerns? (Chapter 4)

♦ How will a school design professional development opportunities that are based on meeting individual growth needs of teachers? (Chapter 5)

♦ How will a school design professional development opportunities based on meeting district goals? (Chapter 6)

♦ How will a school design professional development opportunities based on meeting its specific needs? (Chapter 7)

♦ How will a school select the best tools to implement a professional development design based on building teacher capacity and affecting student learning? (Chapter 8)

♦ How will a school or district evaluate its professional development programs? (Chapter 9)

♦ What have we learned from historical perspectives and current research that will affect our professional development practices and designs? (Chapter 10)

♦ How will future trends and indicators be used to rethink professional development opportunities in schools? (Chapter 11)

(Figure 1.1) provides a conceptual framework of the interactive components supported by research and proven practice. Because of the interactive qualities of the parts, no one element is more important than the others, and, conversely, no one element can be omitted if the design is to be successful. It is of critical importance that the focus be on improving student learning. This is the change from past practice. Prior to the emphasis on standards, educators considered professional development to be whatever someone in the system thought interesting or useful. Without the focus on improving student learning, educators often could not connect what happened in one year with the next. In fact, using "the pendulum swings" as an excuse for waiting for the next change—not doing any serious thinking about the current thrust, because it would be gone next year—is a direct consequence of unfocused professional development practices.

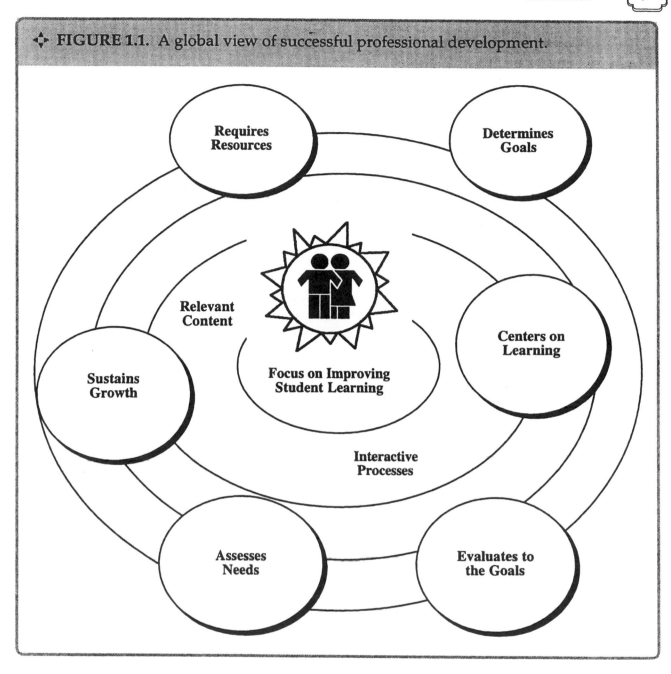

❖ **FIGURE 1.1.** A global view of successful professional development.

Addressing the components illustrated in Figure 1.1 (focuses on improving student learning, determines goals, centers on learning, evaluates to the goals, assesses needs, sustains growth, and requires resources) in a global sense through relevant content and interactive processes provides coherence and sustainability to a professional development plan. If one views a school district's design of professional development over a period of years, one can often see that these key components have been neglected, especially the components of keeping a clear focus on improving student learning and of evaluating procedures to meet the goals.

Elements of Successful Professional Development

If educators have a clear image of what successful professional development entails, such an image will help them evaluate and design their own professional development opportunities. The elements in Table 1.2 are designed as building blocks to help the reader understand the critical global components necessary for developing professional development plans that will bring about change in current educational practice. Although the table depicts an order of importance, the reader should keep in mind that all parts are essential for the total design to be effective. These elements provide a framework for understanding the essential parts of designing quality professional development. Each element will be briefly discussed as regards its importance and its relationship to successful professional development based on research and proven practice.

Focuses on Improving Student Learning

Successful professional development must focus on conditions for improving student learning and achievement. Student success is the ultimate aim and outcome of well-planned professional development (Guskey, 2000; Joyce & Showers, 1995). The needs of all students, especially in our diverse society, must inform all aspects of a professional development design. We cannot afford to lose sight of this goal in the process of designing a professional development program. Professional development work focused on how it will improve student learning will prevent a disconnect from occurring between the purpose of the professional development and the process. Once this overarching goal has been established, the content, processes, materials, and evaluations of professional development efforts can be measured according to whether they support this goal. Components that fail to improve student learning can be dropped, modified, or redesigned (Steiner, as cited in Hassel, 1999).

Districts and schools must hold all professional development plans under the lens of improving student learning and achievement. Teachers, schools, and districts must hold a clear, sustained, systemic focus on specific areas for improving student learning (i.e., literacy) over several (3 to 5 or more) years for lasting change to occur and improvement to be shown (Schmoker, 1996). If learning and professional growth are supported and reinforced, then there cannot be a year-by-year change of focus. Little (1993b) asserts that highly effective schools are those that are able to weather the conflicting policy mandates and practices to which they are subjected and maintain a clear path with well-established goals.

TABLE 1.2   Elements of Successful Professional Development
(Includes Both Content and Process)

FOCUSES ON IMPROVING STUDENT LEARNING

ASSESSES NEED AND ESTABLISHES GOALS

- Emerges from teachers' expressed needs
- Uses data to inform practice and make decisions
- Aligns plans systematically with school and district change efforts and goals
- Bases professional development on a foundation of standards and accountability

CENTERS ON THE LEARNER

- Engages teachers in planning, implementing, reviewing, and revising
- Embeds in real work of the teachers
- Offers choices and levels of learning
- Employs effective teaching and learning strategies
- Has content specific to teaching and assessment of subject matter
- Uses inquiry, dialogue, and reflection to inform practice

SUSTAINS GROWTH

- Supports learning around practice
- Is sustained and intensive
- Expands on knowledge
- Builds on shared knowledge

REQUIRES RESOURCES

Requires administrative support, leadership, and available resources

EVALUATES TO GOALS

Evaluates progress and impact on student learning using data

Recently, there have been signs that districts and schools are truly beginning to understand that there is a need for focus and coherence in their professional development plans if student learning is to improve. Research and experience confirm that the difference for students between a well-prepared teacher and a poorly prepared teacher can be a full level of achievement in a single year (Haycock, 1999). Quality professional development can produce immediate gains in teacher quality, which affects student achievement (Cohen & Hill, 1998). Where does your school or district stand in understanding the true importance of sustaining a focus on improving student learning, both in planning and action taken, through professional development opportunities?

Assesses Needs and Establishes Goals

Emerges From Teachers' Expressed Need. Professional development can emerge from teachers' expressed, and sometimes urgent, need to know. When leaders respond to teachers' expressed professional development needs, which emerge from teachers' daily work with students, the design for professional growth becomes meaningful and immediate (Lieberman & Miller, 1999). Leaders, especially principals, must have the ability to listen to teachers and understand their emerging needs as changes take place and as professional development is adapted to the learning environment. It is difficult for teachers to focus on district-imposed professional development when their immediate concerns are not being addressed. Meeting teacher-felt needs is the foundation for building future professional development plans. A direct connection must be established between the teachers' felt needs and what the students' achievement levels and needs are; this connection can be made by examining student work and allowing teachers to define their areas of needed professional growth (Schmoker, 1996). In order to do this, school leaders must work collaboratively with teachers to provide multiple experiences to help teachers as well as leaders identify their needs, in the areas of both content knowledge and expanding teachers' repertoire of instructional skills to better meet individual student needs (Darling-Hammond & Ball, 1998).

Uses Data to Inform Practice and Make Decisions. Because accountability for student learning is the focus, designers of professional development should use data about student achievement and needs as well as information about teachers' abilities and needs to inform the design. If data analysis does not occur, then professional development plans may be based on misinformation, and training may be initiated that is neither necessary nor useful. Processes must be in place to inform teachers about student achievement data, causing them to analyze the data and look for areas of strength and needed improvement. These assessment processes will show the gaps in student learning and in teacher competence. Then, decisions about what professional development needs to take place are based on a thorough analysis that includes student work, achievement levels, and the alignment with standards. Too often, professional plans are drafted without reviewing data, and prescriptive activities are simply mandated for teachers. The latest fads and programs cannot be sought to fix the problems. Meaningful analysis that requires teachers and leaders to see patterns and trends provides for understanding and informed decision making about professional development needs and plans.

Aligns Plans Systematically With School and District Change Efforts and Goals. If real change and progress is to be accomplished, professional development plans must be aligned systematically with school- and district-wide goals and change efforts. Aligning school and district professional development opportunities sends a clear message about the direction of the district and supports a better use of district resources (Joyce & Showers, 1995). Alignment provides the coherence necessary for long-term commitment to school and district goals and results. How often have school- and district-wide plans lacked focus, jumping from one professional development activity to the next with no aligned, systemic, long-term plan? Aligned school- and district-wide systems and structures need to be in place for effective, career-long professional development (Darling-Hammond & McLaughlin, 1995). Thus, linking professional development to the educational goals of the school and district is essential for achieving significant change (Steiner, as cited in Hassel, 1999).

Bases Professional Development on a Foundation of Standards and Accountability. Professional development plans must be based on a foundation of standards and accountability. Standards provide the starting point for developing plans, a focus, and outcomes for professional development. If educators are committed to students' meeting the standards, then they must have a clear understanding of the content and an ability to teach to the standards. Professional development plans and opportunities must be tied to standards and appropriate assessments; otherwise, the curriculum has no anchor. Teachers must also see a clear link between professional development, student learning, standards, and accountability (Sparks & Hirsh, 1997).

Accountability for the outcomes of professional development is vital in relation to increased student achievement and school improvement. A professional development plan or activity that demonstrates its purpose through specific outcomes tied to school or district goals has a critical way of showing its worth. Educators can no longer afford simply to have a professional development activity without related accountability. If the professional development is valuable, then it should be demonstrated through achievement of clear outcomes. Specific expectations are important for professional development (Guskey, 2000). Participants must know what has been accomplished and what needs to be done. Schools or districts investing in professional development should require results; otherwise, why invest?

Centers on the Learner

Engages Teachers in Planning, Implementing, Reviewing, and Revising. Often professional development is designed by outside experts or district office staff and then imposed on teachers as a quick fix to raise failing student achievement. Unless teachers are engaged in planning, implementing, reviewing, evaluating, and revising professional development plans with their school and district on a regular basis, they will probably not commit to the outcomes (Darling-Hammond & McLaughlin, 1995). Because teachers are the recipients of professional development, they should have significant ownership and a deeper understanding of the plans (Lieberman, 1995a). The development of ownership and commitment to improved practice is important to ensure positive participation by faculty in professional development. Because teachers are affected by change, they must have input into the changes, or there is no meaning in their involvement. Engaged teachers can plan, give feedback, review, and revise professional development based on their working knowledge, understanding of student learning needs, and commitment to the plan. Too often, school leaders undermine the legitimacy and effectiveness of professional development by failing to include participants in planning and delivery (Corcoran, 1995).

Offers Choices and Levels of Learning. A variety of choices and levels of learning in professional development provides participants with options based on their own learning needs. Educators' recognition that "one-size-fits-all" professional development will not meet the needs of all participants is an important concept in designing professional development for the wide range of abilities found within a school or district (Sparks & Hirsh, 1997). Understanding the current developmental level of the participants allows a planner to challenge individuals to improve based on their current abilities within a focused area. Honoring the developmental levels and experiences of teachers through appropriate means is critical to the professional development design. Once teachers and administrators establish the specific needs for learning, then a variety of choices and strategies for learning can be offered to individuals to improve their professional competence. These multiple entry points, based on individual teacher needs and skill levels, will focus professional development in specific areas.

Teachers are tired of professional development that is imposed on them from the top. Such professional development plans are presented as being good for all, rather than being balanced by recognition of individual strengths and areas of personal improvement. Effective professional development has multiple opportunities, is diverse, and provides for an ongoing process as it actively engages the educator in learning. Districts and schools must recognize this complexity and differentiated need to implement successful professional development that meets teachers' needs and improves student performance. Teachers feel a greater sense of commitment to change and more interest in participating in professional development when attention is paid to their assessed needs (Duke et al., as cited in Collins, 1998). This important analysis and understanding of individual as well as school-wide needs make it possible to plan professional development efforts that recognize the teachers' felt needs, content knowledge level, and teacher skill gaps (Guskey, 1999).

Embeds in Real Work of the Teachers. Embedding professional development in the real work of teachers provides for clear connections to their work with students and to the improvement of student achievement. This relevancy and context of professional development allow teachers to inquire, reflect, analyze, and act on their current practice, especially as they examine student work and learning and their ability to provide increased learning for their students. Professional development is not an isolated event that takes place outside the school, but an integrated part of the daily work of teachers. The experiences of learning together emerge from the real work together (Lieberman & Miller, 1999). Such professional development ignites commitment and continual growth based on the unique circumstances of the teacher and the school. It becomes an integral part of a teacher's professional life as the school develops the ecology of a learning community.

However, Guskey (1999) cautions that these professional development needs must be more deeply analyzed to make sure that school-wide (not just individual) needs are accurately identified. This critical analysis requires planning and a team effort by teachers and staff to close common student learning and teacher skill gaps (Guskey, 1999). When professional development is seen as a daily integrated part of a teacher's work life, there is a recognition within the school culture that learning needs, adjustments, seeking out of new ideas and skills, and reflecting on current teaching practices are embedded in the daily life of the teacher and school.

Employs Effective Teaching and Learning Strategies. Understanding the learning styles of participants and providing multiple strategies for learning allow individual learning needs to be met through the professional development process. Educators recognize that not all individuals learn in the same way at the same time. Using a variety of effective learning strategies (e.g., media, the Internet, dramatic presentations, dialogue, or other collaborative processes) enhances the participants' ability to process, understand, and learn new information and skills. This diversification gives participants several pathways to knowing and understanding, which moves well beyond the knowledge level of learning. A variety of techniques can reinforce learning in a number of ways, allowing individuals to process and internalize new information in different contexts with various learning modalities. Professional development plans must include these multiple strategies to recognize learners' developmental, as well as career-level, needs and experiences in order for continuous professional growth to occur (Wood & Thompson, 1993).

Has Content Specific to Teaching and Assessment of Subject Matter. Professional development cannot ignore the integration of specific subject matter content along with teaching and assessment development for teachers. Professional growth opportunities that specifically address how the new information and strategies affect teaching and assessment in particular subject matter areas get to the heart of how the new learning will be implemented. Vague references to applications of new teaching and assessment techniques to content with no examples of what works in the classroom will not advance professional growth. Teachers need rich examples, modeling, practice, and coaching embedded in subject areas. New literacy strategies, such as the use of organizers to focus learning, should be modeled in professional development seminars, practiced in the context of the classroom, and shared with colleagues for feedback and refinement. The more the strategies use actual subject matter content, the greater the learning will be for participants. Including assessment strategies (e.g., running record and personal word lists in reading professional development seminars) provides teachers with specific, integrated strategies to evaluate student progress. Application to the content area gives clear messages about the relationships between content and assessment and how to apply strategies in the classroom (Darling-Hammond, Ancess, & Falk, 1995).

Uses Inquiry, Dialogue, and Reflection to Inform Practice. Cycles of inquiry, dialogue, and reflection provide the means for thoughtful discussion of important learning issues in a school or district. Engaging in a cycle of inquiry requires educators to examine their current practices and outcomes, engage in dialogues about these practices, conduct inquiry into what research and best practices say, and reflect upon what was learned from the study before taking corrective action. Informing practice using these inquiry processes will make a difference for student learning. It is this cycle of inquiry that challenges educational practices and encourages teachers to develop professionally (Darling-Hammond, 1997b; Sagor, 1992; Schmoker, 1996).

Informs Work With Inside and Outside Expertise and Research. Balancing the use of inside and outside expertise and research to inform professional practice in schools and districts is critical (Lieberman & Miller, 1999). The needed and valuable expertise of practitioners within the school, combined with the new knowledge and strategies of outside expertise and research, provides a healthy balance in a system. Informing professional practices by using valued, inside teacher expertise helps provide experiences that sustain the ongoing aspects of professional development in a school. An outside expert can provide new knowledge and even coaching (Joyce & Showers, 1982, 1995, 1996). Teachers then need to practice, reflect on, and refine the strategies over time in their classrooms. Research and outside expertise bring new knowledge and practices to the school setting. This outside expertise and information must be understood and adapted by practitioners to the context of their students and schools. Little change will occur unless current practices are examined and challenged by teachers as new knowledge and strategies are internalized. Utilizing inside expertise (i.e., peer coaches, expert coaches for novices, trainer of trainer models) to help implement, refine, or review practice helps teachers to recognize their own level of expertise and to feel the power of sharing with colleagues on an ongoing basis. Professional practice is balanced and reinforced by the professional development process of combining inside and outside expertise and research (Lieberman & Miller, 1999).

Sustains Growth

Supports Learning Around Practice With Modeling, Coaching, and Problem Solving. New learning must be supported by modeling, coaching, and problem-solving components in order for the new learning to be practiced, reflected on, and integrated into regular use by the learner. Professional development that does not model or include the critical element of ongoing modeling and coaching lacks the continuous support needed for individuals to change practice (Joyce & Showers, 1982, 1995, 1996). If teachers are condemned to onetime or fragmented workshops with little or no modeling, follow-up, coaching, analysis of problems, and adjustment in practice, there will be little change. Just as with sports or music, modeling, practice, coaching, and analysis of performance help hone the skills of the individual. Why should learning new teaching concepts and strategies be different? These crucial elements of modeling, practicing, coaching, and problem solving will end the isolation of teachers and broaden the school into a community of learners in support of teaching and learning (Barth, 1990; Lieberman & Miller, 1999; Little, 1993a; Sparks & Hirsh, 1997). This concept of supporting the "learning organization" (Senge, 1990) within the normal working of a school day gives teachers and administrators the time for the inquiry, reflection, and mentoring necessary for long-term change in practice.

Is Sustained and Intensive With Opportunities for Mastery and Leadership. If individual educators are to continue their personal growth, they must have multiple opportunities for participation with an in-depth approach that is intensive and sustained over a period of time (Darling-Hammond, 1997b). Educators need quality time to master new strategies and new learning by practicing them in their classrooms, reflecting on these practices, and refining their learning. Mastery comes only with study, practice, coaching, feedback, and refinement in a sustained effort. As teachers develop mastery, they can provide leadership in helping others understand the concepts and develop their skills. Encouraging leadership by teachers recognizes their expertise, which can be used to help others, and builds the capacity of the school and district (Lambert, 1998).

Expands on Knowledge of Learning and Development. Continually expanding on teachers' current knowledge about learning and development provides the foundation of lifelong learning for educators. It validates the learning community concept within a school and district. Understanding the developing new research on learning and how it applies to what happens in the classroom helps inform and change practices, leading to increased student achievement. As educators, we can ill afford to retain practices that have not proven to be successful or to avoid the new knowledge being generated around learning and the developmental levels of children (Darling-Hammond & McLaughlin, 1995; Gardner, 1999; Lieberman, 1995a).

Builds on Shared Knowledge of Teachers, Is Collaborative. Professional development must build on the shared knowledge of participants in a collaborative setting. As educators develop plans for professional improvement, they must understand the breadth of knowledge a faculty possesses and plan how to share that knowledge in a collaborative way. When the professional knowledge of teachers is untapped during professional development activities, facilitators create a hostile climate. If outside experts tell, rather than engage, teachers, the opportunity for a collaborative and collective sharing and expanding of baseline knowledge is lost. When leaders recognize the broad knowledge of teachers and commit to constructing collaborative processes to enable teachers to share that knowledge, they will create a culture that nurtures continuous improvement and learning (i.e., action research, cycles of inquiry, trainer of trainer and peer coaching models; Joyce & Showers, 1995, 1996; Sagor, 1992; Sparks & Hirsh, 1997).

Requires Resources

Requires Administrative Support, Leadership, and Available Resources. Administrative support is a key element in successful professional development planning and implementation. When administrators understand the importance of the professional development-plan and how it affects student learning, their support is more easily garnered. Principals can provide support and recognition of the importance of the work through their leadership actions and allocated resources. When administrators support teachers in their professional development work with needed resources, including structured time, they send an important signal that professional development is to be taken seriously (Guskey, 2000; Schmoker, 1996). The leadership of administrators and teachers helps to establish a priority for professional development planning and implementation. Principals and other leaders need to be present and involved in professional development activities to learn, understand, and support the new learnings (Fullan, 1993). Through discourse and engagement in learning, teachers and administrators model a community of learners. Professional development without leadership and direction lacks the necessary commitment on the part of teachers and administrators to carry it out (Little, 1993a). Educators can easily become confused by the "mixed" message that is sent when leaders do not provide support and resources for professional development but still voice an expectation that teachers should learn and implement new strategies to raise student achievement.

Evaluates to Goals

Evaluates Progress and Impact on Student Learning Using Data. Evaluating progress toward the goals of professional development and the impact on student learning is the accountability measure that gives credibility to the importance of continuous professional development. Unless evaluation of progress to date occurs, leaders have no evidence that the professional development is working. A systematic plan to collect data, analyze it, and make changes based on the significance of the data should inform professional development planners (Guskey, 2000). The evaluation process must go deeper than whether participants liked or disliked the activity. It must analyze whether teachers improved their practice and whether the changed practice affected student learning. What difference did the training make in the classroom? Looking long-term at student data and the effect of specific professional development provides important feedback on the investment of a school or district in professional development. This continuous cycle of inquiry into practice causes educators to question current practices based on data and to seek new methods of improving their abilities to increase student achievement (Darling-Hammond, 1997b; Sagor, 1992). A clear evaluation process requires both focused efforts and accountability for progress toward intended outcomes (Guskey, 2000).

Survey of Elements of Successful Professional Development

If schools or districts were to look at research-based elements of successful professional development as a set of questions regarding professional development opportunities, how would they respond? Survey of Elements of Successful Professional Development (Table 1.3) is intended as a tool for analyzing current professional development practices within a school or district. In reality, these elements overlap, repeat, and often occur simultaneously. This assessment tool is intended to lead to reflection about professional development opportunities, not to overwhelm the reader. It is a tool by which key leverage points can be identified in order to improve professional development planning and implementation. By identifying these leverage points (specific elements) for professional development, schools and districts can clarify their goals, strategies, and resources as they focus on student success. The survey provides a baseline assessment of a school or district's professional development practices, which can be used to evaluate the progress toward improving professional development practices and plans.

Conclusion

Transforming schools and increasing student performance is not an easy process. Educators in schools and districts that have a systematic approach to continuous professional development provide a pathway for improving student learning and achievement. Delineating what it means to develop, implement, evaluate, and revise professional development plans has been the intent of the discussion of the elements of successful professional development and the essential questions. Analyzing where your school and district stand in relation to quality professional development and your capacity to increase student learning is an important step to take. Transformation of schools will not happen overnight but must be nurtured over a period of time, with professional development that supports and facilitates the transformational process as teachers and leaders learn, practice, reflect, and grow together.

TABLE 1.3 Survey of Elements of Successful Professional Development

Directions: For each question, circle the number that best represents the answer as it relates to the current professional development program in your school or district based on the following scale:
1 = never; 2 = seldom; 3 = usually; 4 = always.

	Never	*Seldom*	*Usually*	*Always*
1. Is there a focus on improving student learning?	1	2	3	4
2. Does it emerge from teachers' expressed and sometimes urgent need to know?	1	2	3	4
3. Does it use data to inform practice and make decisions about teaching and learning?	1	2	3	4
4. Are the plans aligned systematically with school and district change efforts and goals?	1	2	3	4
5. Is it based on a foundation of standards and accountability?	1	2	3	4
6. Are teachers engaged in planning, implementing, reviewing, evaluating, and revising professional development plans?	1	2	3	4
7. Are individuals offered choices and levels of learning?	1	2	3	4
8. Is the professional development embedded in the real work of the teacher?	1	2	3	4
9. Does the professional development employ effective teaching and learning strategies?	1	2	3	4
10. Does it integrate content specific to teaching and assessment of subject matter?	1	2	3	4
11. Does it involve inquiry, dialogue, and reflection?	1	2	3	4
12. Does it inform work by using inside and outside expertise and research?	1	2	3	4
13. Does it support learning with modeling, coaching, and problem solving around practice?	1	2	3	4
14. Is it sustained and intensive, with opportunities for mastery and leadership?	1	2	3	4
15. Does it expand upon knowledge of learning and development?	1	2	3	4
16. Does it build on shared knowledge of teachers and provide for collaborative interaction?	1	2	3	4
17. Is there administrative support as well as internal leadership and available resources?	1	2	3	4
18. Does it evaluate progress and measure impact on student learning?	1	2	3	4

Total Score: _____ divided by 18 = _____

How does this score on the Elements of Successful Professional Development inform your professional development design and practices?

> ## REALITY CHECK
>
> Transforming schools and increasing student achievement demands high-quality professional development that is meaningful for educators. How is your school or district addressing the elements of successful professional development?

On the Web

The professional educational associations, governmental agencies, and regional educational lab networks listed below can provide on-line resources and links to a variety of professional development current research and practices. "On the Web" resources are intended to provide an ongoing, updated resource for professional development ideas and planning.

Professional Educational Associations

♦ American Educational Research Association: http://www.aera.net

♦ Association for Supervision and Curriculum Development: http://www.ascd.org

♦ National Staff Development Council: http://www.nsdc.org

Government

♦ United States Department of Education: http://www.ed.gov

Regional Educational Lab Network

♦ Links to 10 U.S. Regional Educational Labs: http://www.relnetwork.org

National Reports

National reports provide current perspectives on professional development. Frequently, professional developers search for documents to show others who question the new approach to professional learning, and these Web sites are helpful resources. The documents listed below are important current resources with a national perspective.

♦ Professional Development: Learning From the Best—
   A Toolkit for Schools and Districts Based on the National Awards
   Program for Model Professional Development:
   http://www.ncrel.org/pd

♦ A National Plan for Improving Professional Development—
   National Staff Development Council: http://www.nsdc.org

Focusing Professional Development in a Standards-Based System

Scenario

The principal enters the room with several documents. She distributes the National Standards in Language Arts and Math for the Middle Grades to each of the tables. When her faculty is ready, she begins by describing the process the district will use to convene teachers to rewrite the curriculum so that the adopted standards will be reflected in all schools throughout the district. A few teachers groan. They've been down this path before. A math teacher comments to his colleague, "Someone in the district office gets an idea, and we are expected to make it work with students."

"This is our responsibility as educators," the principal continues, "to make standards work for all students."

Murmurs fill the room. "What does that mean? Who said? What standards? Work for students?"

The principal continues, "The district has decided to implement the adopted standards by next September. Within five years every student graduating from our schools will have learned and mastered the standards approved by the governing board last year. If you want to be a decision maker for the district advocating for what will be taught in your grade level, I suggest you volunteer for one of the district committees. The district will pay a stipend for the committee members, so you can see they are very serious about this. Are there any volunteers? Let me know by four this afternoon if you are interested so that I can e-mail your names to the district office."

Students meeting standards is a major thrust-of the public schools. Too often, however, leaders drop the standards concept on faculties without taking time to explore the urgency of the undertaking, to discuss the implications of standards for all students, or to verbalize the commitment the district will be compelled to make to embed standards in the curriculum. Small wonder that teachers are unable to distinguish the standards movement from any number of thrusts the educational system has made in the last decade.

Pause for a moment to reflect on this essential question.

ESSENTIAL QUESTION

How will schools design and deliver professional development opportunities based on enabling all students to meet the standards?

Why Do We Have the Conversation?

When a nation is truly concerned about the quality of public schools and of the education from kindergarten through high school, standards will be an important part of the conversation. What does implementing standards mean to educators and schools? What do standards mean to students and their learning? How will educators schedule and carry out a professional development design so that the "taught" curriculum, the "written" curriculum, and the "tested" curriculum are aligned with student results? It is more than obvious that every educator must understand the dynamics, implications, and values of a standards-based system before committing to restructuring the school curriculum to increase student achievement.

According to Marsh and Codding (1999), "The most significant role standards play in enhancing learning is in making clear—to students, teachers, parents and the community—the goals for learning" (p. 43). Let us first examine what implementing standards means to different groups, from students and teachers to the entire school community.

Research and Best Practices

District-wide use of standards and the focused efforts of educators to build student capacity to meet the standards has the potential to ensure a quality education for every student in the system. We must be careful, however, not to equate meeting the standards with achieving a passing grade on a test. Brooks and Brooks (1999) argued that "*serious* educational reform targets cognitive changes in students' thinking. *Perceived* educational reform targets numerical changes in students' test scores" (p. 23).

Standards integrated across grade levels and across levels of schooling provide for depth of understanding as well as coherence. With an integrated set of standards, students know what is expected of them. Students also know, for example, that they must accomplish this learning in elementary school because middle schools expect them to arrive able to demonstrate that they have met the elementary standards. Teachers who are assured that students coming into class have met the standards do not have to begin by going over what is old ground for many students. In addition, parents know that the expectations for students in one school are the same as those at schools in another part of town (Marsh & Codding, 1999, p. 44).

Starting with the students' day of graduation and planning backward will give educators a needed perspective. As they retrace the standards process through time, they must focus on students and apply the same question again and again: What do students need to know and be able to do in order to ensure progression and graduation? For this conversation, the authors will not focus on compliance issues related to student conduct and deportment. Educators understand, however, that curriculum is so powerful that the dynamics around information and relationships as they relate to teaching and learning often determine whether a student goes to class, is attentive in class, stays in school, or drops out.

Layering the Work

What is the big picture? Think of the educational system in three layers (see Figure 2.1, Layering the Work of Implementing a Standards-Based System) that, assembled at one time, give an overview of the complexities that must be addressed. Layer 1 is student work, with the educational life of a student at the center. Think of what the student is required to accomplish in the

✧ FIGURE 2.1. Layering the work of implementing a standards-based system.

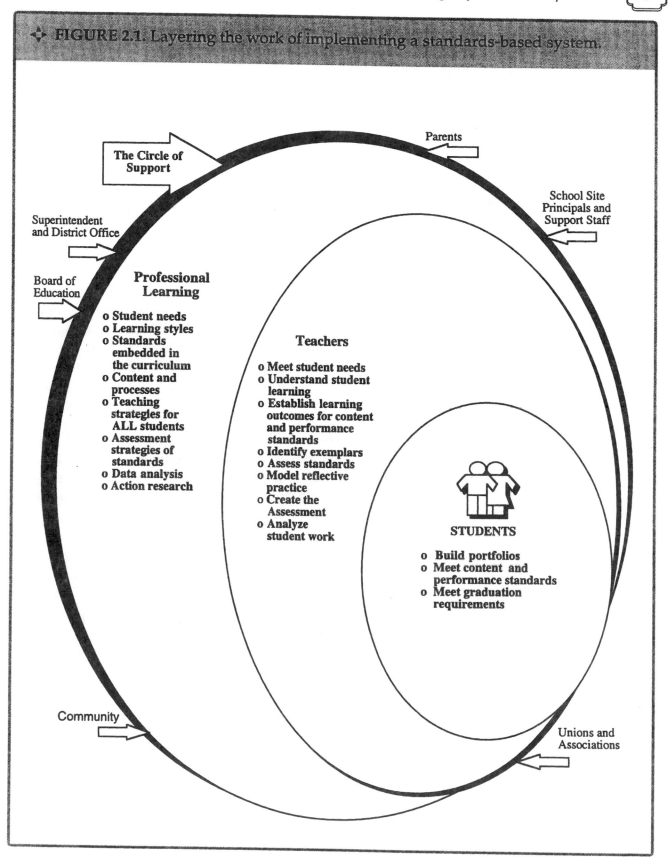

The Circle of Support

Parents

Superintendent and District Office

School Site Principals and Support Staff

Board of Education

Professional Learning

o Student needs
o Learning styles
o Standards embedded in the curriculum
o Content and processes
o Teaching strategies for ALL students
o Assessment strategies of standards
o Data analysis
o Action research

Teachers

o Meet student needs
o Understand student learning
o Establish learning outcomes for content and performance standards
o Identify exemplars
o Assess standards
o Model reflective practice
o Create the Assessment
o Analyze student work

STUDENTS

o Build portfolios
o Meet content and performance standards
o Meet graduation requirements

Community

Unions and Associations

public schools. Layer 2 is the work of the teacher. If student success is a focus, every teacher will be committed to helping every student meet standards. Layer 3 is a plan for professional learning, which is the key to each teacher's continuing capacity to do the work. One area of a teacher's scope of responsibility is teaching content, but if the reader selected each of the topics outlined in a teacher's total work related to student success, no layer would be less complex than the others. Finally, the circle of support surrounds the system as parents, school-site principals and support staff, unions and associations, the community, board of education, superintendent, and district office staff are enlisted to support the work of the teachers to improve student achievement.

Layer 1: Student Work

What is the work of the students? Any senior in a comprehensive high school could complete the information for Layer 1. Students must successfully meet the district standards for their grade level or subject area. In some schools, students build portfolios of their work connected to content and performance standards. Meeting content standards means that students have learned the subject to a level of competency required by the district and are able to demonstrate their performance through classroom assignments, teacher assessments, performance tasks, and standardized measurements. Students are not expected to complete the work unassisted or unsupported. If a student is having difficulty, the professional team agrees to analyze the student's data and determine what strategies will help him or her achieve the standards.

Layer 2: Teacher Work

As with any professional, a teacher's work is as complex and as intricate as the brain of each recipient. Teachers must understand and recognize students' needs and goals. With all the recent research on the functioning of the brain, teachers must have the knowledge of how students learn, which leads directly into teacher work. Designing backward from the standards is a very different way for teachers to think about learning. Teachers become assessors, in that they establish what the students must know to demonstrate proficiency in meeting the standards. They are not thinking about what activities they will facilitate; instead, they are thinking about what students need to learn and do and how they as teachers can prepare their students to reach the required level of proficiency. Teachers sort through data to determine which assessments will help the students. Analyzing student work with colleagues to establish exemplars of performance helps teachers be consistent in answering the question of what level of competency a student must reach to say that he or she has met the standard.

Throughout their classes, teachers model reflective practice as they build life skills in collaboration, problem analysis, problem solving, creative thinking, and technology applications.

The California Standards for the Teaching Profession (California Commission on the Teaching Profession, 1997) begins with "Standards for Engaging and Supporting All Students in Learning" and emphasizes the importance of the classroom:

♦ Teachers build on students' prior knowledge, life experience, and interests to achieve learning goals for all students.

♦ Teachers use a variety of instructional strategies and resources that respond to students' diverse needs.

♦ Teachers facilitate challenging learning experiences for all students in environments that promote autonomy, interaction, and choice.

♦ Teachers actively engage all students in problem solving and critical thinking within and across subject matter areas.

♦ Concepts and skills are taught in ways that encourage students to apply them in real-life contexts that make subject matter meaningful.

♦ Teachers assist all students to become self-directed learners who are able to demonstrate, articulate, and evaluate what they learn. (California Commission on the Teaching Profession, 1997, p. 8)

Layer 3: Professional Learning

Because the work of the teacher is so intense, Layer 3 explores what role teachers themselves are required to play in determining what knowledge, skills, and strategies they must learn to ensure opportunities for student success. In the content area of reading, for example, teachers must know how to assess and prescribe in order to move each student forward at his or her own rate. No teacher can be expected to complete all of the learning tasks relevant to each student in the isolation of the classroom. Collaboration and, especially, the *time* to collaborate are essential to the professional development process.

If we assume a basic human need to succeed at what we do, all teachers require continuous professional development so that they become even more knowledgeable and skillful. One fallacy is to believe and act on the belief that the professional development prescribed for one is the best for every teacher. Districts must guard against embracing models that have their roots in an attitude about the basic incompetence of teachers, who must be forced to improve. Even new information will be received and processed at different levels depending on the experiences of the educators. As the public becomes more demanding about specialized programs for students, teachers will become more demanding about their own needs for specialized knowledge.

Districts Add to the Complexity

The school district makes high-stakes decisions about programs and students, often based on student scores at designated levels on standardized, norm-referenced tests. Frequently, the district controls policies, funding, staffing, and even materials, all of which may contribute to or inhibit successful implementation of standards. Continuous dialogue about standards implementation with the teaching staff and principals is very important so that district mandates and controls, however well intentioned, don't actually impede the work at the sites. Making student achievement a high priority at all levels commits the district to aligning the priorities with the tasks to be accomplished and the resources to support the work.

Student Connections

In addition to district and school expectations for student achievement, educators expect students to make connections to the school. Students connect through sports, clubs, competitions, artistic performances, and special activities linked either to academics or to student interests. The intent is to promote the activities and relationships necessary for each student's success. Because there is a need for belonging, students will connect wherever they can. Through a challenging and interactive academic program, the school has an opportunity to provide positive linking that will benefit students for a lifetime.

Student-Centered Focus

Given the complexity of the outcome for student achievement and subsequent success, educators recognize that it is important to start the work of standards by determining exactly what is required of public school students. When educators start with student needs, they are already refocusing their energies. Traditionally, educators sorted students into those who met and those who did not meet graduation requirements. Now they are focusing on what must be done to help students be successful each step of the way through elementary, middle, and high schools. If students are not successful, teachers commit to reexamining their instruction to determine at what point they could have altered their strategies to reach more students. Committed educators will ask the hard questions: "In what way is the environment I am creating for teaching and learning promoting or inhibiting student success?" and "In what way is the system promoting or inhibiting student success?" Educators with a passion for student success who are willing to confront the system on behalf of students will also have the courage to find the answers and take appropriate actions.

The Circle of Support for Students and Student Achievement

Once the mental model of a standards-based system aligns student work, teacher work, and teacher learning, the next configuration is obvious. Members of the supporting circle—parents, site principals and support staff, the community, superintendent and district offices, boards of education, and unions and associations—play critical roles in this process (see Figure 2.2, The Circle of Support for Students and Student Achievement). Together, they must ensure that each teacher has the opportunity and support for teaching and learning and that each student has the opportunity and support to be successful in meeting the district's adopted standards.

Although teachers continue to define the "success" of students, parents have their own mental model. They want their child to graduate, and many also expect that their children will have assured entry into a university, college, or postsecondary program leading to a career. If achieving standards gets students where they need to go, parents will support the standards. However, if standards are not aligned to the curriculum, to the performance tasks, or to the standardized tests, or if they get in the way of other, more traditional measures of success, such as teacher grades, grade point averages, or SAT tests, parents will probably not support them. The concept of achieving standards in many schools and districts has yet to be included in the mental model parents have of their children's success in the public schools. Because parents are an integral segment in the circle of support for student success, their working knowledge of what constitutes success in the academic system must be a part of every educator's thinking.

The community has its own role to play in supporting the school and student achievement. Without community support of the schools and students, the staff can become demoralized. With the community's support and sustained involvement, schools have greater potential for ensuring each child's success. By law, boards of education are composed of commu-

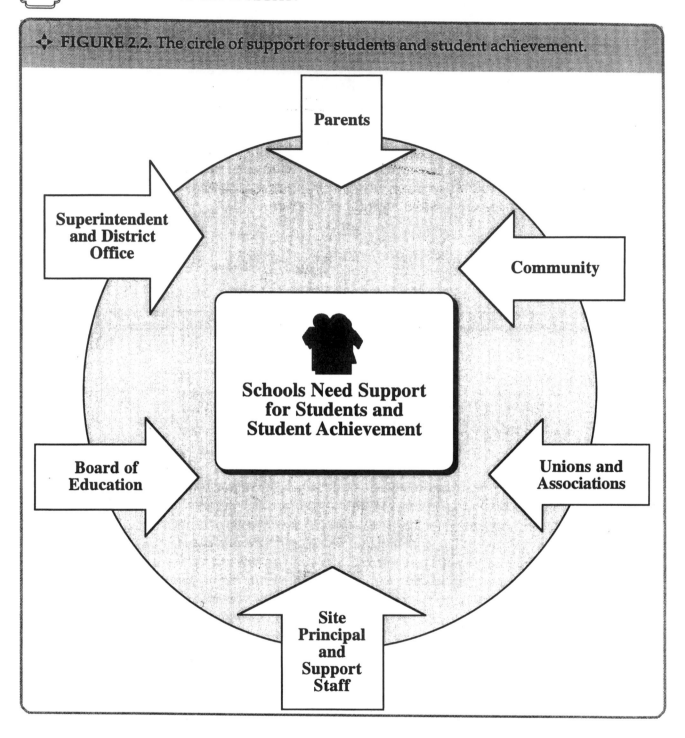

❖ FIGURE 2.2. The circle of support for students and student achievement.

nity members from the school district. Their role is even more extensive than their legal responsibilities for accountability and leadership. They are also responsible for supporting student success. In addition to their visible support of schools, they should model what they want all students to become. A negative, quarreling school board causes the district to lose focus on student achievement as the staff concentrates on survival amidst the storms. A board that is learning to be more effective in supporting teaching and learning is delivering the most important message to their constituents, that the success of all students is important to the board and to their community.

Unions and associations have their roles, too, in supporting changes to improve schools. Their charge to represent their members should not cause them to lose focus on the primary reason all district employees receive paychecks: the success of students and schools. It is imperative that staff members and the associations they endorse through membership have a deep, collective understanding of what a standards-based system means to the quality of education for all students. The circle of support is so important to students that without it, their education is at risk.

Opportunity to Learn

In order to succeed with a standards-based system, each student must have an opportunity to learn. Darling-Hammond (1997b) suggests that we should have the opportunity to learn standards. Opportunity-to-learn standards would establish, for example, that if a state's content standards for science require laboratory work, computers, advanced coursework, or particular content and teaching strategies for science teachers, then resources must be allocated and policies fashioned to give students these entitlements. Such a strategy would leverage both school improvement and school equity, providing a basis for state legislation or litigation where opportunities to learn are not adequately funded (Darling-Hammond, 1997b, p. 279).

Administrators must also accept measures of the context for learning as their particular responsibility. As principals reexamine their schools' infrastructures, they determine what is getting in the way of student and teacher learning. As superintendents reexamine their practices and policies, they decide how they can restructure the district to support and promote student achievement. Are there sufficient materials, resources, coaches, mentors, equipment, technology, and supplementary funds for teachers to do their preparation and classroom work? Without the tools, teachers are working with capacity-restrictive constraints.

Public school teacher Pam Winaker had a supply budget of $50 for the entire year at her middle school in California. She moved to Des Plaines, Illinois, where she had seemingly unlimited supplies to support students and their learning. When she returned to the same school district in California, she was astonished to find that her budget for supplies had not changed from what it had been 2 years previously. Board members appeared not to be conscious of teachers' needs for basic materials such as maps, drawing pencils, and rulers. Such disposables came mostly from her personal budget because of limited district funds. The learning environment could not be favorably compared to her situation in Des Plaines. Perhaps if the California district had adopted standards for the delivery of instruction, the board's recognition of the importance of such supplies would have aligned district resources to teacher and student needs.

It is the responsibility of districts to provide support for teachers in a standards-based system. The superintendent and board must examine all resources and redistribute them according to teaching and learning priorities. Amidst their concerns about materials, facilities, and the physical needs of students, districts that are supportive of students' meeting standards acknowledge that professional development addresses the needs of teachers in classrooms. Professional development focused on student learning and teacher needs will motivate teachers and facilitate student success. Standards of delivery ensure that the learning environment is not a forgotten issue.

The Role of the Board of Education

Who keeps the community informed? The board and the superintendent have another powerful role in this process: keeping the community informed and involved. Boards often ask principals to attend community involvement activities, but in fact, board of education members have a close connection with how the parents and community perceive the schools. It is their task to alert the parents to collaborative opportunities so that parents can support the success of their children.

Should boards also adopt content, performance, and delivery standards as recommended by the superintendent and make certain they are aligned with state requirements? Through district-wide conversations about student performance, the organization achieves consistency of purpose. Boards adopt content, performance, and delivery standards as a systemic validation of the importance of standards to everyone in the district. They also align district policies and procedures so that every facet of the district is supportive of standards-based instruction. In fact, collaboration among schools with common standards and learning goals is a way of cementing district coherence in pursuit of success for all. How a community receives the district's emphasis on the standards is a useful barometer of community pressures and interests. If community members are not supportive of standards, then the district has done an inadequate job of informing them of the potential of a standards-based system and of the consequences of a system without standards.

Even progressive districts sometimes omit a very critical component of student success. The board must adopt standards of professional development to ensure that teachers have opportunities to expand their capacities. Building on the expertise of each teacher should be foremost when planning a comprehensive program in the district. Addressing the combination of teacher and principal capacity along with district capacity will provide a framework for such discussions.

How will boards know when they are successful? As protectors of the district, the superintendent and board must also adopt evaluation designs. Becoming more knowledgeable about the various assessments, the board will be able to put district performance on a particular measure into proper perspective. In California's Berryessa Union School District, Interim Superintendent Pat Stelwagon supported the board's vision of student success by involving parents, teachers, administrators, and community members on action teams. The work was focused on students: (a) student success, (b) student achievement, (c) parent involvement, (d) leadership, (e) communications within and outside the district, and (f) the technology of learning. Teachers claimed compensation for the time invested in the action teams. With an entire district focused on improved student achievement, it is no wonder that this district's students are scoring ahead of districts with similar populations.

A Case Study

Who determines how good is "good enough" both in standards for students and standards of practice? Recently, Berryessa Union School District held district-wide grade-level meetings for teachers to score Performance Assessment Tasks (PAT). This was not an early event in their history: It came after 4 years of working with learning goals and deciding how to assess the outcomes. The district collected data on literacy tests, performance tests, and norm-referenced tests, along with teacher grades. Distributing the data to schools disaggregated by student and teacher prompted the first level of discussion as a professional development activity for the teaching staff. The district then disaggregated the data of Title 1 students who qualified for federal assistance and of English language learners using their proficiency scores. For the first time, teachers were able to look at a collection of data about their own students. They analyzed how other students in the school were achieving as measured by the same instruments. It became readily apparent that multiple measures should be used to assess a student's performance, because several measures can reveal far more about the scope of a student's work than any one measure, even teachers' grades, can. Equally important, the work signaled to the faculty that professional learning, in the form of collaborating to look at student data and student work for purposes of improving instruction, was going to be very different from past professional development experiences.

Professional development based on evaluating how students other than a teacher's own students performed on performance assessment tasks is a key to improving the effectiveness and consistency of the professional staff. The Berryessa district made considerable efforts to align district-wide assessment with curriculum. Teachers who had been isolated in their classrooms or schools had opportunities to compare PAT scores with their grade-level colleagues from a total of eight elementary schools and two middle schools. The conversation about what constitutes unacceptable, acceptable, or exemplary work continued long after the PAT scoring had ended. For the most part, teachers were fully engaged in a professional dialogue that left them both exhausted and exhilarated. Teachers felt that this, in fact, was their real work, and their accusations that the district was unfocused in the use of teachers' professional time were decreasing, especially at the negotiating table. Facilitator Sue Fettchenhauer commented that the conversation in Berryessa had indeed changed from resisting the standards system and the new ways of thinking about assessment to how teachers could be more effective in helping students demonstrate that they had met the standards.

As Berryessa teachers constructed multiple measures of student success, their responsibilities increased. Some schools used portfolio dividers from the National Standards, which established the parameters for building portfolios of student learning. These assessments continued throughout each student's progression through the grades. As a professional development activity, teachers conduct some form of action research in deciding how best to prepare students for improved performance. As the writers observed Berryessa, it became increasingly clear that the teachers and administrators could not have taken the process of change from another district with the intent of replicating it. They had to work through the system by first focusing on the purpose of improved student achievement and then determining what each step would accomplish and how to determine the outcomes. It is, at best, a rigorous, frustrating, consuming, and rewarding process. "Each school community must struggle with new ideas for itself if it is to develop the deep understanding and commitment needed to engage in the continuous problem solving demanded by major changes in practice" (Darling-Hammond, 1997b, p. 217).

Concerns of Teachers in a Standards-Based System

Levels of Understanding

To think more deeply about professional development in a public school system, think about all the teachers in a district. In a single school, some teachers are experienced and have come up through the system. Some have transferred into the district. Some are newly credentialed. In states such as California, a significant number (30,000 in 1998) may have few qualifications other than a college degree. These teachers have also passed a basic skills test and have met eligibility requirements for emergency teaching credentials, according to Don Kairott, former administrator of the Professional Development Unit of the California Department of Education.

Given this situation, why do some districts determine that the same professional development should be provided for the same length of time with the same amount of follow-up for all teachers on a staff? Many articles have been written about new-generation workers. Some managers were amazed to learn that not only were workers not content with being told what to do and how to do it, but that the concept of top-down management did not serve organizations well. Employees wanted to be asked about quality, about creating processes for improving their effectiveness in what they did every day. They wanted to participate in managing themselves and their work. Teachers are no different from these other self-actualizing workers.

Delays in the System

Failure to appreciate the power of deeply held assumptions has undermined many efforts to improve the opportunities for students and teachers to succeed. Changing a system doesn't always work the way educators have planned. A particular high school was moving with great strides in serving students. They had abandoned their former knee-jerk reactions to unsuccessful students and were beginning to use their data to determine why students weren't succeeding. The leadership team interviewed students at all levels about how they responded to the school in general and to learning in particular. They asked focus groups of high school students, "What helps you learn? What gets in your way?"

Based on their data, they searched for alternative ways of scheduling students. Were 45-minute periods detrimental? Would longer blocks of time be advantageous? Would connecting new learning to prior learning be helpful? They began an intensive program for teachers in how to change their teaching strategies to adjust to longer time blocks. They sought support from every adult on campus, forming relationships to assist in the learning process.

And then it happened. A student was killed on campus. Blame was quick to surface. The board was bombarded with demands, which focused on the high school principal. Taller fences, security guards, and school patrols all became higher priorities for funding than the learning process. Disgruntled teachers who were faced with demands for reform by the leadership used the occasion to blame an administration that was more interested in "nosing around the classroom" than attending to the safety of students. The local newspaper attempted to get the facts, and the city newspaper capitalized on the violence. While some parents looked for alternatives to the public school, others voiced their demands for safe schools—in essence, for tighter security. Plans for restructuring and related opportunities for professional development of staff were canceled. The system was in chaos.

Blaming the students, principal, school board, teachers, parents, or the public is out of place in an analysis of this system. Clearly, the parents had deeply held assumptions about their teenagers' safety in the high school. Just as clearly, a living system such as a comprehensive high school operates on many different levels, not one of which can be ignored or underestimated. Although professional development cannot be outside the reality of the context in which teachers live, professional learning focused on helping every student achieve success should not be held hostage during chaos. Had the campus tragedy not happened at that particular time, the school might have had systems in place for dealing with the crisis that ensued, because collaboration with the community was a major goal of the efforts. There had been the potential for school and community to work together to make things happen for students. When this tragedy occurred, traditional reactions to crises surfaced, and the impact on future change efforts was devastating.

Urgent Needs for Information

Several elementary schools are focusing on standards of literacy, with the intent of spending 2 to 2.5 hr each day on literacy-related activities. The writing curriculum is based on benchmarking student learning against the larger outcome—that each student will read at grade level by the end of third grade. With schools where 60 to 80% of the students are speakers of other languages, some entire districts in California, Florida, and Texas are learning and sharing second-language learner strategies in professional development programs for increasing students' abilities to meet the standards. Teachers are analyzing content standards; determining which standards, according to priority criteria, to emphasize; and deciding how to be certain that assessments and benchmarks inform their work throughout the year. This work requires a new level of teacher competence throughout the system.

How do teachers and administrators access knowledge that will transform a group of individuals in private practice to high-performing teams of professionals focused on the work? Personal competence starts with an accurate self-assessment and the self-confidence that whatever I need, I will have access to. A new public yardstick—standardized tests—currently places the responsibility for successful students on teachers. The public is equally ready to blame teachers when students fail. Students, however, can't delay their schooling while teachers wake up the system and become competent through a 5-year plan. When educators renew their credentials or return to the university for a doctorate, ideally they will have access to new knowledge. Because of an urgency for public schools to graduate all students, and because all students must meet the standards to graduate, teachers need access to new knowledge now. Throughout the system, forward-looking districts will nourish cultures of professional access. Web sites, professional libraries, conversations with colleagues, exchanges with other professionals, or, in the best of educational worlds, a multifaceted professional development program supported by the district must address both a teacher's personal mastery and current demands for information, skills, and strategies to connect with all students.

Myths of Professional Development

The first myth, which educators have perpetuated for many years, is that the same program of professional learning is appropriate for all teachers and that once a concept is learned, all teachers will practice the strategy in their classrooms. Entire professional development programs have been implemented based on this assumption. The second myth is that all teachers come to the system with inherent qualities and experiences that prepare them to rigorously examine the cutting edge of research and practices, then to shape these elements into comprehensive strategies to serve all children. Proof that school communities buy into this myth is that programs for professional development continue to be cut as soon as boards face financial hardships. The third myth is that in order for today's students to be successful, each teacher will come to a personal decision that curriculum and strategies need to be different from what he or she saw as a student in K-12 or university classrooms (Figure 2.3).

The First Myth

Is it true that the same program of professional development is appropriate for all teachers and that once the concepts of standards are learned, all teachers will practice the strategies in their classrooms? Few teachers would support this myth, yet districts seem to perpetuate it by having district-wide inservice training that lasts for short periods of time without follow-up systems. When a standards goal is valued, teachers should see system-wide support for implementation. In the same district, there may be a move to provide professional development, for example, in using collaborative teaching strategies to support students in meeting the stan-

❖ FIGURE 2.3. Myths of professional development.

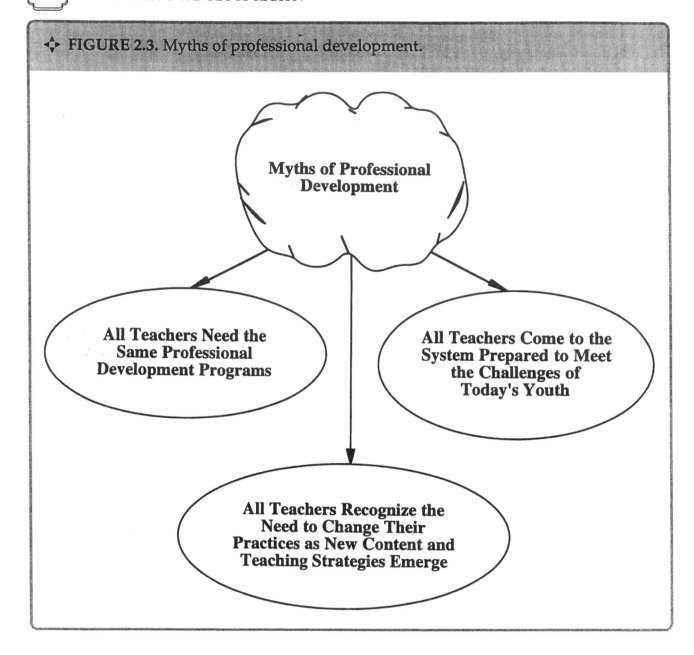

dards. At the same time, the board and top-level management continue to make decisions and pass them down the line. Teachers don't see collaborative strategies modeled or supported at board meetings or at district-wide meetings. The assumption that all teachers need to be instructed in how to teach in a collaborative setting is erroneous, because some may have studied and used the process extensively in other settings. The assumption that all other educators in the district, including the principals and superintendent, need the instruction also may or may not be true. The truth is, however, that when the district places a high value on the collaborative concept, it demonstrates its values through modeling, support, and opportunities to practice throughout the system. When educators internalize the importance of continuous learning and districts demonstrate support for multi-level learning with system-wide follow-through, together they reach a level of commitment that makes a difference for students.

Districts must also be confident that teachers are competent people. This is especially difficult for districts that can't find qualified teachers or administrators to fill their positions, as in many rapidly growing districts in California. Districts must know that the professionally competent educators they hire will have the self-discipline to seek, absorb, and use new knowledge. How will they know that teachers are conscientious, that they will assess their students, and that they won't repeat what is not working for students but will instead seek new strategies for motivating and challenging their classes to take them to higher levels of achievement? Teachers must be flexible in using a toolbox of strategies and must be innovative when working with others to create the settings, the expectations, and the processes for each student's learning. They need feedback on what they do from colleagues in collaborative settings so that together they can seek the best strategies for helping students. Equally important is their professional accountability for helping students meet standards. The professional development program must provide no less for teachers themselves. The professional system must demonstrate support, provide opportunities for teacher mastery and leadership, and be accountable for the time and costs of implementation.

The Second Myth

Who holds the second myth—that teachers come to the system with inherent qualities and experiences that have prepared them to rigorously examine the cutting edge of research, policy, and practices, then to shape these elements into comprehensive strategies to serve all students?

Do teachers feel competent in these areas? Do administrators feel confident that teachers in their schools and districts have these skills? Do citizens feel that teachers in their districts are well-educated professionals, the best they can possibly hire? If the answer is no, educators have a crisis of capacity.

Teaching to the standards is a rigorous discipline requiring a deep knowledge of content and an array of updated strategies for teaching and learning. The need for districts to examine all practices surrounding teaching and learning within a system is obvious. They need to go back as far as the hiring process. For example, rather than assuming that teachers have the aforementioned qualities, public schools must return to the initial screening and interview process. It's important to determine what questions to ask; what demonstrations to see; and what credentials, coursework, and in-depth professional development should be in the background of prospective teachers. In summary, are the teachers about to be hired master learners, capable of teaching to the standards and helping students meet them?

Interview questions may be as specific as: How will you determine what skills and knowledge students are expected to master in your classes this year? How do you use assessment in your curriculum? How will students be evaluated? What happens in your classes if students already meet specific standards when they come to you? What happens when students "don't get it"? How will your instruction be the same or different for each student? What are you learning? Are you engaging in action research? What is your access to learning on the Web?

From the initial conversation about learning, curriculum, and students, the interviewer should ask questions that probe not only the preparation of the teacher, but also the teacher's intent to remain professionally current. District and school interview teams should ask the questions and then find an opportunity to observe as the teacher puts the theory into practice. Some examples include the following:

- What are *your* learning needs?

- What have you mastered, and what are you working on now?

- How do you learn best?

- Describe the professional development that best enabled you to help all your students meet the standards.

- Take the next 15 min to design your own learning, including preferred strategies to attain your goals. What are the elements and the conditions for your success?

- Describe your own standards for professional learning, and tell in what ways those standards are the same as, or different from, standards for student success.

It is common for school boards to require first that students meet standards, and second that teaching and learning be directed to the standards. It is also common for those in the system to become frustrated when significant numbers of students do not meet the standards. Boards and superintendents may conclude that teachers and site administrators have not fulfilled their responsibilities or that sanctions are in order for low-performing schools. Seldom do we hear the more reflective and deeper level of concern: "Maybe they just don't know how to do it." Professional development needs to start with where the teachers and administrators are in their learning and move them as quickly as possible into having the skills to do their work.

Educators are realizing more than ever before that motivating students to meet high standards is not accomplished through tedious, repetitious assignments. Success is achieved through figuring out what makes things work, finding pieces of the puzzle, sharing knowledge, and asking questions. Will my idea work? Who else knows about this? Students check the Net, read recent articles, download a piece of research. They use information in their work; they get feedback and try again as they build their knowledge base. Educators are faced with structuring a culture within a classroom, a school, and a system of public education that allows each student to demonstrate his or her learning. As teachers structure the culture of the classroom, the values they teach and the processes for research, reflection, collaboration, and technology assistance must reflect their own learning in the school setting. In essence, new teachers and principals will become far more demanding when they interview for positions. They will ask, "Where will I find a school that encourages collaboration, continuous learning, team teaching, action research, reflective listening?" Schools and districts that fall short of these expectations will not be able to hire or retain good teachers.

The Third Myth

Administrators do not believe that all teachers will come to personal decisions that, in order for today's students to be successful, curriculum and strategies need to be different from what teachers saw when they were students in the classroom. Some principals have said that they won't live long enough for all teachers to have this revelation. Some teachers feel the same way about their administrators. That's why building a community of learners culture, which we will discuss in Chapter 3, is so important. Even the most knowledgeable teacher struggles to match content with pedagogy. When the struggle is not part of the culture and is therefore not part of the professional development program, the teacher's personal frustration may be submerged into a pattern of "getting by." The difficulties of students may be interpreted as, "I taught the standards, but they just didn't learn them. Oh well, maybe next year's students will be brighter." Copouts are not tolerated in a learning community.

Learners are continuously asking questions about how to be more effective, and they rely on sharing with their colleagues to explore options. How can acknowledgment of their struggles be a key to professional development? Simply expressed, understanding the complexities of the challenge may be motivation for learning. Adults learn primarily on need-to-know criteria. A young high school teacher preparing his first lesson plans may draw from personal experiences in high school and from a textbook about planning lessons. When reality hits and he is facing 80 to 150 students in a day, his requirements change. This is when he needs coaching, because he now has a need to go broader:

♦ What if students don't have the background for my assignments?

♦ What homework will be meaningful?

♦ What if, in collecting data, the computers don't function? Do students understand the processes well enough to continue the research?

♦ What if they don't learn what I teach?

He will soon go deeper:

♦ What is the expected level of student competence to meet the standards?

♦ Will this plan help a student achieve competence?

♦ Are the performance tasks related to the standards?

♦ Will students be able to demonstrate their competence in meeting the standards through the performance tasks I have helped design?

♦ Have I examined student work against exemplars to inform my work?

♦ Do my students understand the expected level of competence?

♦ Will this plan challenge students to a higher level of achievement?

Having an experienced teacher who is trusted by beginning teachers as a reflector and mentor is a luxury, because when teachers need to know, they may not have access to a response that is both timely and appropriate. Even when districts have the foresight to assign a mentor to new teachers, they often do not consider the importance of having the mentor and the new teacher share strategies in a safe environment. Mentors need to have the knowledge and skills to be equipped to focus on teacher quality. New teachers also come with a wealth of knowledge from their recent experiences as students and practicing teachers. At a seminar for elementary teachers, we asked how many had sought the advice of their new teachers about how to connect with students, how to bring new technology to the classroom, or how to relate to single parents. Not 1 in a room of 36 teachers raised a hand. Shared knowledge, it seemed, was a one-way street. "This is my knowledge and I will share it with you" was the way teaching seemed to work.

That is not to say that a beginning teacher doesn't need assistance. They do not come to their classrooms with a built-in cycle of inquiry that takes them from problem to analysis, to plans, to implementation, to data analysis, to a repeat of the cycle. A teacher struggling with pedagogy wants strategies, content, opportunities for reflection and practice, coaching, ways to assess, and—eventually—a sense of mastery so that the next struggle is not so overwhelming. But that isn't all. They want information about how to manage their classrooms, order supplies, determine grades, stay calm, and *survive*. No teacher arrives at a school prepared with all the knowledge and strategies they need for a lifetime of teaching. Continuous professional development for this reason is so very important.

The Uses and Misuses of Professional Development Practices Around Standards

Standards are the theme of this chapter in part because of the uses and misuses of professional development practices around standards for both new and experienced teachers. Policies about how to demand student success or to levy sanctions against those students and their teachers who aren't successful are crafted by lawmakers, often without consulting educators on the front lines. The trend to nationalize the curriculum responds to the public's growing concern about how much, or how little, students are learning in the public schools. Requiring specific content and performance standards to ensure that each student who is graduated successfully meets these rigorous standards has become the goal of public education. The common complaint of "Why aren't kids learning the basics in the public school?" is really a plea for standards. The norm-referenced test with publicly distributed test scores is the next piece of the plan for accountability, because the standardized test reveals each school's success as measured against every other school in the district, state, or nation.

The use of standards is intended to cause a massive rethinking of past and future practices. Aligning curriculum and instruction so that every student is prepared to meet standards may not have been a part of a teacher's preparation at the university. It is therefore the responsibility of districts and schools to do the work of moving teachers from awareness to practice, mastery, and refinement, not only of teaching to the standards, but also of refining the system-wide implications of their enactment.

Understanding content and performance standards that are developed by external entities isn't a high priority with teachers unless the opportunity to examine, make professional decisions about, and personally practice the strategies are part of their ongoing professional development. When teachers acknowledge the dissonance between what they know and what they need to know, they will be prepared for professional learning.

Linda Darling-Hammond (1997b) reported on different effects of two approaches as seen in Kentucky and Vermont:

> Both states set out in the late 1980's to create performance-based assessment systems that would allow more thoughtful evaluation of student learning on more challenging and authentic measures. However, Kentucky's system was framed by a punitive account-ability structure that proposed rewards for schools whose average scores improved by specific ratios each year and sanctions for those whose scores did not improve to the level specified in the statute. Vermont's system was launched with the goal of measuring and reporting student learning, and using the results to focus attention on how instructional improvement should be pursued. The wide involvement of educators in designing and implementing the assessments and a more appropriate use of stakes have made it a powerful tool for improving teaching. (pp. 241-242)

Although there were several differences in the approaches of Kentucky and Vermont, the most significant seemed to be focused on student and teacher learning:

> Vermont's experience illustrates a very different approach, in which a smaller number of performance assessments at a few key developmental points are used to inform educators about student progress. The state assessments include both "on demand" performance tasks and portfolios that are used throughout the school year so that teachers and students can learn from assessment results and continually improve their work. (Darling-Hammond, 1997b, p. 243)

Darling-Hammond (1997b) then points out the very significant choices teachers were then prepared to make about their own professional needs:

> The primary goal is to use assessments and reporting systems to create rich longitudinal information about students' work and progress that supports thoughtful analysis of what is working well and what needs additional attention. . . . Recent evidence indicates that the assessments, along with professional development opportunities associated with them, are positively affecting instruction and stimulating school improvement. (Darling-Hammond, 1997b, pp. 243-245)

Incorporating a set of standards into a teacher's daily work is a major thrust, which requires time to develop and align in a complex system of planning, teaching, assessing, reflecting, redesigning, and starting the cycle once again. Experienced practitioners make daily judgments about student work based on what they deem essential. Advanced Placement high school teachers responsible for students taking national exams for college and university credit use the content articulated by the exam's publishers to focus their curriculum. Students who pass the tests obtain advanced credit and therefore meet the standard. Academies within high schools also appear to be more specific about their exit criteria. Other teachers and their students may not be as clear about their goals or their curriculum as it aligns with the goals. With the new emphasis on standards, both students and educators are accountable for achievement, and failure to meet the standards is a challenge to be met in a way that benefits all students.

Where to Be Fluid and Where to Hold Fast

Where should the program be fluid? Where should districts hold fast? Designing a professional development program with a standards-based accountability system, as educators know, is not an easy or speedy process. The district's superintendent and board need to be very clear about holding to the standards as a way of assessing the achievement and progress of every student in the district, and they need to communicate very clearly what the standards are. A district or school can be flexible about how to embed standards in the curriculum and how they will determine the acceptable performance of each standard; however, the outcome is the same regardless of where the process begins. Each student in the district will meet the standards. As performance standards are developed by states to assess the standards, teachers will continue to be responsible for the preparation of students to demonstrate their competencies.

Analyzing the existing curriculum is an excellent place to begin the standards work. One cohort group of school teams started with each teacher's preparing a mind map with student learning in the center. Teachers were asked by the facilitator what they had learned that improved their instruction and the ability of students to learn content and processes. Some focused on a new math program or a specific teaching strategy. Others pointed to strategies for second-language learners. Next, they transferred the learnings to a timeline on a large wall map.

It was helpful to limit the large map to the past 5 years, with a space reading "before this time" to honor the experiences of older staff. First, teachers put themselves on the graphic according to when they personally had come to the school. After teachers completed their personal timeline and transferred the information to larger wall map, the facilitator announced that they would come back to this at their next meeting. In the interim, the map was placed in the faculty room with pens available so that teachers could add to the map as they thought of all they had learned over the previous 5 years. Individual learning was also important, so teachers added their names or initials behind the significant learnings, even if they were the only ones to participate. They went back to the graphic and highlighted professional development events attended by the majority of the faculty in the previous 5 years. The added knowledge revealed in the graphic enabled the staff to develop a more complete picture of the school and district efforts to date.

They focused on the following reflective questions:

♦ What have you learned?

♦ What are the patterns of your learning?

♦ Has the school's professional development been focused on one area?

♦ Has the district advocated a significant progression of teaching concepts, or has the way been sprinkled with unrelated events?

♦ Have teachers been involved in learning new skills and strategies over time?

♦ Was coaching a part of the plan?

♦ Was collaboration time a part of the plan?

♦ Who were the coaches? Are they still in those roles?

♦ Did participating teachers develop mastery to build the internal capacity of the district? Was this built in as part of the plan?

♦ Did the focus change with a change in administration, or was the learning consistent regardless of leadership changes?

The principal was able to evaluate how his or her predecessors had supported professional growth experiences by reflecting on the answers to these questions as they pertained to other leaders and then to himself or herself. An excellent exercise for principals and teacher leaders is to add "Why or why not?" to the above list. The information gained from this personal research will aid principals in determining how best to support standards-based instruction at the site.

This was also an opportunity to test the district's commitment to a standards-based system for professional teaching and learning.

♦ How does what is on the map relate to a standards-based accountability system?

♦ When did the district adopt content standards?

- ◆ Were teacher, school, and district assessments related to the standards?

- ◆ Did teachers examine student work related to the standards?

These significant findings paved the way for the next steps in the process. Notice the questions that look for alignment of the curriculum with professional learning. This is an issue that is sometimes overlooked by administrators and teacher leaders. Veteran educators remember all too well the professional development activities that had nothing to do with their teaching. People talked at them, and some impressed the audience with their knowledge, but so often that investment of district dollars and human resources never touched a student's life.

Design

When leaders embed standards in the curriculum, they must remember that the greater purpose of professional development design is student achievement. The goal is that standards, as part of a strategic design, will drive the curriculum. The assumption behind the goal is that when standards are reflected in the teaching, learning, and assessment processes, every student will know, understand, and be able to meet the expectations of the school and the school community. These issues, however, must be addressed through a systems approach using connections; relationships; the flow of information; the structures of time; and the identification of each group's role in the process, including students, parents, faculty, community, and the board of education.

The same principle applies to teachers in the system. Teachers must know, understand, and be able to assess the standards that they embed in the curriculum. Because teachers understand the process, they will plan backward from the standards assessment in order to determine their priorities in the classroom. The ability to assess also means that teachers have examined exemplars of student work for each of the standards with their colleagues so that they have a depth of knowledge about expectations for their students. None of this will work if the teachers don't know their content. Teachers' knowledge of content and of how they will assess student learning is what will drive their curricula.

Do teachers conclude that district standards are etched in stone and can no longer be influenced? Do they perceive that their professionalism as teachers, responsible for both curriculum and student learning, no longer matters? Do they feel that when testing comes from the outside, their assessment of individual students no longer has a place in the system? If the answer to these questions is a resounding "Yes!" then the process will fail or, at the very least, will result in polarizing the staff, with unproductive results.

Contrary to what some state administrators—who view standards as the same as building codes—would have us believe, standards are the result of a collaborative process at the district and site levels. Their implementation needs interactive processes to keep them alive in the system. As teachers form their own concepts of how to teach to the standards and from the standards, they share their perspectives with principals and colleagues, and the standards take on the clarity of a shared vision.

The system components associated with standards are important:

1. Teachers use standards and performance assessment as the basis for their everyday classroom planning. Standards drive the curriculum.

2. Parents hear the language of standards and assessment used by all educators in the district as the foundation of teaching and learning in every grade level, in every content area, in every school.

3. Students know what is expected of them and how their work will be assessed.

4. Teachers and administrators communicate to parents why standards are important, which standards their children will be expected to meet, and the expected performance as evidence of their success.

5. As students and parents see evidence that the standards are attainable, the conversation about what the student has accomplished and what he or she needs to accomplish takes on added importance.

6. As teachers recognize each student's performance, the enthusiasm caused by individual achievement will be self-reinforcing.

Analysis

Teachers start with the standards and how they will be assessed. They plan backward using student assessment as their guide. Once they have decided how the standards will be assessed, they align their curriculum with the appropriate benchmarks to the assessment. If they have not developed specific performance tasks based on the standards or benchmarked their activities toward achieving specific standards, they will need time to complete these tasks. Collaborative time is a major consideration as teachers perform their assessments, examine student work, select exemplars, and use the exemplars with students so that everyone is very clear about what the expectations are. Looking at the resulting student data is a critical piece of

❖ **FIGURE 2.4. System components associated with standards.**

- Standards and performance assessment are the basis for everyday classroom planning.

- The language of standards and assessment is used by all educators as the foundation of teaching and learning at every grade level, in every content area, in every school.

- Students know what is expected of them and how their work will be assessed.

The Purpose Is to Improve Student Achievement

- Teachers and administrators communicate to parents why standards are important, what standards their children are expected to meet, and the expected performance that will be evidence of their success.

- Students and parents understand that standards are attainable by seeing evidence of what the student has accomplished and what needs to be accomplished.

- Teachers recognize each student's performance knowing that enthusiasm caused by individual achievement will be self-reinforcing.

teachers' professional growth, because doing so will tell the instructors what parts of the curriculum need to be adjusted, abandoned, or rewritten. An important component of the process is that teachers decide how professional development in the school or district will help to fill in the gaps of their knowledge and skills to do this very complex work.

Pitfalls and Strategies

Implementing a standards-based system is challenging, difficult, and rewarding work. Principals and teacher leaders should foresee troubled waters when the faculty is in transition. Ideally, knowing some of the pitfalls can better prepare leaders for working through some of the more common difficulties (see Table 2.1, Pitfalls and Strategies for Implementing a Standards-Based System, for a summary).

1. Teachers may be confused about district, state, and national standards. Which standards are *the* standards? In a professional development setting, facilitators should schedule an opportunity for review and discussion of the different sets of standards, the exemplars, and the assessments. Teachers should know how they are similar, how each has components teachers can use, and how each integrates the assessment performance into the curriculum. Some schools have presented to the faculty only the standards they intend to use so that they don't "muddy the waters." Because the national standards have so many well-designed components, including examples of student work, curriculum leaders at every level need opportunities to review them with their clusters of teachers, and districts need to make them available in a reference library for professional use. Districts should not deny all the research that went into the documents to teachers who wish to examine the different standards to inform their own professional practices.

2. Individuals or the group may jump to the attitude of "Why have standards?" As time becomes more closely guarded, education will always have principals who want to "just do it!" When schools are developing learning communities, leaders will assign time to this topic for a full discussion so that teachers will know why they are professionally responsible for developing strategies so that *all* students perform to meet the standards. They will understand both the public's demands and how educators have responded. To those teachers who don't think it is possible for all students to meet standards, the leaders can draw examples from other participants. Successful strategies for bringing low-performing students up to standard do not emerge from a vacuum. Every teacher has strategies that work for some students, some of the time. That is why collaborative

discussions are essential to a learning community, so that teachers can build on the knowledge and expertise of colleagues.

3. The discussion feels abstract and isolated from concrete next steps. After spending time with young teachers who are raising families and starting teaching careers while dealing with the ordinary stresses of other people, including medical emergencies, transportation problems, and computer-generated snarls, principals should be prepared for impatience at whatever does not relate to the classroom. From a philosophical foundation, leaders should move quickly to looking at specific standards for content at grade levels relevant to the participants. Teachers with busy schedules will want to get into the specifics of "my classes" and "what I can or will do." Teachers who are ready will then move to grades above and below so that they have an idea of the expectations in both directions.

4. Statements about the standards blame young people or are based on an assumption that there's nothing that the teachers can do (e.g., "those kids just don't try, they don't want to learn"). Asking teachers to think of the names of one student who is sailing through the requirements and one who is struggling will help ground them in the expectations of specific standards appropriate to the grade level. Leaders can then brainstorm strategies in small groups for teaching one standard or one small component of a standard to a low-performing student. The professionalism of teachers is positively challenged when the learning of a targeted student is at stake.

5. The discussion keeps returning to the resources we need instead of the curriculum we are looking at together. Teachers will return to the needs that they have, because resources are often insufficient to accomplish the work. It is natural that they should want the best resources for the tasks ahead. Leaders understand that the needs of one staff member may or may not reflect a priority of needs of all teachers, and usually the distribution of resources does not allow for granting each teacher's requests. Chart the needs that arise, prioritize them, and get consensus for referral to the leadership team that monitors the budget. Continue with the group, using texts and resources currently available.

6. The discussion gets stuck on how to keep records on standards or components of the standards met by individual students. Chart the record-keeping needs and share with other schools. Often other teachers have developed strategies for record keeping that they can share with colleagues. Some districts have revised their report cards to align with a standards-based system. They have involved the teachers in the process and have agreed to field test before fully adopting the new system. Several software programs are geared to the National Standards and their record keeping. Sometimes a resource person in the school, district, or regional

TABLE 2.1 Pitfalls and Strategies for Implementing a Standards-Based System

Common Pattern	Strategy
1. Teachers may be confused about district, state, and national standards.	1. Provide opportunities to review standards, exemplars, and assessments of the three sets.
2. Individuals or the group may jump to "why have standards?"	2. Assign time to this topic for a full discussion of why educators are responsible for developing strategies so that all students perform to meet the standards. Draw examples from participants of successful strategies used to bring low-performing students up to standard.
3. The discussion feels abstract and isolated from concrete next steps.	3. Look at specific standards for content and grade levels relevant to participants. Teachers with busy schedules will want to get into the specifics of "my classes" and "what I can or will do."
4. Statements about the standards blame young people or are based on an assumption that there's nothing teachers can do (e.g., "those kids just don't try, they don't want to learn")	4. Ask teachers to name students and match them with specific standards appropriate to their grade level. Brainstorm with your group strategies for teaching one standard to that student. The professionalism of teachers is positively challenged when the learning of a targeted student is at stake.
5. The discussion keeps returning to the resources we need instead of the curriculum we are looking at together.	5. Chart the needs that arise, prioritize, and reach consensus. Refer to budget review team. Continue by using texts and resources currently available.

6. The discussion gets stuck on how to keep records on standards or components of the standards met by individual students.	6. Chart the record-keeping needs. Several software programs are geared to the National Standards and their record keeping. Some districts have revised their report cards to align with a standards-based system.
7. People want to see what other schools and districts have done to revise their curricula to meet the standards.	7. Chart these needs. Teachers will never know what is out there if they don't ask. Participants should be aware, however, that setting priorities among the standards is a district and school responsibility. Also, as teachers successfully devise content and strategies to address the standards, the curriculum will change.
8. Teachers are confused about how to use content and assessment in their teaching to support standards.	8. Performance measures of the standards inform instruction. When students are not able to meet the standards, teachers will examine student work to determine if content and instructional strategies should be revised so that students will be successful.
9. The group is hesitant to say things because teachers don't want to be blamed for student performance. This prevents honest dialogue and examination of the data.	9. Reconnect to the norms you established with the group about being open and not blaming. Emphasize that the purpose of working with standards is to help students. This is important work that needs our best unrestricted thinking.
10. The group feels depressed by the enormity of the task.	10. Start with sharing successful strategies used at a time when students were motivated and able to achieve. Build on these successes when teachers collaborate to rewrite curriculum so that students are able to meet the standards.

service center can research these ideas if schools can clarify their specific needs.

7. People want to see what other schools and districts have done to revise their curriculum to meet the standards. Chart these needs. Teachers will never know what is out there if they don't ask. Teachers may want to search the Internet for schools that have revised their standards-based curriculum. If e-mail addresses are given to teachers and administrators, it will be easy to ask these other schools for information about their processes. Few schools have a sufficient budget to support sending their entire curriculum upon request, so be prepared either to ask for examples or to define what you are requesting when contacting the district office. Often district curriculum and instruction directors have access to other districts' related documents. Participants should be aware, however, that setting priorities among the standards is a district and school responsibility. As teachers successfully devise content and strategies to address the standards, the curriculum will change.

8. Teachers are confused about how to use content and assessment in their teaching to support standards. When teachers say that students have met the standards, student performance is the assessment. These performance tests of the standards will inform instruction. That is, when students are not able to meet a standard, teachers will examine student work to determine if the content and instructional strategies they have used should be revised. Their goal is that students will be successful. Continuously examining curriculum to determine if it supports student success is the work of a teacher. Once again, doing this work in isolation is not the most productive pathway because colleagues, based on their own experiences, can often think of different strategies than what the teacher has used.

9. The group is hesitant to say things because teachers don't want to be blamed for student performance. This prevents honest dialogue and examination of the data. Third-grade teachers, for example, may be reluctant to meet with fourth-grade teachers who in the past have criticized students' lack of preparation coming into the fourth grade as the main cause of failure in their upper-level classes. Blaming serves no useful purpose. It is important to reconnect to the norms the group established at the beginning of school about being open, agreeing to listen, and not blaming others. Leaders who emphasize that the purpose of having standards is to enable all students to achieve set the stage for collaborative efforts. Working from a common vision of student achievement is an important commitment that requires a staff's best, uncluttered thinking.

10. The group feels depressed by the enormity of the task. Those who understand a standards-based system will be very aware of the amount of

work ahead, because prior efforts may not have required that teachers continuously research new approaches to teaching and learning. Teaching to enable all students to meet the standards is a major change in direction. To encourage the faculty, team leaders may start by asking their colleagues to capture successful strategies when students were motivated and able to achieve. Building on these successes when working with standards will enable the faculty to become keenly aware of what helps learning and of what strategies do not work for students. Teachers, discovering gaps in their pedagogy, will commit to seeking new ways to be more effective. In order for all students to meet the standards, the faculty will require many opportunities to collaborate as they examine student work and revise their approaches according to results.

Conclusion

For teachers involved in the everyday business of classroom preparation and teaching content, the thought of doing the work involved in setting standards and assessing them may be overwhelming, especially if they think they must do everything on their own. Establishing a culture of collaboration should lighten the load of standards-based instruction, not add to the weight on the shoulders of professional staff. Teachers should be encouraged to form teams and partnerships for purposes of classroom preparation, implementation, and performance assessment. When they begin to trust each other that the work will be as good as, or better than, they could have done in isolation, the fermentation process will be working. As the district supports these efforts with professional development, including human and financial resources for follow-through strategies, the timeline for implementation of standards in the district will become a reality.

REALITY CHECK

When districts focus on standards for student achievement, how can they be assured that professional development designs support the achievement of the performance goals?

On the Web

Grant Wiggins has one of the best sites (http://ubd.ascd.org/index.html) for working on standards. The Understanding by Design Web site, as developed by Grant Wiggins and Jay McTighe (1998), is complete, user-friendly, and research based in its approach to curricular design.

The Center on Learning, Assessment, and School Structure (*http://www.classdesign.org*) stores and retrieves curricular units, assessment tasks, and rubrics in a searchable database. Viewers are welcome to print any unit, task, or rubric in the database. It also has access to state standards on-line.

In addition to these resources, many states have placed their own standards on-line, where they can be easily accessed through states' departments of education.

Creating the Culture
for a Learning Community

When two teachers walked to their cars after the first day of school, their conversation would have surprised some staffs and alarmed others.

"I'm glad I could come to Redwood Hills after doing my student teaching here last year, but I'm worried. I'm going to have my hands full with this class."

"Oh really? That's too bad."

"Do you think I should ask the third-grade teacher for some ideas? She had most of these kids last year!"

"I wouldn't. She'd say they shouldn't have hired you if you can't do the job."

"Would she really say that about me?"

"Maybe not to your face, but she harped about a new teacher last year, and he's no longer here."

"So where do I go if I need help?"

"Well, I'll help you when I can, but I've never taught fourth grade."

"Thanks, anyway. I'll see what I can find on the Web when I pick up my e-mail tonight. Maybe I can use Google or Yahoo to search for a chat room for new teachers."

"It's worth a try. See you tomorrow."

"Sure. See you tomorrow."

- Pause for a moment to reflect
on this essential question.

ESSENTIAL QUESTION

How will a school design professional
development opportunities and policies that are based on
student achievement while shaping the school culture
and the learning community to sustain the efforts?

Why Do We Have the Conversation?

When the culture of an organization is collaborative, each teacher has a built-in network of support. The role of the leader is not only to select the right people to be part of the organization, but to create an environment where they can succeed. In a learning community, the leader encourages all educators to develop a mind-set of collaboration, shared inquiry, and teamwork and then formalizes the structures necessary to support them. New teachers and teachers new to a system are particularly at risk without a network of support. When the system provides what they need through, for example, coaching, mentoring, buddy systems, university partnerships, collaborative teams, or other on-site programs, the investment a district makes in the new teacher has potential for long-term rewards.

Linda Lambert, Deborah Walker, and their colleagues (1995) point to the new "enlightenment" with the advent of the learning community in the 1980s, which advanced some challenging assumptions, including the fact that achievement is increased when the culture of the school supports learning for both students and adults. They supported the fact that new norms need to be developed that foster collaboration and shared inquiry. The first movement to place a high value on teacher growth linked teacher and student learning. "Collaborative teaching methods that promote learning for all students are applied to the organizational processes that characterize the school, so that the school becomes a learning organization (a continually renewing place to live and work)" (Lambert et al., 1995, p. 15). When a school lives in a culture of learning and working together, not only do educators rely more on each other's strengths, but also they are less reluctant to identify missing expertise. Collaborative interaction is not a sign of lack of knowledge in a professional setting. It is evidence of both faculty strength and a healthy school climate.

Sharon D. Kruse (1999) discusses being a new teacher in the only portable classroom at an elementary school in a Seattle suburb, half a football field away from the rest of the building: "What I gained in autonomy, independence, and opportunity for personal growth, I paid for in a loss of cooperative relationships, collegial support, and collaborative interaction" (p. 14). The second part of her article describes her new learning after she moved from the portable to the main building: "In the 'real' school building teachers may be closer to the bathrooms, but many are no less isolated, alone, and unsupported than I'd been in my portable" (Kruse, 1999, p. 14). The realization was sobering for a new teacher who could project a professional career with no hope of receiving any collegial support in the future.

If we endorse the premises that we are living in chaotic times, that as educators we are isolated, that more is expected of us, and that we expect more from our careers than ever before, what can we do?

One important step is to formalize professional development policies that include collaborative interaction as a part of any new learning. In addition, schools must include collaborative time for teachers and administrators so that these educators have opportunities to be with other professionals. In a university class of 35 teachers, we asked participants to think of a team that they were members of at their site. Two students reported that they were not members of any team. Puzzled, we asked if they were at least part of grade-level or content teams. Again, the answer was negative. Even today, with the widely published research on collaborative inquiry in quality organizations, we still found principals who didn't acknowledge the power of teacher collaboration to improve student learning by formalizing collaborative time.

Educators are seeking a more expansive definition of professional success. The old strategies for teaching and learning aren't enough. More students should be graduating from high school with the skills and knowledge to succeed in their chosen university or career fields. Teachers have to connect successfully with all students and create value in the system for them. These are huge demands on educators of today. Teachers and administrators must not withhold professional expertise from each other. They should be interacting and collaborating locally and nationally to figure out how it is possible for them to serve all the students in their schools.

Who has the time to make all of this happen? No one, unless the expectations, resources, scheduled opportunities, rewards, and recognition for collaborative action are built into school and district culture.

Boards of education and school administrators may push so hard to implement standards and raise test scores that they forget to put equal pressure on the system for high-quality professional learning and a collaborative environment. They are asking teachers to run a race by increasing the stride, yet when the stride gets too long, the heel hits the ground at a bracing angle and acts as a brake to the long-distance runner. When educators strive to teach all standards to all students without professional learning to sharpen their teaching and partnership strategies, their race toward student achievement may act as a brake on their success.

Research and Best Practices

The opportunity to work in a culture of learning and growing is one that has to be shaped by all levels of the organization. Researchers have identified characteristics of a collaborative school culture with norms and expectations that support change and improvement, including the following (Saphier & King, 1985):

- Collegiality with peers

- Experimentation in the workplace

- High expectations for self and students

- Trust and confidence in interactions

- Tangible support from administration and peers

- Reaching out to a knowledge base

- Appreciation and recognition, both personal and professional

- Caring, celebration, and humor in the workplace

- Involvement in decision making at the governance level

- Protection of what's important in the workplace

- Honest, open communication

- Meaningful traditions

Experiences in working with teachers also led the writers to a list of what many teachers cannot or will not do in a school culture. They are reluctant to close down a current system to start another, totally new one. They don't voluntarily change the culture of a school in which they are experienced, comfortable, and secure. They won't envision, develop, implement, and sustain a new culture until there is support in the system for doing so. In impossible situations, we have seen teachers withdraw from leadership positions because of the stressful circumstances of trying to change themselves and their colleagues as they challenge the existing culture of a school. Some lose interest in their profession and seek other outlets for their initiative and creativity; others change positions or take on different roles and responsibilities. A few leave education to try different careers, and others retire early. Educators must understand how to build a culture of learning in which each staff member of the school is simultaneously a teacher, learner, and leader so that every member of the school community is able to demonstrate that his or her school is about learning and success.

The Role of Leaders in a Learning Culture

So what then is the role of the administrator or teacher leader in a learning culture? First, the role of the leader is to put people in touch with their values, the reason they became educators, the reason they chose teaching over business or the other professions, and the reason they are in a school with other professional colleagues. Bringing talk about values to the surface is important in a culture. Thomas Sergiovanni (1992) summarizes,

> The evidence seems clear: self-interest is not powerful enough to account fully for human motivation. We are also driven by what we believe is right and good, by how we feel about things, and by the norms that emerge from our connections with other people. (p. 23)

It is through these values that teachers act in the best interests of students.

Second, a leader must encourage a culture of interactive collaboration and professional networking to be certain that teachers have opportunities to share and benefit from their colleagues' best thinking. We see excellent teachers engaging students in high levels of group learning and performance, but their colleagues, some teaching in the same building, have never had the opportunity to observe each other's classes or learn from peers in a professional environment. "If teachers' interests and motivations lie at the heart of successful efforts to enhance classroom practices, then the professional networks that engage teachers comprise promising vehicles for change" (Lieberman & Miller, 1991, p. 78).

Third, leaders must model effective listening and learning throughout the organization. If we are truly helping students advance in their learning, we must be models as learners. Some of our best teachers may be colleagues engaged in their own action research. Moreover, students need to see how teamwork, collaboration, and action research work for their teachers. As students prepare for multiple careers, they are also preparing for a lifetime of relationships and interactions that would be greatly enhanced by observing their teachers modeling the behaviors that are expected from students. Roland Barth (1990) uses the analogy of an oxygen mask in the airplane. Passengers traveling with small children are instructed to put the oxygen over their own faces first and only then to place the mask on their children's faces. He continues,

> Principals, preoccupied with expected outcomes, desperately want teachers to breathe in new ideas, yet do not themselves engage in visible, serious learning. Teachers badly want their students to learn to perform at grade level, yet seldom reveal themselves to children as learners. (Barth, 1990, p. 42)

In a learning community, people of all generations and all positions are learners, simultaneously.

The Role of Teachers in a Learning Culture

The role of a teacher in a learning culture is to create a climate of high expectations for teachers and students and a culture of working together to achieve the high expectations for both. Teamwork and collaboration are necessary, because the job of an educator in creating and delivering curriculum is too difficult to accomplish alone. Teachers need to reevaluate the time they spend alone preparing to educate students and balance that time with enlisting the best thinking of more than one professional about how to approach a lesson, a unit, or a standard or to help a student who is not prepared to handle the content.

To test our theory about how little many districts currently invest in collaborative activities, we asked teachers in a training seminar to estimate the following:

1. How much time they spent preparing for classes in a week.

2. How much time they spent preparing outside of school in a week.

3. How much time they spent discussing their work with colleagues.

4. How much time they invested in collaboration, dividing their work among colleagues, and discussing the work they received from other team members.

The answers were revealing. When asked how many had spent 50% or more of their class preparation time collaborating with colleagues, the number of hands in a room of 31 teachers was zero. When the question was changed to "How many spend at least 40%, 30%, 20%, of your time collaborating?" still no hands were raised. When the question about the percentage of time dropped to 10% of preparation time in collaboration, we had four raised hands. All others spent less than 10% of their preparation time in collaboration.

How should we have predicted these findings? We could have looked at how these teachers came through the educational system or their struggles with "cooperative learning" as a teaching strategy. Teachers were embarrassed to admit that they couldn't "control a class" or that they had given too many high grades. How others prepared for teaching, taught integrated units, or assessed cooperative learning were often well-guarded secrets.

Teaching has often been referred to as a lonely profession. In fact, Leiberman and Miller (1991) state,

> It is no longer necessary to comment on the isolation factor in relation to teaching. For too long, teachers, unlike most other professionals, have been compartmentalized, much like workers in a cottage industry, with few opportunities for meaningful and sustained interactions with one another. (pp. 249-250)

The truth is that the teachers we questioned did not collaborate as a strategy for classroom preparation. Did they prefer not to collaborate; did they not know how to effectively collaborate; did they have no consistent opportunity to collaborate, as Lieberman and Miller (1991) confirmed in their research; or did they just not value collaboration as a link to classroom effectiveness? Whatever the reason, the conclusions were clear: Collaborations were not a norm in this district, and without an intensive effort and support on the part of the administrators and faculty leaders, the comfortable pattern of isolation established from years of modeling and practice would not be broken. The reasons for teachers to collaborate must be so compelling that teachers will be willing to stretch beyond their paradigm of professional expectations, beyond the boundaries they have set for their collegial involvement.

Evidence of a Learning Community

So how does one create the culture of a learning community? One exasperated teacher was very cynical: "A learning community as opposed to what?" he asked. Underlying this comment was his claim that schools have always been learning communities. We, the authors, disagree. Schools are too often filled with private practitioners who infrequently communicate about student learning. In one middle school, the young teachers were so concerned about their isolation in the classroom that they started weekly meetings. They even identified their need by referring to the participants as a support group. Topics varied from "What are the laws regarding a student's right to privacy when a teacher discusses every detail of his learning problems, including his family history, for all staff and guests to hear in the faculty room?" to "Why is talking about diversity in our school a taboo subject? Is it really because 'it isn't an issue' or is it because we don't want to discuss the teacher's role in student failure?" In a learning community, the questions would be placed in front of the entire staff for dialogue and inquiry to occur. In essence, a staff that does not seek opportunities to discuss the big issues of teaching and learning is operating in a learning vacuum.

It is also very obvious to the authors when introducing new concepts to educators whether the educators' intent is to learn or to protect themselves from any learning that might disrupt the way they teach or administer the schools. The signs of a learning school community are observable to everyone, because they are deeply embedded in a school's culture. They form evidence of a learning community because they shape the environment in which teachers are learners and also leaders. The overview presented in Figure 3.1, Evidence of a Culture of Learning, will help teachers and principals see how all the practices fit together to form a learning community that is deeply embedded in the culture of the school.

Evidence of a Culture of Learning Survey

How do educators define evidence of a culture of learning? They look for actions in their schools that reveal the tremendous energy generated by a staff continuously engaged in learning. School leaders can use the Evidence of a Culture of Learning Survey (Table 3.1) as a way to heighten awareness of staff about what it takes to be a learning community.

Educators living and working in a learning community could add many more practices to the above list. A learning community evolves, just as individuals continue to grow, change, and reshape themselves based on their new learning.

A learning community is a natural extension of professional effectiveness for teachers and principals. Educators are aware of the larger system that they need to connect with, but they may not be aware of the advan-

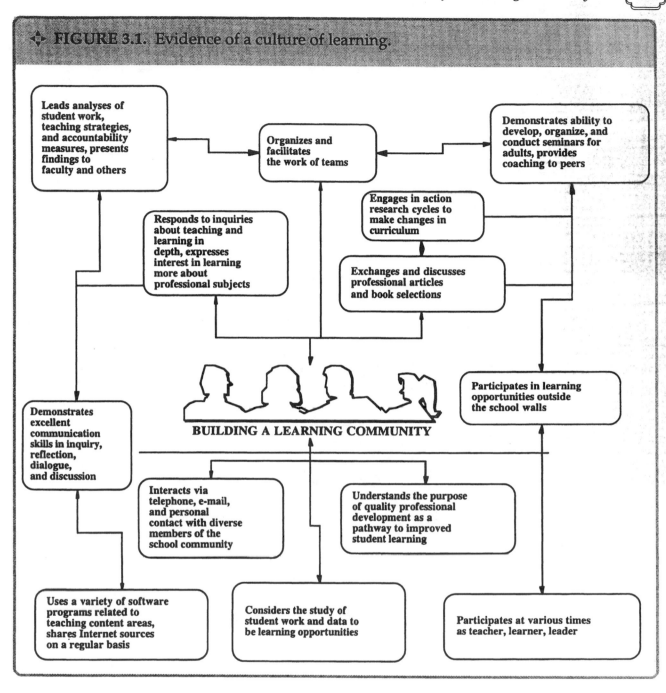

❖ FIGURE 3.1. Evidence of a culture of learning.

tages of building a learning community that reaches beyond the school grounds in order to increase student achievement. What a tremendous opportunity to walk the talk of education by modeling teaching and learning at every level. There are some challenges to engaging others in a commitment to build a learning community. Principals and teachers have committed their professional energies to increasing student achievement through working with their faculties and their communities to build and sustain this support system for students. The 10 pitfalls discussed in the fol-

TABLE 3.1   Evidence of a Culture of Learning Survey

Directions: For each question, circle the number that best represents the answer as it relates to the current professional development program in your school or district based on the following scale:
1 = never; 2 = seldom; 3 = usually; 4 = always.

	Never	Seldom	Usually	Always
1. Do faculty members lead analyses of student work, student learning, and student success in relation to the standards; facilitate discussions of teaching strategies and accountability measures; and present findings to faculty and other members of the school community?	1	2	3	4
2. Is there evidence of the faculty's excellent communication skills in reflection, inquiry, dialogue, and discussion?	1	2	3	4
3. When teachers use a variety of software programs related to teaching content areas, do they share sources and Web sites on a regular basis?	1	2	3	4
4. Do teachers and administrators respond to inquiries about teaching and learning in depth or express the need to learn more about professional subjects?	1	2	3	4
5. Do teacher leaders have a demonstrated ability to organize, develop, and conduct training for adults? A willingness to provide coaching to peers?	1	2	3	4
6. Do teachers feel a shared responsibility for each other's learning?	1	2	3	4
7. Do faculty members demonstrate the ability to interact via telephone, e-mail, and personal contact with all other members of the school community, including classified staff, peer teachers, and administrators, as well as parents and other community members?	1	2	3	4

lowing section are built on their experiences and on some of the actions they took to meet the challenges.

Challenging Common Pitfalls to Building a Learning Community

In schools and districts, leaders may see subcultures forming that are unhealthy for the organization. In schools, one manifestation is individuals' exerting their energies against what the school as a whole has defined as its purpose, for example, improving student achievement. At the begin-

TABLE 3.1 Continued

	Never	Seldom	Usually	Always
8. Do teacher leaders organize and facilitate the work of teams?	1	2	3	4
9. Do teachers engage in action research cycles to make changes in their curriculum?	1	2	3	4
10. Do faculty members consider the study of student work in relation to the standards and student data as learning opportunities? As quality professional development?	1	2	3	4
11. Do teachers and administrators exchange and discuss professional articles and book selections? When the training is in the school and teachers or administrators are asked to read a selection and identify concepts that will inform their work, do they participate?	1	2	3	4
12. Do staff members demonstrate that their involvement in quality professional development is a pathway to improved student learning?	1	2	3	4
13. Do faculty members demonstrate the ability to develop, organize, and conduct seminars for adults and provide peer-coaching opportunities?	1	2	3	4
14. Do staff members participate in learning opportunities outside the school walls?	1	2	3	4
15. Do teachers and administrators participate as teachers, learners, and leaders?	1	2	3	4

ning of the standards movement, for example, some faculty members decided that what they were doing in their classrooms was more important than teaching to the standards. Initially, they did not believe that standards benefited students. They later understood that by having the entire district focus on students' meeting standards, students were, in fact, guaranteed a quality education from every teacher in every school. Understanding the rationale, most teachers subsequently discarded their objections and joined collaborative efforts to preserve the best of what they were doing while embedding the standards and assessments into the curriculum. Few educators would say that they are in the profession for other reasons than to help students be successful. The first line of reasoning, therefore, should be "What is the benefit to students?" There are other pitfalls to building a learning community (see Table 3.2, Challenging Common Pitfalls to Building a Learning Community).

TABLE 3.2   Challenging Common Pitfalls in Building a Learning Community

Common Pattern	Strategy
1. The same people discredit the discussion of changing our school's culture to become a learning community.	1. First, be clear about the purpose—to improve student learning by modeling learning. When the discussion is focused on how we learn instead of how we need to change, the energy will be positively placed. After addressing how we learn, identify how one would know if this were a "learning" school. Then you can identify what is in place now and what needs to happen.
2. The group or particular individuals are stuck on "the way we do things around here."	2. Be very concrete about "the way WE do things," and be specific about who is included and who is not in the we. When faculty understand "privilege"—who has it and who does not, who agrees with them and who does not—they will be more receptive to new ideas.
3. The discussion about culture feels abstract and isolated from our school.	3. Take the culture survey (Table 3.1) available for schools to use in the initial determination of a need to change. Using an instrument developed externally will provide a helpful objectivity when it is time to study the data.
4. Decisions based on who is valued and who is not are damaging to students.	4. In small groups, review major decisions of the last 2 to 3 years and pull out the assumptions on which they were based. Then test the "assumptions" made by the small group with the rest of the faculty. You must use data to validate your conclusions.
5. The discussion keeps coming back to how poor the students are and how the parents don't really care about their kids.	5. Use data to substantiate the concerns. Is it a valid assumption that parents who fail to attend 8-to-5 parent meetings don't care about their children? Look at data and ask parents who can speak personally to errors in reasoning to attend the meeting.

A common concern in attempting to build a learning community is that some staff members discredit the concept. Using the same approach of asking the question "What will benefit students?" is as valid for building a learning community as it is for embedding standards in the curriculum. First, leaders must be clear about the purpose—to improve student learning by modeling learning. When the discussion is focused on how we learn instead of how we need to change, the energy can be positively placed. After addressing the issues around how adults and students learn, the staff can identify how outsiders would know if this were a "learning" school. As the conversation progresses, the faculty can identify what is in place now and what needs to happen.

A second pitfall is that sometimes individuals are stuck in "the way we do things around here." Leaders should be very concrete about "the way

TABLE 3.2   Continued

Common Pattern	*Strategy*
6. People don't want to hear about what other schools and districts have done to change their cultures.	6. Facts are very helpful. Conduct a survey of the school community about their perceptions of the school. Ask them the location of the best school in the state. Then invite a number of new community members and new faculty to talk about first impressions of your school. People must first see a need to change before they will look at how to change.
7. The group is confused about how to help students learn by changing the school culture.	7. Chart the attributes of an ideal community, one in which every person is a learner. Ask, "What would you see? How would students improve their achievement if all were learners? What models would they need?"
8. The group is hesitant to say things that might be taken as offensive to teachers who have been at the school for a long time.	8. Open communications are free of put-downs, and at the same time, they offer an equal voice to everyone in the room. Use an outside facilitator and prompt him or her to give equal weight to voices heard in the room. Charting responses and looking for patterns is also helpful.
9. Most teachers are disconnected from the school community.	9. Use your school advisory council or any group with involvement from both faculty and community to address this concern. Discuss ways to bring the faculty and community together to learn from each other, and be clear about expectations that this will happen.
10. The press continuously criticizes the school and its environment.	10. Develop good relationships with education reporters. How do other schools get better press? Work with the faculty and school community about how to turn this around.

WE do things." They will have to be specific about who is and is not included in the *we*. When faculty members understand "privilege"—who has it and who does not or who agrees with them and who does not—they may be more receptive to new ideas. Senior teachers get used to the benefits of knowing how a system operates and of therefore being able to use it or circumvent it. Sometimes they do not see that they are excluding others from professional decision making by using their influence against new ideas. That is exactly why the learning community concept, where everyone learns from everyone else, is so critical to a healthy organization. The continuous efforts of leaders to surface new ways of thinking and acting to benefit students are the building blocks of an open, learning school community.

A third pitfall is that the discussion of a learning community feels too abstract and isolated from the daily work of schools. Data are always useful because they take the discussion from what individuals say in a faculty meeting to looking at what everyone believes to be true about the school. Leaders can offer a survey about how adults in the school function as leaders and learners. Table 3.1, Evidence of a Culture of Learning Survey, for example, determines a need for change. Using an instrument developed externally will provide helpful objectivity when it is time to study the resulting data.

Some teachers have admitted that they are deeply concerned about the learning of those students who want to learn and that they are a little concerned about students who don't express the same interest. The fourth pitfall of a learning community—problems with who is valued and who is not—can be damaging to students. This bias becomes the basis of many decisions in the school, especially regarding additional opportunities for students as well as the treatment of absences and disciplinary measures. One way to face the biases in a school is through using professional development time to review major decisions of the last 2 to 3 years with those who were involved and affected. Small groups can pull out the assumptions on which the decisions were based. Then they can test the assumptions made by their small group with the rest of the faculty. For example, did adding more "time-out" periods for disciplinary reasons cause changes in student or teacher behavior? All must use data to validate their conclusions. As faculty develop more trust, they can engage in the same process regarding decisions made by the faculty that have affected teachers in various ways. Locating the missing voices at a school is one way to begin rebuilding the culture to focus on the achievement of all students.

Blaming is out of place in a learning community, yet it is difficult for humans to resist blaming others for the current state of affairs. The fifth pitfall to building a learning community is teachers' blaming parents. Using data to substantiate concerns about unsupportive parents is important to all teachers who blame parents for students' lack of performance in the classroom. For parents who fail to attend 8-to-5 parent meetings, is the assumption valid that they don't care about their children? An open dialogue with parents, who can speak personally about attitudes in the community, should lead to ideas about how school and community members can collaborate to resolve the issues. This collaboration is a way for educators, students, and parents to learn together for the common purpose of improving student achievement.

The sixth pitfall is that some educators resist hearing about what other schools and districts have done to change their culture. They are only concerned about their unique school. Using a survey that involves students' and community members' responses to questions about the school is a helpful place to start. The leadership team could conduct a survey of the school community about perceptions of the school. They could ask community members the location of the best school in the state and how they personally identified the "best." They could then invite a number of new community members and new faculty to talk openly about first impressions of their current school. After recording the data, the team will meet to look for patterns. People must first see a need to change before they will look at how to change.

Staff may be confused about how to help students learn by changing the school culture. This dilemma is the seventh pitfall to building a learning community. In response, the facilitators can chart the attributes of an ideal community where every person is a learner. "What would you see the principal and teachers doing? What would you see students doing? How would other staff members and parents demonstrate their learning? How would students improve their achievement if all were learners? What models would they need?" Working from a clear, shared vision of the ideal helps to clarify the goal.

When members of the group are hesitant to say things that might be taken as offensive to teachers who have been at the school for a long time, the pitfall may be that individuals don't feel as if they have status in the school. Open communications are free of put-downs and also offer an equal voice to everyone in the room. Openness also means that people are committed to learning communication skills that will help them discuss what is best for students without offending others or accepting fault. The intent is not that the faculty will agree or remain silent, but that they will know how to disagree without being disagreeable. At times, it helps to use an outside facilitator who is prompted to give equal weight to voices heard in the room. Charting responses and looking for patterns are helpful processes when seeking objectivity about highly charged issues.

The ninth pitfall is when teachers are disconnected from the school community. Leaders can use the school advisory council or any group with involvement from both faculty and community to address this concern. They should discuss ways to bring the faculty and community together to learn from each other. It is important for leaders to be clear about expectations that this will happen. The learning community is not composed of a select group. The entire school community's teaching and learning efforts will prepare them to sustain their focus on student achievement.

The 10th pitfall to building a learning community is when the press continuously criticizes the school. It's difficult to be open to a community when the media report the worst about the school environment. As the school staff builds its culture, leaders must also develop good relationships with education reporters. Faculty, principals, and community leaders can research how to get better press. This is another opportunity for collaboration, as members learn together how to rebuild their school's image in support of students and their place of learning.

Meeting the challenges of public education is the work of professional educators. When the work is the most challenging, the desire to succeed takes on an intensity that keeps educators moving through the rough times. The work is too important and too challenging for an individual or school to tackle alone. Building a learning community is like weaving a safety net for students that will also "catch" educators who occasionally waver at the heights of teaching and learning.

What a tremendous task to sift through new knowledge about teaching strategies, learning patterns, and content-specific information and at the same time to stay in touch with all the environmental changes that have profound effects on students and their learning. Some educators assume that the challenge to reform their schools into learning communities is too great. It is a challenge worth accepting, however, because the consequences of stagnant school communities are too damaging to students. When Roland Barth first revealed his personal vision of a good school in 1990, he built his community on the concept of continuous learning:

> A major responsibility of adults in a community of learners is to actively engage in their own learning, to make their learning visible to youngsters and to other adults alike, to enjoy and celebrate this learning and to sustain it over time even—especially—when swamped by the demands of others and by their work. (Barth, 1990, p. 162)

Our Learning Horizons

When Peter Senge's *The Fifth Discipline: The Art and Practice of the Learning Organization* was published in 1990, he explored the delusion of learning from experience:

> But what happens when we can no longer observe the consequences of our actions? What happens if the primary consequences of our actions are in the distant future or in a distant part of the larger system within which we operate? We each have a "learning horizon," a breadth of vision in time and space within which we assess our effectiveness. When our actions have consequences beyond our learning horizon, it becomes impossible to learn from direct experience. (Senge, 1990, p. 23)

The struggle to build a learning culture for schools may be the result of this myopia, not caring to see the consequences of our actions. We cannot assume that one teacher's failure with a student will be remedied at some later time in some other classroom or, worse yet, that it doesn't matter. Before schools had standards in place, middle school teachers may not have been overly concerned that students were failing in high school. With standards, we now see our responsibility for ensuring a student's success no matter where he or she is in the system. Students must demonstrate their learning, because the schools hold them accountable so that they will enter the next phase of their academic preparation with the skills, knowledge, and performance capability expected of them. When students were passed from one grade level to the next without demonstrated competence, teachers could predict failure at the next level, and they were usually right. When a student's failure to meet standards is directly linked to a teacher's capacity to teach, the need to understand more about teaching and learning, to expand a teacher's horizon, becomes a very high priority for public school teachers, their principals, and their districts. Without continuous opportunities for all teachers to expand their knowledge and skills, schools have little chance of succeeding (Darling-Hammond, 1997b, pp. 270-273).

Personal Expectations of Professional Development

While interviewing a middle school teacher who was with a group looking at student work, we were surprised that she found it interesting for about 5 minutes, then expressed to us that it was a waste of her time. When later she met with the same group during time designated for professional development to examine student work and assess it against a standard of performance rubric, she found it tremendously valuable. What had changed? The first conversation had no substantive implications for her work; the purpose had not been established. The second conversation directly connected her to the effectiveness of her teaching in ensuring that students achieved an acceptable level of performance aligned to the content standard. She began to analyze her own work. "What did I do that helped students achieve the standard? What did I do that appeared to be more or less effective for students? How do I know that to be true?" Everything in her language arts classes came under scrutiny—homework, field trips, library help classes, research projects, critical essays, participation in plays, interpretation of poetry. The strategies were now focused on the results—achieving the standards. When she was able to analyze the data and scrutinize her own performance, she was also able to determine what she needed to improve her personal effectiveness. Then she met with colleagues to analyze student performance across the grade levels. As she returned to her team, her conversation changed from "What do I have to attend this year for my professional development credits?" to "I need to target critical thinking and expository writing as my greatest needs for professional development this year. Why don't we all consider these areas, especially since students across grade levels were weak in their performances of these standards?"

She had used the data to analyze student needs and determine her expectations of their improved performance. She then analyzed her teaching ("How did I teach this standard, when, and with what performance expectation?") and built her professional development expectations ("This is what I need to be more effective"). To determine if she was effective in learning the new strategies, she will again analyze student data. Consider this model, which is illustrated in Figure 3.2, Personal Expectations of Professional Development:

Analyze student data → Determine student needs → Determine expectations for improved student performance → Determine personal needs → Seek inside or outside professional development → Try new strategies → Analyze student data to determine effectiveness in using the strategies.

School-Wide Expectations for Professional Development

Because she based her professional development request on personal and grade-level performances, she and the other teachers are in a position to set up an improvement design for the school with whatever strategies they choose (see Figure 3.3, School-Wide Expectations for Professional Development, for an illustration of this pattern).

Identify personal needs for professional development → Determine school-wide needs → Agree on expected student performance → Identify content-specific strategies → Plan professional development → Try new strategies → Examine student data for improved performance.

She has the professional encouragement to assess her own teaching strategies based on what the group has learned. As others on the team assess *their* own strategies, or variations on the strategies, the conversation when they analyze student performance again will be even richer.

Collaborative Action Research

Action research, another collaborative model, is a pathway to student achievement. Action research should not be planned, conducted, or

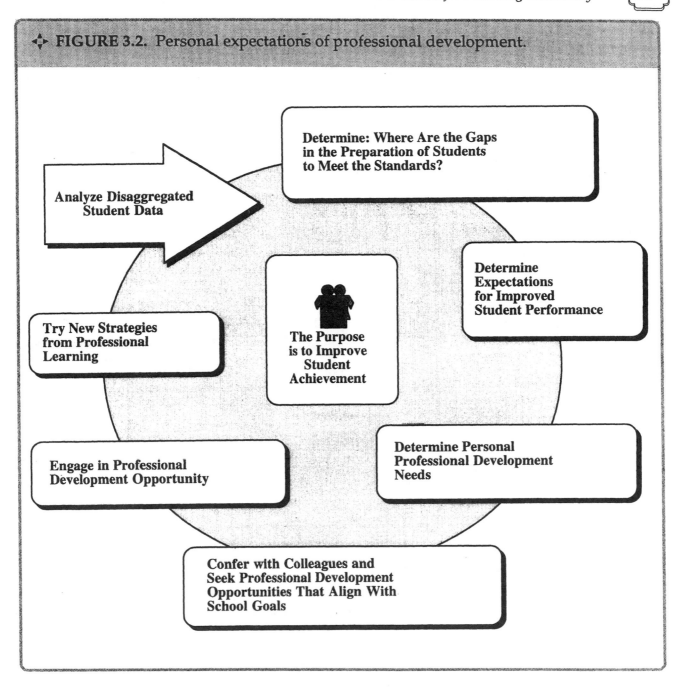

❖ FIGURE 3.2. Personal expectations of professional development.

reported in isolation. When teachers decide to conduct action research as a group or team, the experiences are far more enduring. After agreeing on their expectations of student performance, teachers confirm each other's findings when they analyze data, collaborate to test one another's hypotheses, and examine data together to plan for the next cycle. If the need exists for additional professional development, they determine what that will be, when it will happen, and how they will apply their new knowledge to increase student achievement.

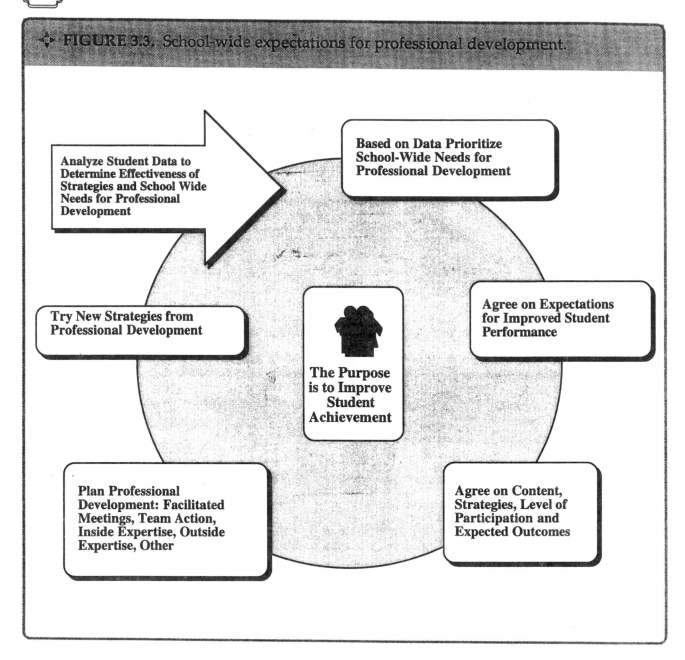

❖ **FIGURE 3.3.** School-wide expectations for professional development.

Apply personal knowledge to student needs → Analyze student performance data → Form hypotheses about what worked or did not work → Examine the evidence to verify hypotheses, plan the next cycle for action research → Include a design for collecting evidence → Determine the need for new content or knowledge strategies → Return to the cycle for applying personal knowledge to student needs (see Figure 3.4, Collaborative action research as professional development).

The missing links for educators in the past have been (a) a culture that has clarity of focus on student performance, and (b) a culture that supports

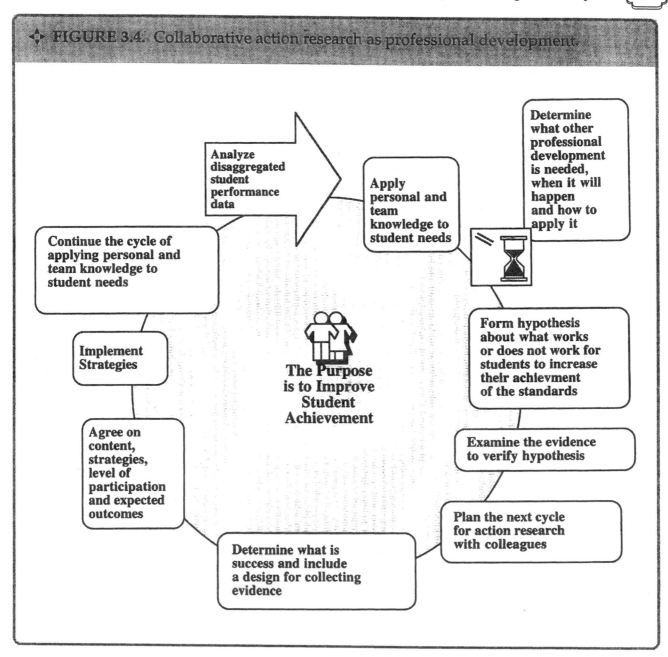

♦ FIGURE 3.4. Collaborative action research as professional development.

each educator's acceptance of personal responsibility for student performance throughout the system.

As long as teachers were encouraged by the district and state to live with uncorrected myopia about long-term student performance and achievement, they absolved themselves of personal responsibility. Although teachers decried the lack of preparation of students coming into their classes and celebrated the success of those who "made it" through their classes, they did not connect the two as being related to each teacher's responsibility for each student in current and future terms. Teachers may not acknowledge, for example, that changing attitudes, strategies, preparation in strategic areas, knowledge of content and how to teach it, and a willingness to learn all of the above could make major differences in the short- and long-term academic lives of students.

We have seen that myopia in high schools. We know of ninth-grade language arts teachers who have firmly expressed their unwillingness to teach reading, despite the fact that 500 of 1,200 students are scoring in the lowest quartile of a standardized literacy test. The personal concern on the part of the teachers is the need for immediate new knowledge without the opportunity to learn, practice, or master the concepts. They have not recognized the urgency of the situation so that they can plan how to proceed. The myopia on the part of the district is not seeing that having new expectations of teachers means supporting them with professional opportunities that include information about content and strategies and about new standards and how to measure them, as well as access to coaching.

Educators have shifted from their view of students as passive recipients of classroom instruction to a concern with what schools must do to help students learn and be successful. In a student-centered school, the focus, obviously, is the latter. Teachers will not be afraid to confront these new challenges in the culture of a learning community. They will not be reluctant to risk their professional reputations on trying something new. Based on their experiences with a learning community, teachers know that they will be supported and encouraged to take risks on behalf of students, even if not all ventures are successful.

Where to Be Fluid and Where to Hold Fast

School faculties must be like high-performing teams—certain of the goal; focused on the outcome; aware of every member's role; confident of others' skills; willing to learn from the statistics; trusting themselves and others to do their jobs; and confident that, with all the team working together, students will succeed. The culture must reflect and support these qualities so that high-performing teams can accomplish their purpose.

So where are we fixed in concrete? Educators must acknowledge that learning is what they do; it's nonnegotiable. They must continue to work toward a culture of learning and leading at every level. And where are they fluid? Teachers should be free to assess their professional development needs based on student performance and school-wide data. They are encouraged to search for professional development content and strategies that align with their goals while meeting the needs and goals of the school and district. In essence, once the goal is agreed upon, teachers play a key role in determining the learning pathways they will take to accomplish the goal. They are also willing to be accountable for their learning and to demonstrate the impact on student success. The culture of continuous learning and improvement is essential to public education professionals and the students they serve.

Conclusion

Will each professional involved in the public schools make a commitment to caring relationships, conscious valuing, and the academic success of all students? Will imagination, intellectual drive, curiosity, and a desire for success be exhibited daily by students, as well as by adults involved with students? Considering the complex world we live in, the answer to both questions must be affirmative. Teachers, principals, and all other staff involved with students can create the best possible environment for student learning and student success. By modeling the very academic and social behaviors they expect students to exhibit, teachers demonstrate commitment to the culture of a learning community that will result in an optimal climate for student success.

REALITY CHECK

How will reshaping the culture through professional development enable a school to develop a learning community focused on improving student achievement? Is one a natural outgrowth of the other?

On the Web

Access to information has changed dramatically for teachers. Educators have entire bodies of research available at their computers—lesson plans, subject-specific information, teaching strategies, and assessment formats.

Teachers can enter chat rooms to discuss attention deficit disorders among children ages 9 to 11, or they can go to university researchers for the latest diagnoses and medication.

Using the word *culture*, we found 2,737,944 matches, including throat culture, tissue culture, and aboriginal art and culture, as well as cultures of states and countries. We even found a message board under Interculture with discussions about matters of state, royalty, and immigration. Narrowing the search brought us to more familiar territory. Using the search words *school culture*, we found 531,716 matches. Although admittedly, we did not search even a tenth of the sites, the surfing brought us to three interesting areas:

♦ National Staff Development Council (NSDC): http://www.nsdc.org

♦ California School Leadership Academy (CSLA): http://www.csla.org

♦ North Central Regional Educational Laboratory (NCREL): http://www.ncrel.org/pathways.htm

We chose the NSDC because of the extensive work in this field by Dennis Sparks and Stephanie Hirsh, as reported also in their book, *A New Vision for Staff Development* (1997).

The CSLA is important because it supports a 2- to 3-year comprehensive professional development program for school leaders. In existence as a result of school reform legislation since 1985, school leaders practice strategies for building a culture of a learning community focused on student success. When visiting this site, click on the Foundation II program to review the curriculum for changing schools in support of powerful learning. For information about how to change schools using on-site members of the school community, click on School Leadership Teams. The Executive Leadership Center is a program for superintendents to learn about restructuring districts for student success.

We spent considerable time at the NCREL (1999) site visiting Pathways to School Improvement. We found articles and quotes from giants of our profession, such as Linda Darling-Hammond (1997a), Kent Peterson (1994), and Terrance Deal and Kent Peterson (1993), to name a few. In addition, a bibliography (http://www.ncrel.org/sdrs/areas/issues/educatrs/leadrshp/le0petab.htm) included annotations of works by Michael Fullan and Andy Hargreaves, as well as of Peterson and Deal. The Pathways page focuses on current issues and includes the following: overview, goals, action options, implementation pitfalls, different points of view, and illustrative cases of schools and their leaders throughout the north central region of the United States, as well as an extensive list of resources.

Addressing Teacher Work Concerns Through Professional Development

The principal was sitting at her desk writing her "back to school" letter when Franklin walked into the office.

"Didn't mean to disturb you, Tracy," Franklin said with a smile. "I stopped by to see how the opening of school is shaping up. Is everything about finished?"

"Hi Franklin! How was your summer? Thanks for stopping by." Tracy was delighted to see him. "I knew you'd want everything in place for the opening. Your department will be pleased. The science lab is state of the art, just as you folks planned it, and the portables will be used for prelab planning lectures as well as classrooms." Tracy continued thoughtfully, "Wish I felt as positive about other situations."

"What's up?" Franklin noticed the concern.

"It's the staff newsletter. Teachers are mandated to attend another district inservice that appears to have nothing to do with our needs here at the site."

"Oh no. Not again." Franklin's voice was louder. "I thought we made it very clear to district folks last year that they can't have it both ways. They can't expect us to implement standards and assessment in every classroom, bring every student in our classes up to standard, and still invest a day of expensive staff time going to inservice training that has nothing to do with teaching and learning."

Tracy hesitated, seeing Franklin's reaction. "I guess they know what they're doing. Some of this training is mandated by the state, and our funding depends on meeting the requirements. Maybe you and I just don't have the big picture."

"Maybe not, but I wish the state would get its act together and decide which direction we really are going."

"Take it easy, Franklin. Wait until we have a completed agenda. Come on. We'll both feel better when we see your department's new lab. It's a beauty. Students have both the lab facility and new computers to support their experiments. Give me a second. I'll snag the keys and we can take a look. Do you have time?"

"Sure. Getting back to why we're in this profession always feels right to me. I'll reserve judgment about the inservice until we get an official agenda; then we'll look at next steps."

"Good idea, Franklin. Back in a minute." Tracy left her office to retrieve a set of keys from the contractor. She always tried to support district actions, but sometimes they just didn't align with her ideas about professional development and student success.

***Pause for a moment to reflect
on this essential question.***

ESSENTIAL QUESTION

How will a school design professional
development opportunities that are based
on meeting teacher work concerns?

Why Do We Have the Conversation?

As teachers continue their learning to improve the curriculum, instruction, and assessment for increased student achievement, their work concerns must be met in the design of professional development programs. Teachers should see professional development not only as a district mandate but, more importantly, as effectively embedded in their daily lives, providing continuous professional growth opportunities (Bull & Buechler, 1996; Lieberman & Miller, 1999). The traditional professional development model of onetime training workshops delivered by an outside expert with no follow-up is outdated. In fact, it never was an effective approach to adult learning. A broader and more complex approach to professional development needs to encompass ongoing sustained research, reflection, analysis of data, discussion, peer coaching, mentoring, collaborative planning, problem solving, and involvement in decision making by teachers.

As a district addresses teachers' work concerns and makes professional development plans to incorporate those concerns, it recognizes teachers and validates the importance of their needs. The issue of their work concerns must influence the planning process and professional learning activities as they are developed. Recognizing and dealing with these concerns in professional development planning allows teachers to participate, take ownership, and understand the purpose. Teachers need professional development that has a coherent focus rather than fragmented activities with little meaning for actual application in the classroom to improve student learning. Shanker (1990) captures the importance of why we should address teacher work concerns in the following statement:

> Every teacher in America's public schools has taken inservice courses, workshops, and training programs. But as universal as the practice has been, so is the disappointment among teachers and management as to the usefulness of most staff development experiences. (p. 91)

Why does this type of professional development practice continue to be perpetuated in our schools and districts? How can we better address teacher work concerns in context with professional development planning and improving student achievement?

Research and Best Practices

Professional development of teachers is central to successful educational reform. The numerous educational reforms facing teachers daily in the classroom include new curricula and instructional strategies; rigorous academic standards for all students; use of multiple measures of student achievement (i.e., standardized tests, portfolios, and performance-based assessments); diversity of student needs (disabilities, languages, cultures, and experiences); technology uses in the classroom; and the new demands of site-based management. Teachers need numerous opportunities and the means to learn new approaches to stay professionally current. Professional development must provide the learning that teachers need to improve instruction, meet student needs, and accelerate achievement. Approaching professional development through the lens of teacher work concerns encourages the designers to collaborate with teachers. As they gain a broader perspective of teachers' needs, professional development designers will begin to validate the relationship between professional development and increased student achievement. Helping teachers expand their repertoire of content knowledge and strategies is meaningful professional growth in the context of teachers' working conditions and concerns.

Researchers have reached a clear consensus that onetime workshops for teachers are ineffective. The content is not transferred to the classroom, nor does it affect student achievement (Joyce & Showers, 1995). Instead of sporadic, fragmented workshops, professional development must move beyond the current series of teacher-training workshops to embedding ongoing professional development in the daily work of teachers (Lieberman & Miller, 1999). Opportunities for learning, observation, practice, feedback, coaching, and reflection on practice need to be integrated parts of a teacher's work. Using systems thinking helps us understand that the school should be the focus of professional development, where teachers interact with each other around issues of learning and achievement, and the district supports the site focus in numerous ways. Districts must know how to address the unique challenges of a school site to meet teachers' and students' unique learning needs. When professional development at the site level is tied to a school improvement plan, teachers and administrators can implement a coherent program that takes into consideration their particular needs and how these needs will be addressed.

For a better understanding of research and practices centered on teacher work concerns in relation to professional development, three major areas of concern need to be addressed: (a) roles and responsibilities, (b) conditions of professional development, and (c) processes for professional development.

Roles and Responsibilities

In the past, school employees had the luxury of assuming that most professional development responsibilities belonged to someone else. Principals and teachers could look to a central office staff member who planned, coordinated, and sometimes even presented professional development programs. Whatever the case, it was possible for virtually all district employees to view professional development as someone else's job.

Today, the concept of job-embedded staff development has come to mean that educators in many roles—superintendents, assistant superintendents, curriculum supervisors, principals, and teacher leaders, among others—must all see themselves as teachers of adults and must view the development of others as one of their most important responsibilities. (Sparks & Hirsh, 1997, p. 83)

If professional development is focused at the school level so that teachers can meet classroom improvement targets, the roles and responsibilities for teachers must evolve from isolation in their classrooms to involvement in the larger school-wide view of improvement and professional development. Recognizing the individual roles of teachers in the larger school organization has proven to be critical for schools to reform and improve (Elmore, 1996). Researchers have found that teachers' individual efforts, in random isolation, have not provided the power to move student achievement and school improvement in significant ways (Darling-Hammond & McLaughlin, 1995). Nor have district-level initiatives that vary from year to year made a consistent impact on schools, teachers, and student achievement (Little, 1993a).

Professional development must consistently focus on an overall vision and plan for school improvement that both teachers and administrators understand and make a commitment to carry out. Even the process of developing a coherent vision is itself a form of professional development. Expanding the roles and responsibilities of teachers in professional development will be a key to future student success and to the ongoing growth of teachers. Ownership of their own professional development is an important step for teachers in both their roles and responsibilities to the profession. The study by Joyce et al. (1989) of governance issues in professional development confirmed that professional development programs jointly governed (by individual staff, schools, and the district) were considered valuable by educators because involvement and decisions had been made democratically.

Currently, teachers may be offered a broad range of professional development activities by the district's professional development department in a "buffet style" or in a series of workshops that have no clear focus for the teacher's professional growth needs or key school improvement goals. In the traditional model of professional development, the role of the teacher is usually as a passive participant or sometimes as a presenter of activities at a workshop. How often have we heard the following: "The district organizes professional development, and we don't go because it is not relevant to where we are and what our needs are." The evolving vision of professional development requires multiple roles for the teacher. Teachers should be designers, leaders, and presenters as well as participants in professional development (Lieberman & Miller, 1999). McLaughlin (1994) emphasized that meaningful professional development takes place not during workshops and inservice day presentations, but in the context of professional communities that have been locally developed to be responsive to teachers' needs. Successful professional development is no longer the domain of a district-level supervisor; instead, it is organized to give teachers the authority and resources to take charge of their own learning (Little, 1993b).

Expanding the roles of teachers in professional development processes will include increased attention to their roles as: (a) school learning community members, (b) teacher leaders, and (c) coaches. These new roles, their responsibilities, and what they entail will recognize teachers, their expertise, and their ability to lead and share professionally to expand teachers' capacity to help students achieve (Lieberman, 1995a). Each of these roles will be discussed for its significance.

School Learning Community Member

Site-based professional development involves expanding the role of the classroom teacher as a member of the larger school learning community. As learning community members, teachers must see their roles and their professional development integrated into support of the overall school improvement plan. The ownership of responsibility for professional development is at the school site level, where specific problems, needs, and possibilities are understood. It only makes sense that teachers involved in the design of their own professional development programs will meet their unique school and student needs (Little, 1993b). As active members of the school learning community, teachers can make professional development an ongoing part of the overall school improvement plan so that it is aligned with both school and district goals (McLaughlin, 1994). Teachers will see the emerging coherence of professional development tied to the school plan and to the work of the school learning community as evidence of a focused, not fragmented, effort. As a member of the school learning community, each teacher has a role in helping the school keep its focus and carry out its goals for student success. As a school learns together in professional development settings, teachers and principals must agree that their focused efforts to study, learn, implement, reflect, and refine practices will result in improved student achievement (Lieberman & Miller, 1999).

Within a school's learning community, the individual professional growth of teachers will still be present and supported as long as these individual opportunities are seen as aligned with the larger plan for school learning and improvement. As teachers engage with colleagues in planning, discussing, practicing, reflecting, and sharing through professional development activities, their concerns about relevant, meaningful professional learning will be addressed. There are multiple ways for teachers to collaborate and learn in professional development settings (small groups, grade-level teams, faculty meetings, and connections to outside subject matter state and national networks and professional associations) to inform their practice.

> The point of school-based professional development is that the needs of each school, as defined by the staff at that school, play a major role in determining the form that professional development will take. The school is the starting point for professional development planning, not a fortress with unbreachable walls. (Bull & Buechler, 1996, p. 9)

Thus as learners and colleagues within a school learning community, teachers help shape their own professional growth and view it as "continuous growth in professional practice" based on their unique circumstances and needs. The learning community nurtures teachers' inquiry into their practices and challenges and supports them to improve their practices to achieve student success.

Teacher Leader

Teachers will take on new instructional leadership roles with professional development as members or chairpersons of school improvement site councils or at the district level as members of school improvement teams, expert presenters, teacher leaders, coaches, facilitators, mentors, and problem solvers. Teacher leadership roles may be formal or informal, but it is important that teachers accept and seek leadership roles as professionals taking responsibility for what is happening in the teaching profession and that they value their own ongoing professional learning in the larger context as well as at their schools.

Teachers must share in the leadership role of determining professional growth rather than attending sessions imposed upon them by others. Teachers may choose to use outside consultants and experts to help initiate or guide change efforts at their school, or they may capitalize on the expertise of teachers within their own school or district. Even mandated legislation should include shared leadership between teachers and administrators to determine the implementation of "hows" and "whens" of their professional development. Participation in leadership roles demonstrates a collaborative leadership process that gives teachers structured opportunities to participate in decision making. Further, such participation models democratic shared leadership and decision making, which builds ownership and commitment for teachers in a school improvement process. "Teachers who are leaders lead within and beyond the classroom, influence others toward improved educational practice, and identify with and contribute to a community of teacher teachers" (Katzenmeyer & Moller, 1996, p. 6). Teachers, as leaders, enact their beliefs daily through their interactions with other teachers, students, parents, and the principal. Leaders must clearly communicate their expectations and voice their strong beliefs about children and schooling. "Principals and teachers in schools that are in the midst of change are finding that as they do their work, they are blurring boundaries and forging new connections between leading, learning, and teaching. Their schools are leadership dense organizations" (Lieberman & Miller, 1999, p. 46). The ideal is that teacher leadership becomes so embedded in a school that when a principal leaves, teacher leaders are able to carry on the change process and provide continuity to the work. The principal can cultivate a culture of teacher leadership by listening, engaging, and empowering teachers to deal with professional learning concerns. In doing this, a principal sends a clear message that teacher concerns matter and that teacher knowledge and experience count. In small steps, the foundation for new forms of leadership in schools can be constructed. Principals must always be attentive to the learning needs of both students and teachers. In collaboration with the faculty, they provide a wide variety of opportunities for growth and development. Every teacher must have the opportunity to learn, and learning can be led by others than just the principal or outside experts. As districts give more leadership and decision-making authority to teachers, an important, untapped leadership resource will be released for improved student learning. The old paradigm of deciding in an administrative vacuum what is good for teachers does not work. Teachers as professionals need and want to be leaders and participants in their own professional learning and growth.

Coach

The teacher's role as coach has emerged as a powerful means of individual and school organizational development. The importance of using teacher coaching as a follow-up to new learning has increased the implementation of new concepts and strategies by teachers. The ongoing coaching support has definitely led to improved student achievement. Teacher as coach makes the theory, demonstration, practice, and feedback elements to support growth more meaningful, because they come from a peer as ongoing support for the new learning and application in the classroom. Educators have all experienced how difficult change can be. Even with the best intentions, new information and strategies get filed away for possible future use unless coaching support takes place. The support of a teacher in the role of coach increases individual teacher's or teams of teachers' use of new learnings by 85%. The research by Joyce and Showers (1995) substantiates the importance of coaching and feedback and demonstrates that the level of use of new learnings by teachers in their classrooms depends on the type of training procedures used by the coaches. Table 4.1, Level of Impact of Professional Development, shows the relationship between types of professional development strategies used and the level of impact on concept understanding, skill attainment, and application by teachers.

TABLE 4.1 Level of Impact of Professional Development

Professional Development Type	Level of Impact (%)		
	Concept Understanding	*Skill Attainment*	*Application*
Presentation of theory	85	15	5
Modeling	85	18	5–10
Practice and feedback	85	80	10–15
Coaching	90	90	80–90

Adapted from the research of Joyce and Showers (e.g., 1995).

Teachers as coaches are able to increase their understandings of the use of skills within their classrooms. Coaching allows teachers to observe each other; give feedback and support; share ideas, lessons, and materials; discuss problems and concerns; and develop curricula together. The isolation of the individual classroom is broken down because professional development through coaching can happen during school hours. Training of coaches can be done by an outside expert, but a cadre of schoolteacher coaches can train new coaches and share the coaching role. Coaches claim they learn as much about teaching as the teachers they coach (Joyce & Showers, 1995). The reflection and discussion of classroom observations allow both the teacher and the coach to reflect on teaching practices and to hone their skills to improve instruction for students. The coach's follow-up of the learning activities reinforces new learnings and also models correct implementation within the classroom. Time is needed for teachers to absorb and practice new ideas or strategies and adapt them to their classrooms. Teachers as coaches help reinforce and refine the new knowledge and sustain the professional development change process for the teacher.

Sparks's study (1986) of professional development activities on the performance of teachers helps substantiate the importance of teacher peer coaching. The study looked at three types of professional development activities on the performance of teachers: workshops alone, workshops plus coaching by the trainer, and workshops plus peer coaching. The research found that teachers who were coached by peers improved more than those who were coached by experts and that both improved more than teachers who attended the workshop alone. Sparks (1986) came to the following conclusions regarding teacher peer coaching experiences:

♦ Teachers rarely get to see one another in action, and just watching a colleague teach may have been a powerful learning experience.

♦ Peer coaches had to analyze the behavior of other teachers, which may have helped them analyze their own behavior more accurately.

♦ Structured interactions with other teachers may have led to a heightened sense of trust and esprit de corps.

It is interesting to note that Joyce and Showers (1995), in their most recent research, have reversed their definition of *coach*. The coach is the teacher, not the observer, and the observer is learning from the teacher—not observing the teacher for feedback, but learning from the observed teacher and reflecting on his or her own practice. Joyce and Showers (1995) explained that they no longer include formal feedback as a component of peer coaching; instead, they emphasize other aspects of peer coaching in peer study teams, where the primary activity is the collaborative planning and development of curriculum and instruction in pursuit of shared goals. Their research raises questions about what feedback means in the coaching process, but their work reinforces the importance of the interaction of collaboration and learning opportunities of peers around their teaching activities.

Understanding these new roles and responsibilities for teachers within the creation of professional development designs is critical. Teachers and their work concerns cannot be ignored, because teachers are the vital links between students and learning. Expanding teachers' roles and responsibilities helps expand the participation of teachers in defining their own professional development, thus making teaching more of a profession.

Conditions of Professional Development

Teacher work concerns usually focus on the conditions under which professional development is provided. Questions about time, trust, collaboration, incentives and recognition, resources, and leadership and policy issues arise when teachers view professional development plans and opportunities (see Figure 4.1). These important conditions for professional development raise questions that should be addressed in designing and meeting the conditional requirements for high-quality professional development:

♦ Will the training be worth my time preparing for a substitute and the time lost with my students?

♦ Who says we have to attend the training and why?

♦ How relevant is the training to my classroom and students? Is it all theory, or are there practical applications?

◆ FIGURE 4.1. Conditions for professional development.

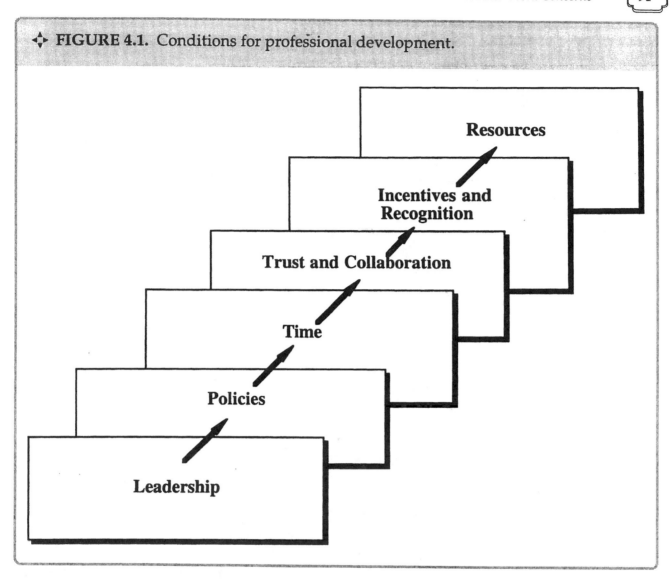

- ◆ Will the strategies work in my classroom, and how will I have time to prepare to use my new knowledge and strategies?

- ◆ What incentives or recognition can I expect, or is it expected that I will do this above and beyond my classroom duties?

- ◆ What resources and materials are available after the training to help me implement the new knowledge in the classroom?

- ◆ Who is providing the leadership and follow-up to the professional development?

- ◆ What policies are in place that promote high-quality professional development opportunities?

Leadership and Policy

"Effective staff development requires strong leadership in order to obtain continuing support and to motivate all staff, school board members, parents, and the community to be advocates for continuous improvement" (National Staff Development Council, 1995, p. 5). Leadership and advocacy for continuous learning are critical to the professional development and maintenance of an effective school. Only if professional development is embedded in the philosophy, leadership, and organizational structure of schools and district can a culture of continuous growth thrive (Loucks-Horsely et al., 1987). Leadership and policy coherence can keep schools from being inundated with conflicting demands as they strive to improve and focus their professional development efforts (Little, 1993b). Ideally, school, district, and state improvement plans are coordinated into a seamless whole, targeted at increasing student learning. Equally important are the district's infrastructure of policies and its commitment of leadership to support continued professional development for teachers. School board policies are enacted to facilitate school-based improvement and to eliminate barriers to professional development. Teachers clearly understand the impact of these district policies and leadership actions on professional development plans. They are tangible evidence of how important professional growth is among district priorities.

It is important for leaders of a district to view continuous professional growth as essential to district and school goals to raise student achievement levels. As an integral part of any district's strategic plan, school boards should enact policies and standards to promote ongoing, quality professional development (Darling-Hammond & McLaughlin, 1995). These policies will provide a guide for planning and implementing new strategies to increase student learning. Policies must create significant roles for teachers in many areas of practice that have previously been managed by others, including setting standards, developing curriculum and assessments, and evaluating practices.

Further, policies must focus on stimulating the environment that nurtures high-quality learning communities of teachers, rather than on particular institutional structures and processes. Policymakers should focus on the richness and relevance of the variety and means for teachers to learn in the context of their school environment (Darling-Hammond & McLaughlin, 1995). The leadership and policy environment of a district sends a clear message to teachers and should be examined as evidence that districts have, or don't have, high expectations for school improvement.

Time

Reforms conducted on the fringes of the school day will never become an integral part of the school (Purnell & Hill, 1992). In talking with teachers, we found that adequate time for professional development is one of their chief concerns. Time to be involved in professional development training, discussions, decision making, study or task groups or teams, action research inquiry, and collaboration draws the teacher. When, on top of the regular school day schedule and the time needed to correct homework and plan lessons for the next unit, will it be done? How can teachers find time for continuous professional development and learning when their normal days are consumed with all their demanding teaching responsibilities? Time needs to be scheduled for teachers to work together. Individual teachers may take summer or semester courses or workshops, but these are separate, discrete activities based on the individual teacher's motivation and use of personal time. Schools must structure time for professional learning within the regular school calendar, or they must expand the school calendar, if teachers are to have quality time for professional development.

What are the options available for increasing professional development time for teachers and meeting their work concerns? Research and proven practice provide several models for reallocating time within the existing school calendar or by expanding the school year and calendar. Each possible option will be briefly discussed in the following section: (a) accumulated or banked time, (b) alternative grouping, (c) alternative scheduling, (d) expanded staffing, (e) school-university partnerships, (f) expanded professional development hours and days, and (g) expanded school calendar and year.

Accumulated or Banked Time. Increasing instructional minutes during the week to accumulate or bank release minutes can be used as a block of time each week for professional development. Some states require waivers to implement this strategy. Schools using banked time have developed effective block time each week or month to do substantial intense professional development work with their teachers.

Alternative Grouping. Working with colleagues, teachers bring students together in large groups rather than single classes to provide free time for designated teachers. Team teaching, regularly scheduled assemblies, or community service learning offer means to free teachers and to expand the time available for professional development.

Alternative Scheduling. Altering the master schedule to give teams of teachers common planning time for professional development and collaboration is another action a principal can take to provide quality time. This alternative scheduling can be done under different configurations, such as (a) common planning time, at the start or end of the day; (b) use of block scheduling, with teacher-scheduled prep periods; and (c) adding an extra period to the schedule, so that blocks of time can be available at different times of the day for different teams of teachers.

Expanded Staffing. A school can use regular substitute teachers to free teachers to work on their professional development during the school day. This may include the use of a floating substitute who can move from class to class within a school, releasing teachers for observations, coaching, mentoring, or other types of job-embedded professional development activities. This floating substitute should be a regular who knows the curriculum and students well enough to carry on regular learning activities in the classroom while the teacher is involved in professional development. A further way to expand staff is for administrators to occasionally volunteer to release teachers as a demonstration of clear support for their professional development work. Administrative leaders who help expand staff time for important work by substituting in the classroom also learn themselves by teaching and participating in learning with the students in the classroom.

School-University Partnership. This approach is very comprehensive and allows for university students or faculty to cover teachers' classrooms. Professional development activities tied to school-university partnerships inform teachers and university practice in a reciprocal way, as those involved share university research and classroom practice. Teachers, student teachers, and university faculty work together on teaching and learning issues that expand their knowledge and abilities. These types of partnerships play an enriching role for both the school and the university in a systematic way.

Expanded Professional Development Hours and Days. Districts can extend the teachers' contract to include additional hours or days for professional development. The extended contract buys time during the summer for workshops, seminars, curriculum development, and planning, and during the school year the contract adds hours for follow-up. It also buys time for coaching and collaboration, providing the needed time for learning and concept implementation for teachers. Collaboration time for purposes of writing curriculum and refining assessment strategies is also an excellent investment for schools.

Expanded School Calendar and Year. The option of expanding the school calendar should be explored more extensively than it has been to date, because it could provide quality time for professional development without having teachers leave their classrooms and students. More districts and schools should explore the use of a single-track year-round calendar that shortens the summer vacations and expands periodic breaks during the school year; these breaks can then be used for professional development activities (see Figure 4.2).

✧ **FIGURE 4.2.** Traditional versus year-round calendar.

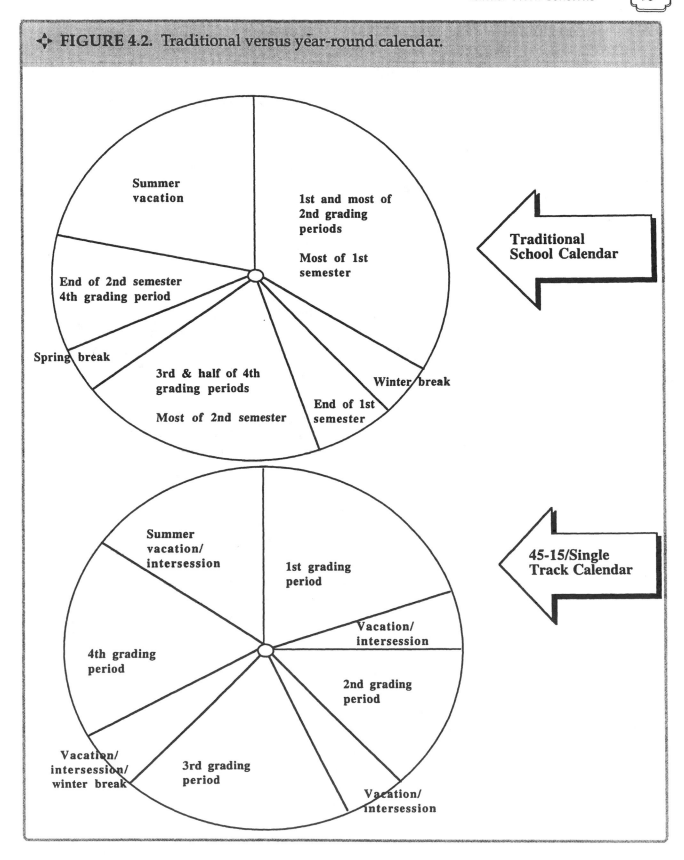

The other benefit of the single-track, year-round calendar—besides teachers' professional development—is increased learning for students. It is an important recognition of the amount of learning loss students experience over the summer. Learning loss is less for students with shorter summer breaks (Cooper, Nye, Charlton, Lindsay, & Greathouse, 1996). In addition, teachers use less time reteaching material or establishing classroom management when students have not had an extended 3-month summer break from learning and school. The single-track calendar illustrated in Figure 4.2, with periodic breaks and the shorter summer break, could be used for professional development. Continuous learning for teachers and students is better served by a single-track, year-round calendar than the traditional school calendar. The traditional school calendar has its roots in our agrarian history, when students worked in the fields to harvest the crops. Educators should take a serious look at the school calendar year and how it is used. Finding the time for continuous professional development over the entire year is a strong possibility in a revised school calendar year.

Given all of the above considerations for the use of time for professional development, educators are reminded that there are constraints to be negotiated in the change process. The legislature, the state department of education, the teachers' union (including bargaining agreements), the school board and community, and district policies are all fluid parts of a changing system. The use of time must be addressed if teachers are to transform schools and learning for students (National Commission on Time and Learning, 1994). Time is an essential factor in turning schools into continuous learning communities. If educators and boards refuse to tackle alternative schedules, they are stuck with what they have had in the past: periodic, shallow, or episodic professional development activities that have little or no sustaining effect on a teacher's practice in the classroom.

Time is an important element for continuous learning. Adequate time for professional learning must be allotted. Teachers may be required by their state to take a certain number of professional development hours to renew their teaching licenses, or they may earn salary increases for taking college units or advanced degrees. This is a catch-as-catch-can system. The patchwork nature of this model of professional development will have to change. Continuous learning opportunities must become part of teachers' everyday working lives and part of every school's institutional priorities. Administrators and teachers will have to develop an ethos of inquiry, as Bull and Buechler (1996) described:

Examining their own practices and trying new ones;

Learning about subject matter, instructional methods, and student development;

Questioning what they learn in light of their own experience;

Thinking deeply about overall school improvement; and

Working together to enact that improvement. (Bull & Buechler, 1996, p. 22)

Time is the critical element that must be provided if these things are to happen.

Trust and Collaboration

Trust and collaboration are hallmark conditions that must be present for learning communities to develop and for teachers to grow, but these are not easy conditions to establish. Most schools are organized in ways that isolate teachers so that collaboration is not easily established or sustained. Working within their classrooms on a daily basis with students, teachers do not have a lot of time for interacting with colleagues or developing trust with other teachers and administrators. Teachers' experiences and their collective understanding of trust and collaboration vary. The skills associated with continuous collegial interactions must be nurtured within the school. Professional development, like school reform efforts in general, works best as a collaborative effort when teachers, administrators, classified staff, students, and parents trust one another and can work together over a sustained period of time.

As schools become learning communities, trust and collaboration are developed and modeled. Teachers need structured opportunities to collaborate on decisions, problems, and new ideas within an atmosphere of mutual trust and respect. Even motivated teachers are unlikely to sustain innovations in their own classrooms without the support, trust, and involvement of colleagues. The school as a whole is even less likely to improve without productive interactions and trusting relationships among the teachers.

Trust must permeate the organization in order for teachers to collaborate and take charge of their own professional development. Administrators help to promote trust by providing support for teachers' efforts, helping them stay focused on student achievement, and giving them leadership and power to carry out change efforts. Teachers need to trust each other as they work together for school improvement. Coaching requires the ultimate trust of receiving feedback and reflecting. Trust can take fear out of the context for learning. Teachers must believe that they can learn new ways to teach and assess. Beliefs are built on trusting people, including their integrity and commitment. Like collaboration, trust must be nurtured step by step and must be reinforced constantly by leaders and teachers at the school and district level.

Personal conversations, well-planned meetings, school newsletters, newspaper articles, site councils, up-to-date Web sites, and a continuous information flow during emergencies build trust with parents and the community. Parents need to know what changes are taking place within the school that will affect their children, and schools need to solicit and consider parents' feedback before implementing major changes. Parents need to trust that teachers and administrators will retool constantly, as do other professionals (doctors, lawyers, and engineers), to keep up with changing times and expanding knowledge. Parents understand that as professionals, teachers cannot operate with knowledge they gained when they graduated from college two or more decades ago to meet the needs of today's students. Just as doctors don't operate on the knowledge they had when they left medical school 30 years ago, teachers cannot effectively function without updating their skills. Parents must trust that when teachers are involved in professional development, they are developing skills and abilities to meet the learning needs of their students. They should be informed about the relevance of new knowledge in the following areas:

- Instructional strategies and how students learn

- Uses of technology

- Changes in student population and greater diversity—and how teachers will meet these changing needs

- New demands on schools to create informed citizens and productive workers

When teachers leave their classrooms for continued learning, parents must trust that teachers' professional growth will ultimately benefit their children.

Collaboration is never easy, and breaking down isolation is difficult. Fullan (1993) discusses the issues of isolation, autonomy, and collaboration. Teachers guard their solitude, because it gives them a territory to call their own, provides them with an opportunity to get work done, and shields them from unwanted scrutiny. Although leaders understand a teacher's desire to work alone, one teacher cannot meet the increased academic performance needs of students without reaping the benefits of intellectual support from colleagues who share research, analyze student work together, use technology, develop new curricula, and update their teaching strategies.

Hargreaves and Dawe (1990) cautioned against "contrived collegiality," when administrators impose superficial forms of collaboration on a school culture that is still isolationist at heart. Schools need to foster genuine collaboration that stems from committing to shared goals and recognizing the necessity to work together to achieve them. Again, common time to work together is a means of fostering collaboration among teachers when they work as grade-level teams sharing lessons, creating team units, or reading a book together and reflecting on its implications for their school.

Collaboration is also evident when committee members use consensus building to make decisions on curriculum or school budgets. As mentioned before, two of the most powerful forms of teacher collaboration are involvement in designing and implementing professional development and peer coaching. In the context of their work together, learning skills in such areas as group facilitation, conflict management, and other group process skills helps develop and sustain teachers. Their collaborative efforts break the norm of isolation found in schools. Different schools approach collaboration development in various ways, but it is important for teachers and the principal to acknowledge the significance of collaborative work as they nurture the relationships that strengthen collaboration.

Collaboration within the school is important; however, collaboration should extend beyond the school to inform teacher practice. Teachers can collaborate at the district level with other teachers who share their concerns and restraints. Through state or national collegial networks, such as the National Writing Project (or other subject matter projects) or the Coalition of Essential Schools (educational philosophies and instructional methods), teachers and principals can share problems and successes that transcend the boundaries of districts or regions. Their involvement provides them with opportunities to develop, implement, and discuss new approaches in a safe and supportive environment. Networks provide members with opportunities to attend conference; publish articles; and exchange information through discussions, correspondence, electronic listservs, newsgroups, and other formats. Teachers can interact with experts and peers at different times by exchanging e-mail, asking questions, sharing experiences, and discussing issues. The community of learners in networks reduces teacher isolation and increases collaboration without regard to location and time.

Incentives and Recognition

Most teachers are intrinsically motivated to keep learning, but how is this motivation sustained for teachers throughout their careers? What incentives or recognition will be meaningful for teachers? Recognition in its various forms acknowledges from within the school and district the valuable work of teachers. Teachers often respond that time and appreciation, as well as being treated as professionals, are ways to recognize their efforts for continuous professional development. Treating teachers professionally and recognizing their efforts may include providing materials, a dinner, or refreshments at an activity they are sponsoring; providing release time to work with others on a unit of curriculum; or giving formal recognition at a school board meeting. Stipends; supplementary materials related to a training they attended; or equipment, such as computers or software for participating in development activities, are incentives for teachers that provide real and visible rewards for their work in professional growth. These incentives recognize that the teacher has participated in and is open to new learning. Publicly recognizing teachers' professional development efforts without creating animosity is important.

Time, however, remains the greatest incentive that teachers need. Building time for quality professional development within a teacher's workday or year is crucial. Superintendents and principals who commit to recognizing and honoring teachers for their continued learning for school improvement legitimize professional learning in the eyes of teachers, administrators, parents, and communities.

Resources

Teachers need access to adequate as well as enriching resources such as research; effective practices from inside and outside their schools; assistance by accomplished practitioners as coaches; and creative ideas of experts on subject matter, instructional methods, and school organization. Resources are fundamental to supporting reform efforts and influence teacher and administrator abilities to implement change (Guskey, 2000). Lack of resources or spreading resources so thin that they have little impact may hinder the implementation of a well-designed professional development plan. Targeting resources where they can have the greatest effect is a strategic way of using limited resources in schools and districts. Without the proper resources, teachers can become disillusioned with the innovations because materials, books, supplies, equipment, software, technology, or facilities are not available to help them implement what they have learned and are ready to apply.

Professional development cannot take place without the proper resources being made available to teachers in the implementation stage. Use of the computer and the links it can make for teachers electronically are barely explored resources for information and assistance. Using listservs and e-mail allows teachers with common interests to share information and ideas, but for these to be useful, teachers need consistently functioning, up-to-date technology and easy access. Again, nothing is more frustrating for a motivated and passionate teacher trying to implement new strategies than a lack of the proper resources. Leaders must assure teachers that their professional development work is important by providing the necessary resources and support.

Processes for Professional Development

Teachers are interested in the processes or the "hows" of professional development, so that they have opportunities to acquire and reflect on new

TABLE 4.2 Professional Development Processes: Impact and Use

Type	Length	Level of Use	Level of Impact
Onetime workshop	Episodic, one time	Awareness of new idea or strategy	Little or none; less than 5%
Series of workshops	2-3 days	Awareness, practice	Beginning use; less than 5%
Series of workshops	3 months to 1 year	Awareness, practice; beginning implementation	Implementation; developmental level
Practice, feedback, coaching	Ongoing	Ongoing coaching	Continued use
Job embedded	Daily	Research into practice; observation, reflection	Inquiry into practice
Cycle of inquiry; action research	Ongoing	Research into practice	Study of issue; understanding outcomes
Networks	Periodic	Awareness and sharing reflection	Reinforces work
Conferences	Periodic	Awareness and sharing	Little or none
Summer institutes	Periodic	Awareness, development, practice, reflection	Little or none

knowledge, strategies, and behaviors. Teachers need to think about their own professional development, school-wide improvement, and the level of impact that professional development processes will have on their own practices. Table 4.2, Professional Development Processes: Impact and Use, serves as a guide when considering different types of professional development activities and how they affect a teacher's practice.

Each type of professional development has a purpose and a level of impact, both of which must be weighed in the overall design for school and student improvement. Multiple processes must be used for a sustained effect so that new knowledge and strategies can be applied and evaluated in the teacher's classroom. Balance and infusion of ideas from the "outside expertise" as well as "inside expertise" should be used to inform professional practice within the school setting (see Figure 4.3). Lieberman and Miller (1999) describe this balance as taking on three organizational forms: direct teaching (workshops), learning in school, and learning out of school. These organizational forms for professional development provide for support and pressure, coupled with multiple entry points that are sensitive to teachers' career stages, and offer many opportunities to grow professionally (Lieberman & Miller, 1999). It is important to understand how profes-

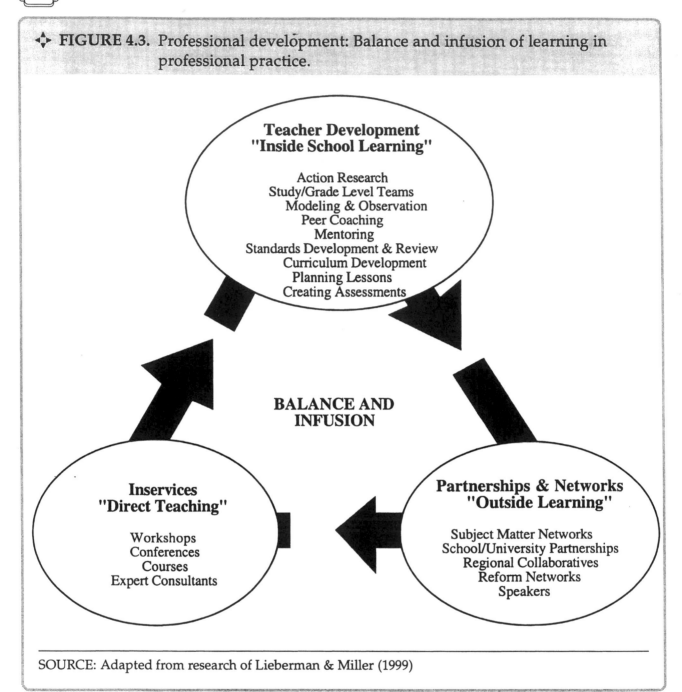

◆ FIGURE 4.3. Professional development: Balance and infusion of learning in professional practice.

SOURCE: Adapted from research of Lieberman & Miller (1999)

sional development activities interact, connect, and build on past experiences and present needs and when outside expertise and research are needed to inform and enhance professional learning within the school.

We hope that the days of disconnected professional development events staged for teacher learning are gone. The coherence of a balanced and infused professional development plan supports the overall school improvement efforts in a systemic way. Educators should view Figure 4.3, Professional Development: Balance and Infusion of Learning in Professional Practice, in relation to their school's professional development plan. What insights do you gain about balance and infusion in your school's professional learning? What would other teachers within your school say about the balance and infusion of professional development practices?

Using Figure 4.3 as a tool, a school could survey and assess the status of each teacher's professional learning (direct, inside, and outside). These data could be used to inform the school-wide professional development plan. Too often, assumptions are made about where teachers and administrators need to grow professionally, but there is a failure to assess the current status of learning of individuals within the school. Such an assessment could provide valuable information for professional growth that meets the learning needs rather than prescribing activities that are inappropriate. Also, it could serve as a resource for information about which teachers have expertise or experience with specific curricula, instructional strategies, or assessments that could be shared within the school and district. Tapping the knowledge base of a school's teaching force not only validates teachers' expertise, but also provides a rich resource for shared knowledge within a school and district.

Conclusion

Professional development planners must take teachers' work concerns seriously if they are to have a significant impact on the continued professional learning of teachers. Recognizing the roles and responsibilities, conditions, and processes of professional development from the perspective of teachers' work concerns provides insights into how professional development is envisioned, planned, and carried out for school improvement. Teachers must be given leadership roles and responsibilities (teacher leader, coach, mentor, etc.) that provide them with the opportunities to lead, present, evaluate, and reflect on their professional learning and growth. By addressing teacher work concerns around the conditions of professional development (leadership and policies, time, trust and collaboration, incentives and recognition, resources), a school can plan how to meet the concerns raised by the conditions. To develop a well-designed school professional development plan, teachers and principals should determine together how to respond to teachers' work concerns. To incorporate a variety of processes and forms for professional development available to a school, teachers can access both "inside" and "outside" sources. When educators recognize the potential of meeting the reality of teacher work concerns through professional development plans and activities, they will have developed a foundation on which to build continuous professional learning for all teachers.

REALITY CHECK

If teachers' work concerns are legitimate, how will
you recognize the issues and address them in developing
your site or district professional development plans?

On the Web

Web resources are available to address professional development opportunities in relation to "teacher work concerns." This list of Web sites provides on-line resources and links to a variety of professional development research and proven practices that relate to teachers' professional development and work concerns.

Professional Educational Associations and Centers

♦ Association for Supervision and Curriculum Development: http://www.ascd.org (see Professional Development and Classroom Leadership Online)

♦ National Staff Development Council: http://www.nsdc.org

♦ Phi Delta Kappan: http://www.pdkintl.org

♦ American Federation of Teachers: http://www.aft.org

♦ National Education Association: http://www.nea.org

♦ National Board for Professional Teaching Standards: http://www.nbpts.org

♦ National Center for Research on Teacher Learning: http://www.crtl.msu.edu

♦ National Center for Restructuring Education, Schools, and Teaching: http://www.tc.columbia.edu/~ncrest

◆ National Teacher Policy Institute: http://www.teachnet.org/ntpi

National Reports

◆ Professional Development: Learning From the Best—A Toolkit for Schools and Districts Based on the National Awards Program for Model Professional Development: http://www.ncrel.org/pd

◆ Prisoners of Time:
http://www.emich.edu/public/emu-origrams/tlc/Better3.html

◆ What Matters Most:
http://www.tc.columbia.edu/~teachcomm/Conference-99Quality

Promoting Individual Growth Through Professional Learning

Scenario

Three teachers left the school to have dinner together before attending a parent advisory board meeting scheduled later that evening.

"What did you think of the inservice on reading last week?" Maria asked the others as they waited for the signal to cross the street. "Wasn't it great?"

Janna was quick to respond. "I thought it was terrific. It's just what we needed. It's time we approached reading skills as a whole school, instead of trying to figure it out all by ourselves."

Dan wasn't so sure. He waited until they were across the street and away from traffic before he responded. "I liked the inservice, especially because it focused on our practices in teaching reading, and I really enjoyed the part where we talked to each other about how our students were doing in each of the skill areas. It's just that . . . well, I'm not certain I want three more meetings with the same focus on reading skills. I have a master's degree in reading and a reading specialist credential. At this time I personally need more work with science and how to integrate reading and science so that students meet the standards in both areas. If I understood the inservice program, the intent for next week is to practice diagnostic skills. No offense, Janna and Maria, but I really don't need that."

Maria was sympathetic. "I understand, Dan. I appreciate having professional development focused on teacher needs, but we'll never be able to meet every teacher's needs in the same inservice. It doesn't look as if we have choices about which are in line with your and my individual levels of expertise or experience. Now that's a goal for the next decade's agenda. Maybe meeting our individual needs will be a priority then."

Dan smiled. "Of course. I can wait until January 1, but not much longer."

Janna looked anxiously at Maria. "Are you certain our needs will be met that soon? I'm desperate for some help with estimation in math. You are going to be on the planning committee. Just give us some assurances."

"Sure. I think I will take that on right after I raise my four children. The youngest is three. Can you wait that long?"

"Do we have a choice?" Dan asked. "Let's have dinner. Now there is something we can count on," he added as the three entered the restaurant.

Pause for a moment to reflect on this essential question.

ESSENTIAL QUESTION

How will a school design professional development opportunities that are based on meeting the individual growth needs of a teacher?

Why Do We Have the Conversation?

The demand for individual teachers to be professionally current considering their individual strengths and needs for improvement is critical in today's schools. Teachers have never before been met with the demands of such diverse student needs, standards requirements, and accountability for student learning. To stay professionally current, teachers need personalized plans of professional development that are designed to meet their individual growth needs in the context of their schools.

Traditionally the dominant form of staff development in most school districts has been either training or large-group awareness sessions. Teachers and administrators leave their jobs to attend workshops that may range from an hour or two to several days spread over a number of months. Critics have long argued that this "sit and get" form of staff development, in which educators are passive recipients of received wisdom from an "expert," has produced little lasting change in the classroom. (Sparks & Hirsh, 1997, p. 52)

Districts and schools have begun to recognize that one-size-fits-all professional development activities do not focus on the individual needs of teachers or on where teachers are in their career paths. By recognizing the importance of individual professional development plans, a district and school can demonstrate that they value the depth and maturity of each teacher and their desires for continued personal growth. The district and school need to seek balance with district-school professional development for teachers to meet goals and individual needs and abilities. Recognizing the knowledge and experiences of individuals, principals, and district leaders can provide opportunities for teachers to help design and integrate their own ongoing professional development plans. By encouraging ownership and responsibility for continuous learning and growth, principals and superintendents are able to recognize teachers as professionals in an educational organization that values their professionalism.

Professional educators, like consumers of new products, demand options. Teachers also want to exercise their professionalism by filtering new information through their knowledge of what is best for their students. By exploring options, they will control opportunities they deem essential for their personal growth. Individual learning plans should be designed so that self-directed learning becomes an integral part of the teacher's overall plan. Finally, teachers must address how to align the needs of the school community with their own individual growth in ways that lead to student success and whole-school achievement. The goal is not to seek a comfort level for professionals, but to help them become increasingly competent in working with students and to improve achievement. Individual development, aligned with goals and needs of the district, supports systemic change and improvement. How often do educators see individual professional growth plans aligned with the goals of their districts? While continuing to focus on the benefits, not only to individual teachers but to students and the school as a whole, a principal can foster individual professional growth plans leading to increased teacher competence in the classroom.

Research and Best Practices

Individual professional development plans link learning to the immediate and real problems faced by teachers. Professional development designed by the individual teacher assumes that the most powerful learning is that which occurs in response to the current needs of a teacher. It allows for immediate application, experimentation, and adaptation in the classroom by the teacher (Sparks & Hirsh, 1997). Recognizing and supporting individually guided professional development provides opportunities for principals or superintendents to help each teacher's growth in unique ways while still supporting overall school improvement goals (Tracy & Schuttenberg, 1990). The self-directed model is designed to assist both the individual and the school organization in achieving mutually agreed-upon goals of increased student achievement.

Helping teachers not only design but be accountable for their own learning and professional development is critical to the process. Supporting teachers as they develop individual pathways to learning provides each teacher with freedom of choice, but also with clear expectations that their efforts must focus on students and help increase student success.

> A variety of delivery patterns and growth opportunities which are clearly laid out have the most potential for satisfying the diverse needs of any school staff while remaining congruent with a larger frame. Professional development choices need to be goal-directed and have some common thread which enhances previous experiences while developing new learnings. (Lipton & Greenblatt, 1992, p. 24)

Supporting Individual Pathways and Adult Learning

By supporting individual pathways for professional development, the school can model a learning community approach to teacher growth. As teachers design their own professional growth, they model for others life-long learning habits as members of a vibrant school learning community. These individual pathways must honor what we know about adult learning and the implications for professional development:

♦ Adults will commit to learning when they believe that the objectives are realistic and important for their personal and professional needs. They need to see that what they learn through professional development is relevant and applicable to their day-to-day activities and problems.

♦ Adults want to be the origin of their own learning and should therefore have some control over the what, who, how, why, when, and where of their learning, as long as it meets the criterion of increasing teacher capacity to affect student achievement.

♦ Adults will resist activities that they see as an attack on their competence. Professional development must be structured to provide support from peers and to reduce the fear of judgment.

♦ Adult learners need direct, concrete experiences for applying what they have learned to their work.

♦ Adult learners do not automatically transfer learning into daily practice. Coaching and other kinds of follow-up support are needed so that the learning is sustained.

♦ Adults need to receive feedback on the results of their efforts. Professional development activities must include opportunities for individuals to practice new skills and receive structured, helpful feedback.

♦ Adults should participate in small-group activities during the learning process. By providing opportunities to share, reflect, and generalize their learning and experiences, these small groups help adult learners move from simply understanding the new materials to the desired levels of application, analysis, synthesis, and evaluation.

♦ Adult learners come to the learning process with self-direction and a wide range of previous experiences, knowledge, interests, and competencies. This diversity must be accommodated in the planning and implementation of professional development.

♦ Adults enjoy novelty and variety in their learning experiences, and learning opportunities need to reflect these critical attributes of quality professional development. (Joyce & Shower, 1995; Little, 1993a; National Staff Development Council, 1995; Speck, 1996)

Individually guided professional development plans should recognize these adult learning needs and provide a means for meeting the diversity of needs, interests, and learning styles of teachers within a school. The school reform efforts focus on individualizing and personalizing learning. What better way to model this for teachers than by promoting and honoring the depth of an individual teacher's own professional development plan? Providing opportunities for teachers to exercise professional judgment about their learning empowers them as professionals to reflect on their practices and needs for improvement. Nothing sends a clearer message than the district's articulation of what is important in professional development. Individualized professional development and school-based changes are mutually supportive. One without the other renders either strategy unattainable. Together, they create a climate to support more effective learning for both students and teachers. Practiced together and balanced, they will transform schools into learning communities.

The design of individual professional development plans cannot be vague. Otherwise, the commitment of individual teachers to carry out their professional development plans lapses into good intentions, and something always forestalls their carrying out the plans. Teachers should analyze their current status as professionals, their classroom needs, the needs of their students, and the data that are available regarding student learning and achievement. Using this analysis as a starting point, teachers can develop the beginning elements of their individualized plans. Planning for professional growth does not consist of teachers' picking a workshop here and there. Individual professional development plans need to be structured with specific goals, which need to be met by specific actions on the part of the teacher. For example, a teacher might select participation in a series of grade-level meetings to examine student written work to determine the strengths and weaknesses of her writing curriculum. Or, if most students are failing estimation on the math exams, it is obvious that the teacher needs to include estimation as part of the curriculum and needs strategies for teaching this concept. Individual teachers may use professional development time to research training for themselves and later to embed appropriate learning and assessment strategies into the curriculum to meet their students' deficiencies. Assuming that raising math scores is a district goal, the principal as well as the teachers will be able to see the alignment of intentions, actions, and district goals and yet still meet individual teacher learning needs and abilities.

As professionals, teachers also need to look deeply into where they are in their career and where they should continue to develop. Individualized professional growth is not haphazard; instead, it is well planned and includes reflection time. Administrators should provide appropriate support for teachers to carry out their individualized plans. Administrators also help by focusing the teacher on the overall school and district goals that the individualized plan will help promote. It is this *balance* that must be kept in focus—between *individualizing* to meet a teacher's learning needs and working *together interdependently* to improve the school and student achievement.

Career stages and developmental needs of teachers are critical pieces in an individual's professional development process. By reviewing where they are in their careers and assessing their developmental needs, teachers will have a better understanding of how to keep themselves professionally current, excited about teaching, and moving toward appropriate goals. Table 5.1, Career Stages and Developmental Needs, is a tool for teachers to examine their developmental needs based on their career experiences. After reviewing the career stages, principals, too, will have a better understanding of teachers' developmental needs. These needs are very different for teachers in the first, formative years in the classroom versus senior teachers a few years from retirement. This individualized assessment of where teachers are in their careers honors teachers as professionals and

TABLE 5.1   Career Stages and Developmental Needs

Career Stage	Developmental Needs
Formative years (1-2 years)	Survival stage—Needs to learn day-to-day operations of classroom and school
Building years (3-5 years)	Building stage—Developing confidence in work and multifaceted role of teaching
Striving years (5-8 years)	Striving stage—Seeking to develop professionally and to achieve high job satisfaction
Crisis periods (varies)	Teacher burnout and need for renewal
Complacency (varies)	Complacency sets in, and innovation is low
Career wind-down (varies)	High status as a teacher without exerting much effort
Career end (varies)	Retirement

Based on the work of Burden (1982); Burke, Christensen, and Fessler (1984); Christensen, Burke, Fessler, and Hagstrom (1983); Feiman and Floden (1980); Newman, Dornburg, Dubois, and Kranz (1980); and Ponticell and Zepeda (1996).

creates the expectation for creative, needs-based individual professional growth plans designed and owned by teachers.

Designing Individualized Professional Development

As individual teachers design their personal professional development plans, Figure 5.1, Personal Cycle of Inquiry: Individualized Professional Development, will help focus the effort. The Personal Cycle of Inquiry invites teachers to complete a needs assessment, determine a focus, create a plan, carry out the plan, apply new learning in the classroom, reflect on the application, and evaluate the learning outcomes. The cycle is effective when used to inform teachers of their ongoing needs and plans for continuous growth and application of learning. As each step of the Personal Cycle of Inquiry is accomplished, the teacher has deepened his or her understanding of content and strategies, applied the new learning, and reflected on it, including analyzing its effectiveness with students. Too often, the professional development plans of individuals consist of series of activities with little application or reflection as to how the information and strategies

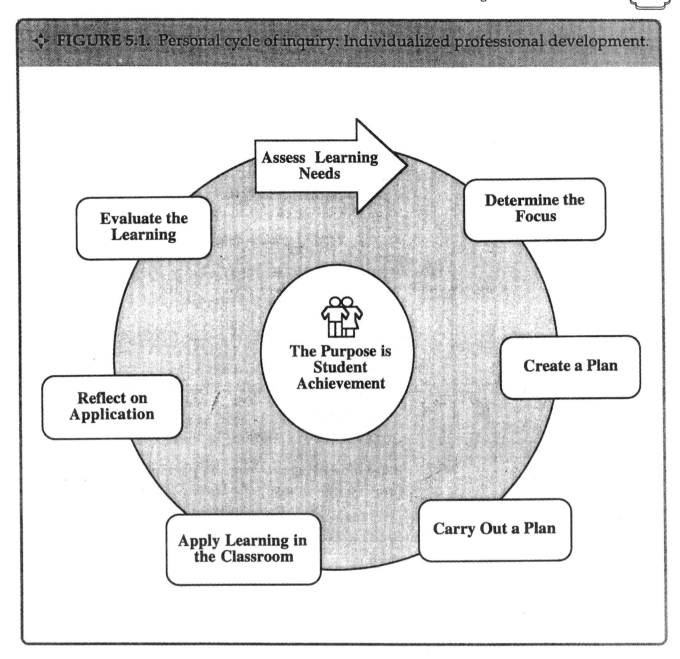

FIGURE 5.1. Personal cycle of inquiry: Individualized professional development.

will be used back in the classroom. With a clear plan of action, teachers can make intelligent and reasoned judgments on appropriate professional development opportunities that will meet their professional development goals in a systematic way. Each of the areas within the Personal Cycle of Inquiry: Individualized Professional Development will be reviewed by first raising a series of important questions and then discussing the importance of the area to keeping a clear focus for the individualized professional development plan on increasing student achievement.

The Personal Cycle of Inquiry

ASSESS LEARNING NEEDS

Where am I in my career?

What are my students' needs and achievement levels?

What data have I analyzed?

How am I prepared to meet my students' needs?

What are my school goals, and how do they relate
to my professional learning needs?

What do I want to learn as a teacher
to improve my students' achievement?

What are the priority areas I need to develop as a teacher
in order to increase my students' achievement?

Assess Learning Needs

In using the Personal Cycle of Inquiry, teachers must first look at where they are in their professional careers and where they want to grow professionally. Career stages and developmental levels are important factors in the needs assessment process for teachers. The needs assessment process allows a teacher to identify areas for growth, as related to classroom and student needs as well as overall school goals. This process helps to prioritize what is important for the teacher to focus on, because the vision of what needs to be learned and how it must be demonstrated is very clear. When teachers are empowered to assess their own learning needs and then to determine appropriate avenues for their development, they take ownership of the assessment and planning process.

DETERMINE THE FOCUS

Where will I focus my development?
Who will help me clarify the focus of my work?
Will my focused work help students to achieve?
How will my focus help promote school-wide and district goals?
How will I know?

Determine the Focus

Developing a clear focus for the professional development plan helps teachers stay centered on their professional growth. Too often, teachers can become distracted by the dailiness of schoolwork and fail to find the time to focus on their own growth needs. By creating a clear focus, teachers can target their efforts in professional development. The focus should emphasize impact on student achievement, which is the heart of every teacher's work.

CREATE A PLAN

What are my plans for carrying out my focused work?

What resources and support do I have to help me?

What connections can I make with others
to help develop my plan or our plans?

Create a Plan

Planning allows teachers and administrators to focus the professional development work with a clear process so that it can be carried out. Without a plan, teachers can drift from one focus to another without any validation for their efforts. A plan helps teachers reach a destination and clarifies how to spend their professional development time. The professional development plan becomes a road map for the teacher and allows for focus and depth of understanding to occur.

CARRY OUT A PLAN

How will I determine the professional development opportunities that best meet my needs and plans?

How will I schedule and carry out the professional development plan?

Carry Out a Plan

Professional development activities with a clearly defined plan become an important means of carrying out a teacher's focus. A thoughtful plan, with the specific types of professional development activities laid out, provides a systematic means of reaching the teacher's professional growth goals.

APPLY LEARNING IN THE CLASSROOM

What are my plans for applying the new learning to my classroom?

What will be different for students as a result of the plan when applied in the classroom?

How can I involve others in helping me plan the integration of these new ideas and concepts with the current curriculum?

How will the new learning affect my students?

Will it address their needs?

Apply Learning in the Classroom

How the teacher applies new learning and insights back in the classroom after a professional development seminar on content or strategies is critical. Without application and adjustments to specific classroom settings, teachers will not experience the power and influence of new information. The new learning must fit with identified student learning needs and must be tailored to an individual teacher's classroom situation. Professional development opportunities that plan coaching and feedback can help teachers as they apply new learnings in their classrooms, so that the new practice is understood, refined, used, and assessed on a regular basis.

REFLECT ON APPLICATION

How will I reflect on my learning and application
of ideas in the classroom?

How will I know that the application of these learnings
will improve student learning?

What difference has my professional learning
had on my classroom and student learning?

How have I expanded my repertoire as a teacher?

Reflect on Application

Reflection on the application and practice of new learning is important if teachers are to fully understand the impact level of a new concept or strategy. After implementing a new practice, a teacher needs additional professional development time to reflect on the success of the implementation and to determine if it met the intended outcomes. Reflective questions can help focus the work: Was the strategy implemented correctly? Were the right resources used? Were the processes clear? How did it align what is written in the curriculum with what was taught and assessed?

Reflection on the new learning and its application in the classroom allows teachers time to see what influence the professional development had on themselves and the impact on students. Reflections are more effective if shared with colleagues who used the same information or strategies.

A variety of implementation experiences will surface. This reflection process allows individual teachers to understand if their situations are unique and to compare experiences with others who have had the same difficulties or successes. Not only does reflection cause the curriculum and teacher behavior to change, but these changes also affect student learning and achievement.

EVALUATE THE LEARNING

How will I know that I have met my focus and goals?

How will my new learnings influence my future growth?

Given my current level of professional knowledge, what plans can I now make for additional growth?

Evaluate the Learning

Knowing whether the professional development's focus was appropriate, the follow-up plan was feasible, and the activities were relevant, as well as whether it had the potential to make a difference for students, is important for teachers to assess. Evaluation of how far a teacher has grown is an important part of the individualized professional development process. Evaluation and self-assessment provide new knowledge of what has been learned and of what a teacher needs as a continued or expanded area of focused growth. Too often, an educator experiences professional growth activities but never has follow-through or evaluates whether or not the activities were effective or how they fit into his or her overall plan to gain expertise. Evaluation sets the stage for an ongoing process of professional development and meeting goals. The results of the evaluation process provide information with which teachers can begin to design their next steps in the quest to keep professionally current.

Table 5.2, The Guiding Questions: Professional Development Personal Cycle of Inquiry, is provided for teachers to use in developing their own professional development plans. These guiding questions, which summarize the Cycle of Inquiry, will help teachers determine their own cycle of inquiry into their teaching practices and to plan their own individualized professional growth. The questions will help individual teachers determine needs, prioritize, plan, and evaluate their own learning.

TABLE 5.2   Guiding Questions: Professional Development Personal Cycle of Inquiry

Teacher Name: _____ School Year: _____

Assess learning needs

♦ Where am I in my career?

♦ What are my students' needs and achievement levels?

♦ What data have I analyzed?

♦ How am I prepared to meet my students' needs?

♦ What are my school goals, and how do they relate to my professional learning needs?

♦ What do I want to learn as a teacher to improve my students' achievement?

♦ What are the priority areas I need to develop as a teacher in order to increase my students' achievement?

Determine the focus

♦ Where will I focus my development?

♦ Who will help me clarify the focus of my work?

♦ Will my focused work help students to achieve?

♦ How will my focus help promote school-wide and district goals?

♦ How will I know?

Create a plan

♦ What are my plans for carrying out my focused work?

♦ What resources and support do I have to help me?

♦ What connections can I make with others to help develop my plan or our plans?

Carry out a plan

♦ How will I determine the professional development opportunities that best meet my needs and plans?

♦ How will I schedule and carry out the professional development plan?

Apply learning in the classroom

♦ What are my plans for applying the new learning to my classroom?

♦ What will be different for students as a result of the plan when applied in the classroom?

♦ How can I involve others in helping me plan the integration of these new ideas and concepts with the current curriculum?

TABLE 5.2 Continued

Teacher Name: _____ School Year: _____

♦ How will the new learning affect my students?

♦ Will it address their needs?

Reflect on application

♦ How will I reflect on my learning and application of ideas in the classroom?

♦ How will I know that the application of these learnings will improve student learning?

♦ What difference has my professional learning had on my classroom and student learning?

♦ How have I expanded my repertoire as a teacher?

Evaluate the learning

♦ How will I know that I have met my focus and goals?

♦ How will my new learnings influence my future growth?

♦ Given my current level of professional knowledge, what plans can I now make for additional growth?

Conclusion

By honoring teachers' individual professional growth plans, the principal and superintendent encourage them to be the initiators of their own professional growth. When the district understands and provides opportunities for teachers and other professionals to design their growth plans based on individual needs within the boundaries of school and district goals, it creates a culture of self-improvement, supporting teachers' individual growth needs and recognizing their development as professionals. For teachers and administrators to stay professionally current and meet the needs of diverse student populations, districts must pledge their support for educators to pursue lifelong learning.

REALITY CHECK

Given educators' diverse needs for professional growth
as well as the district's determination to improve student
achievement, what assumptions can we make
about the most effective design for individual professional
development in relation to school improvement?

On the Web

Resources for the individualized professional growth needs of teachers may be searched for on the Web in a variety of ways. The following Web resources provide information on the Regional Educational Lab Networks and their specialties, general teacher resources sites, and specific subject matter area resources sites; finally, there are important search engines that can assist teachers in their search for professional development opportunities to meet their specific needs.

Regional Educational Lab Network

The Regional Educational Lab Network (http://www.relnetwork.org) provides links to 10 U.S. Regional Educational Labs:

- Appalachian Educational Laboratory (specialty: rural education): http://www.ael.org

- North Central Regional Educational Laboratory (specialty: technology): http://www.ncrel.org

- Northwest Regional Educational Laboratory (specialty: school change process): http://www.nwrel.org

- Western Regional Educational Laboratory (specialty: assessment and accountability): http://www.wested.org

- Mid-Continent Regional Educational Laboratory (specialty: curriculum, learning, and instruction): http://www.mcrel.org

- Pacific Region Educational Laboratory (specialty: language and cultural diversity): http://www.prel.org

- Northeast and Islands Laboratory at Brown University (specialty: language and cultural diversity): http://www.lab.brown.edu

- Mid-Atlantic Laboratory for Student Success (specialty: urban education): http://www.temple.edu/departments/LSS

- SouthEastern Regional Vision for Education (specialty: early childhood education): http://www.serve.org

- Southwest Education Development Laboratory (specialty: language and cultural diversity): http://www.sedl.org

Teacher Resource Sites

- Teachnet (a teacher support network): www.teachnet.com

- Library-in-the-Sky for Teachers (user-friendly index of more than 6,300 education sites—organized by disciplines): www.nwrel.org/sky/teacher.html

- Libraryspot (this efficient site offers links to best library and references sites; reading room has a collection of on-line journals): www.libraryspot.com

- Collaborative Lesson Archive (practical lesson plans from fellow teachers): http://faldo.atmos.uiuc.edu/CLA

- The Art Teacher Connection (ideas and lesson plans): www.primenet.com/~arted

- Carol Hurst's Children's Literature Site (a great site!): www.carolhurst.com

- Awesome Library (access to just about anything you need): www.neat-schoolhouse.org

- The Internet Public Library (one of the largest searchable collections of links): www.ipl.org

- Curriculum Web (information and links): www.curriculumweb.org/cw

- Educator's Toolkit (information in a variety of areas): www.eagle.ca/!matink

- Web Sites and Resources for Teachers (links and more links): www.csun.edu/~vceed009

- Mailbox Companion (lesson plans): http://
  www.themailboxcompanion.com/members/int/repros/trip.html

- Busy Teachers' Web Site (helps K-12 teachers find direct source
  materials, lesson plans, classroom activities):
  www.ceismc.gatech.edu/BusyT

- Classroom Connect (searchable directory of educational sites and
  resources for teacher ideas): www.classroom.net

- Education World (lots of lesson-planning and curriculum
  resources): www.education-world.com

Specific Subject Matter Sites

Math Sites

- Arithmetic (ideas, lessons plans, software, and math games):
  http://forum.swarthmore.edu/arithmetic

- KidsBank.Com! (money, banking, and investing):
  www.kidsbank.com

- Math Magic (games and ideas):
  http://forum.swarthmore.edu/mathmagic

- Geometry Center (geometry ideas): www.geom.umn.edu

- The Math Forum (answers to just about anything you want to
  know about mathematics): http://forum.swarthmore.edu

- MegaMath (a site for both teachers and students):
  http://www/c3.lanl.gov/mega-math

- Teacher2Teacher (post a question, and other teachers can respond
  with math help and lesson plans):
  http://forum.swarthmore.edu/t2t

- SAMI (Science and Math Initiative, a one-stop shopping stop for
  math and science resources):
  http://www.learner.org/content/k12/sami/lessons/shtml

- Eisenhower National Clearinghouse for Mathematics and Science
  Education (exemplary K-12 programs for teaching science and
  math): www.enc.org

Science Sites

- National Science Teachers Association (an organization for the professional growth of teachers; many links): http://www.nsta.org

- ◆ K-12 Science (lessons plans, science fair projects, links to experts, lots of science ideas and projects): www.scicentral.com/k-12/index.html

- ◆ Exploratorium (science experiments): www.exploratorium.edu

- ◆ Plant Earth (a great amount of information on physics): http://www.nosc.mil/plant_earth/physics.html

- ◆ Science Adventures (reach hundreds of museums, science centers, planetariums, zoos, aquariums, aviaries, and nature centers across the United States): www.scienceadventures.org

- ◆ National Aeronautics and Space Administration (NASA) Educator Resource Center (access to NASA materials): www.vasc.mus.va.us/erc

- ◆ Bill Nye the Science Guy (a great Web site that parallels the television show): http://nyelabs.kcts.org

- ◆ Science Learning Network (wonderful resources for teachers, including lessons plans): http://www.sln.org

Social Studies Sites

- ◆ History/Social Studies for K-12 Teachers (access to lesson plans and teachers' advice): www.execpc.com/~dboals

- ◆ Lesson Plans and Activities—Social Studies (sources of social studies inspiration): www.mcrel.org/resouces/links/sslessons.asp

- ◆ Lesson Plans and Resources for Social Studies Teachers (compiles lesson plans on all aspects of social studies): www.csun.edu/~hcedu013/index.html

- ◆ Country Studies (information on countries from the Library of Congress): http://lcweb2.loc.gov/frd/cs/cshome.html

- ◆ GeoNet Game (an interactive geography game): www.hmco.com/hmco/school/geo/indexhi.html

- ◆ White House Tour for Kids: www2.whitehouse.gov/WHKIDS/html/kidshome.html

- ◆ This Day in History (famous events for every day of the year): www.historychannelcom/historychannel/thisday

- ◆ Internet Public Library Culture-Quest World Tour Page (information on many cultures): www.ipl.org/youth/cquest

- ◆ World Safari (changes every month): www.supersurf.com

♦ Electronic Field Trip to the United Nations (includes class activities): www.pbs.org/tal/un/index.html

♦ Around the World in 80 Clicks (explore 80 different places): www.coolsite.com/arworld.html

Language Arts Sites

♦ CyberGuides (provides step-by-step guides for teaching core literature works K-12): www.sdcoe.k12.ca.us/score/cyk3.html

♦ Academy Curricular Exchange (tons of ideas and plans): http://ofcn.org/cyber.serv/academy/ace/lang/elem.html

♦ Literary HyperCalendar (literary events for every day): www.yasuda-u.ac.jp/LitCalendar.html

♦ Creative Futures (kids write about technology): www.ozemail.com.au/!michaels/future.html

♦ Internet Public Library—Youth Division (a perfect place for on-line research at a kid's level): http://ipl.sils.umich.edu/youth

♦ Children's Literature Web Guide (many references and reviews to help you plan language arts lessons): http://www.ucalgary.cal!dkbrown/index.html

♦ New York Times Learning Network (daily news source and learning-teaching companion to the *New York Times*): www.nytimes.com/learning

Search Engines

♦ Google: http://www.google.com

♦ Infoseek: http://www.infoseek.com

♦ Dogpile: http://www.dogpile.com

♦ MetaCrawler: http://www.metacrawler.com

♦ Education World: http://db.education-world.com/perl/browse

♦ Northernlight: http://www.northernlight.com

♦ Inference Find: http://inferencefind.com

Challenging Districts Sustain Professional Growth

Scenario

Three members of the district—the assistant superintendent of instruction, the elementary principal, and the middle school principal—met to discuss why the standards movement had stalled in the schools. The assistant superintendent began the conversation. "I wish I knew how to get through to the teachers that this standards movement is the most important thing to happen to the public schools in the last decade."

The elementary principal was ready to speak. "If anyone forgets about standards, it's the district office and even site administrators. We ask teachers to completely rewrite their curricula with embedded standards, determine the assessment, set exemplars, examine student work, and learn new instructional strategies to connect with all kids. Then we go on with everything else we've always asked them to do, without ever acknowledging the enormity of the commitment to standards."

The middle school principal looked thoughtful. "The congestion on the streets is terrible today. I almost didn't get here on time." Now that you've mentioned the standards, I have to draw an analogy. It's like we're all stuck in traffic. The light has changed but we can't get going.

The assistant superintendent looked out the window. "Not a bad analogy, Dave. Maybe we do need to pause and figure this one out. It's too important to treat lightly." Seeing the cars now stalled in both lanes, she turned to the principals.

"Maybe we need to reroute traffic to get where we-need to go. Let's meet with the lead teachers right away to see how we can really support what we are asking them to do at the sites. Invite some leaders at your schools and get them subs for the morning. I'll see all of you at the Pancake House for breakfast on Tuesday morning at 7:30. I'm buying."

**Pause for a moment to reflect
on this essential question.**

ESSENTIAL QUESTION

How will a school design professional development opportunities based on meeting district goals?

Why Do We Have the Conversation?

Although the impetus for reform may come from either the school or the district, reform is not sustainable without support from the district office for professional learning. Nor will the public acknowledge a reformed or successful district without observing significant improvement in student achievement, school by school. Educators are not knowledgeable about how to develop learning communities or how to support reform throughout an entire district. A district that sustains change efforts, in which every school is connecting with all students and in which all students are meeting standards and demonstrating proficiency, is difficult to find.

> After over thirty years of working at the problem of change in schools, I have come to the conclusion that change is peculiarly difficult in schools because the schools, and the school districts of which they are typically a part, lack the capacities needed to support and sustain change efforts. Even in private companies when these capacities are often present, change is difficult; in public

school systems, where they are usually absent, real change is nearly impossible. Regardless of this observation, I have not given up on the idea that schools can be, and should be, changed in fundamental ways. If changes are to occur, however, those who lead must come to understand that to change schools and what occurs in classrooms, reformers must first introduce the changes needed to enhance the capacity of the educational system to support and sustain change in the schools. (Schlechty, 1997, pp. 80-81)

Case Study: A School's Need for District Support

An example of a school's commitment to change is Gilroy High School in California. Excited about their school, located in the fruit-, vegetable-, and garlic-producing farmlands of northern California, the school had received a major restructuring grant from the state, and staff members were already redefining their roles in school reform. They formed a leadership team with established roles and responsibilities. A team member agreed to be the "researcher," who read professional articles about reform efforts along with the team. He then summarized the articles, distributed copies to the staff to keep them informed, and filed a copy for future reference. One member was the "evaluator" and became the accountability conscience of the team, reminding them of the need both to ground their proposals in data and to conduct evaluative studies as they progressed. For informed presentations to their faculty, board of education, and state funding agency, they needed to present hard data in such a way that others could understand their direction. They had a "historian," so that their work was never wasted or lost in someone's notes. They also assigned rotating roles of "recorder," "facilitator," and "reporter." The teachers on the team were well grounded in curricular areas, and the principal never missed a meeting with his team to support, inform, and sometimes guide the discussions of practices they wished to change or professional development opportunities they intended to incorporate. They presented their plans to the Gilroy Unified Board of Education, who would be responsible for approving many of their changes, including the class schedule. The principal and superintendent suggested daylong informational sessions to keep the board fully advised of their plans. Eventually, the team brought Dr. Philip Schlechty to work with them, starting with a joint session in cooperation with two other restructuring high schools. They invited superintendents, district office personnel, and boards of education along with their high school leadership teams to meet with Dr. Schlechty and become better informed about his work in Kentucky and other states. They hoped to learn more about the process of reform and what to expect in results. One young faculty member was astounded at the time required for his involvement in the effort. He complained to one of the authors, a facilitator at a meeting of school leadership teams, "I teach my classes; I teach my peers; I teach my principal; and now I must teach the Board of Education?"

Boards want to hear from teachers and students to bring reality to the district reports about how their priorities for dollars affect students in the classroom. In addition, they need to understand the systemic support that schools need to sustain major reform. The caution for boards of education is that if a board supports only one school's reform, other schools in the system will probably not move ahead. They will wait to see what happens to the school that confronted the need for change. Like the lead goose in the V formation taking the beating of adverse winds and storms, the school that stays in the lead of reform will soon tire. It needs another school to step into the lead position while it moves wearily to the end of the V and is held aloft in part by the momentum of the rest moving in synchronization. Synchronizing the movement of all schools to focus on student achievement and continuous teacher preparation constitutes the work of the superintendent in concert with and supported by the board of education.

> In spite of the fact that there are numerous examples of "schools that work," few examples can be found of school districts where all the schools work as well as the community would like. . . . Exemplary school districts are harder to find than exemplary schools within school districts that seem to be failing. Further, when exemplary districts do appear, they tend to be relatively small or to consist of clusters of schools in larger school districts such as East Harlem District 4 in New York City which includes the highly praised Central Park East Secondary School. Indeed, much of the early research on effective schools was based on locating schools that worked inside school districts that did not. (Schlechty, 1997, p. 77)

Research and Best Practices

In 1973 Peter Drucker, in his landmark book entitled *Management: Tasks—Responsibilities—Practices*, devoted an entire chapter to effective boards. Drucker addressed three functions of the board; in summary, they are to fulfill the role as a review organ to counsel, advise, and deliberate with top management about the organization's business; to remove top management that fails to perform; and to serve as a public and community relations entity. Drucker was concerned at that time with top management's efforts to get rid of boards in the business world, because he feared that if large corporations did not have boards who had the company's best interests in mind, then government would step in and appoint boards. "Such an imposed board will attempt to control top management and to dictate direction and decision" (Drucker, 1973, pp. 631-632).

Over the years, organizations have made several attempts to identify the work of boards of education. One of the problems has been that when special interests groups elect board members, their interests are tied to their sponsors instead of to student achievement. Single-interest board members who do not set priorities for the district based on the success of all students have frustrated conscientious teachers and administrators. Other boards have been known to expend valuable resources on negotiated agreements that the district cannot possibly meet. Their penalty, unfortunately, is merely that they do not run for additional elected terms. The district staff members, on the other hand, are left to face the consequences of the lack of focus and direction.

The authors have also worked with boards that have made courageous decisions to support change efforts in the schools. They used strategic planning processes as well as district-generated future scenarios to make informed decisions about potential directions for the organization. As a result of the process and new understandings about how to bring about changes in schools, they instituted learning opportunities for students, teachers, and parents of the community. These efforts may not be sufficient in the eyes of legislators, however. With sanctions against low-performing schools, the California legislature, for example, is moving in the direction of state-assigned school, district, and board governance. Furthermore, ever since Chicago citizens opted for governing boards for each school instead of one board of education for the district, schools and districts have been waiting to see what will happen to traditionally elected boards and to the ways they establish learning priorities for teachers and students.

All reform efforts—adoption of standards and assessment objectives, federal initiatives, state mandates, political change—highlight the need for professional development policies in the district. Included in the policies should be the professional growth of board members—a need that is just as real as the need for teachers, administrators, and classified staff to achieve greater competence in their positions. When boards expand their own capacities to keep up, not only with the changes of school populations, but also with changes in teaching and learning, they are better prepared to support a district-wide focus on student achievement with professional development dollars for teachers.

District Efforts to Build Capacity and Sustain Professional Growth

The Learning Cycle

District staffs who believe that professional learning and growth will make it possible for the district to continue to improve should demonstrate the practice to their schools and public. They become responsible for collecting accurate data on student achievement to use in decision making and in establishing reinforcing cycles of learning for themselves, other educators, and students in the schools. To demonstrate their commitment to action research and the learning cycle, districts model the process by reporting both the process and the results to the schools and the public. Aligning their actions to the purpose of increasing student achievement, districts plan their cycles of learning as follows:

+ Consider the data

+ Develop objectives

+ Decide the outcomes aligned to the purpose

+ Plan the assessment

+ Prioritize the activities to align with the purpose and objectives

+ Reject the unaligned activities

+ Establish benchmarks with roles, responsibilities, and timelines

+ Implement the actions

+ Study the results

+ Reflect

+ Adjust

+ Continue with the next cycle, beginning once again with considering the data (see Figure 6.1)

It is sometimes difficult for district teams to realize that there is no major difference between the use of learning cycles to support schools and asking teachers and principals to use learning cycles to improve student achievement. When they "walk the talk," others will understand the level of commitment they are making to professional learning and student achievement.

❖ **FIGURE 6.1.** Planning cycle for districts.

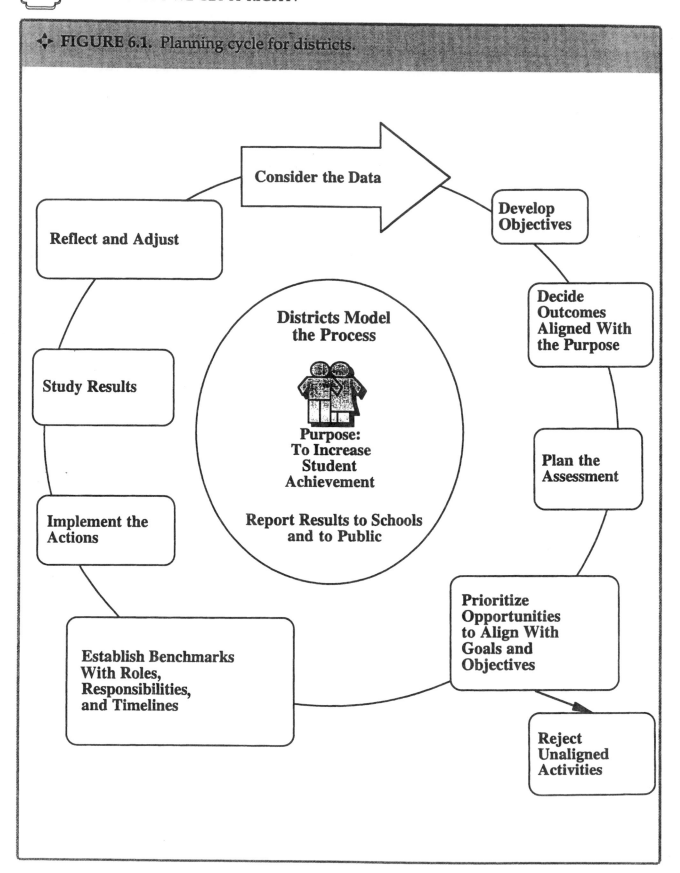

Consider the Data

Develop Objectives

Reflect and Adjust

Decide Outcomes Aligned With the Purpose

Study Results

Districts Model the Process

Purpose: To Increase Student Achievement

Report Results to Schools and to Public

Plan the Assessment

Implement the Actions

Prioritize Opportunities to Align With Goals and Objectives

Establish Benchmarks With Roles, Responsibilities, and Timelines

Reject Unaligned Activities

Districts sometime think that they can plan each teacher's role and professional growth in the change process. The difference is between planning—and then handing off the plan for someone else to do—and planning personal actions to support schools. Handing off a completed plan has no power for the users, and although the energy may have been high during the brainstorming ideas period, the energy for carrying out the plan is usually very low when teachers are not involved in shaping the initiative. Whether districts are developing parent information and communication networks or assisting schools in developing new curricula, the cyclical nature of performance and assessment should be their mental model.

Planning Processes Sustain Growth

Strategic plans can result in a major curricular thrust in which teachers revise their district grade-level expectations of students and in which assessments are used to determine whether or not students should be promoted or graduated. In one district, the board conducted an extensive informational campaign so that the major change in this district was that more parents became aware of the expectations of teachers. This, in itself, was not sufficient, because although the expectations were in place, no plan accompanied them for supporting teachers to change instruction to be certain all students could meet the standards. Saying to one student who expects to be promoted or graduated, "You made it," and to another, "You didn't, so try harder next time," is an old way of thinking that supports the theory of sort and select instead of the goal that every student will succeed. In a similar vein, saying to all teachers, "Teach all students to meet the standards," without asking them what they need to learn to be able to adjust or significantly change their instruction is also an invalid approach to reform.

Case Study: A System-Wide Effort

Contrast the above traditional planning processes with California's Berryessa Union School District's implementation of their goals. The Berryessa board and superintendent made a number of commitments. First, they adopted goals centered on student achievement, so that no matter what the area, they used student achievement as a measure of the district's success. Second, in their mission statement, they included supporting partnerships with the school community—staff, students, parents, and local business and community members. Third, they made learning a priority of the district at all levels for all members of the school community. They lived their mission statement when they gave professional growth credit for membership on action teams for student success formed around their goals. Parents, teachers, classified staff, administrators, and community as members of collaborative action teams were asked to sustain the work in the district. Fourth, they kept the same goals for several years so that they could sustain the focus of the district. Fifth, each collaborative action team had multiple schools represented, so that they could strategically position the district to retain its focus no matter what other directives were imposed on the district from the state or local community.

At a 2-day seminar at the start of the school year, collaborative action team members started their planning with the following resolution:

Every student has the right

♦ to be held to high expectations and standards,

♦ to have access to the latest technology in the learning environment,

♦ to expect the highest quality of thinking and behavior from the staff, experience good teaching and appropriate instruction,

♦ to be safe and secure,

♦ to be listened to, heard and understood.

—*Berryessa Union School District Student Rights*

Thinking of professional development in traditional ways, administrators would not have considered the time spent on these district-wide action teams as viable alternatives to seat time at a reading seminar. As teachers served on these teams, however, their knowledge of the district and of the power of setting goals together contributed significantly to their personal and professional growth. Interestingly, many school representatives were also teacher leaders at their sites, responsible for convening grade-level meetings, deciding how to invest their professional development days, and reviewing data to set goals for student achievement. The superintendent challenged the teams to have very specific objectives. On student achievement, for example, the action team's statement began, "Starting in June 1998, the number of students who are below the district standards in reading will be reduced by 10%." The plan also included how the team would measure success.

The team's actions included "review assessment data, identify students who are below standards (have not met standards), develop strategies (by individual teacher and grade level), and assess students at least every eight weeks to monitor progress towards meeting standards." To emphasize the importance of these goals, the action teams individually reported to the board of education in January and May 1999 and in February and May 2000.

Following Ann Lieberman's recommendations for seeking both internal and external balance in professional learning (Lieberman & Miller, 1999), the superintendent decided that sponsoring teams centered on the board's goals was not the only strategy needed by the district. The superintendent sponsored leaders who enrolled in the Foundation Program of the California School Leadership Academy (CSLA), a major player in the professional development area for significant changes at the school site resulting in student success. The Academy was an outgrowth of Senate Bill 813, major school reform legislation in California that included among its articles the professional growth of administrators. During 2 to 3 years of professional development seminars, participants, who can also be teacher leaders, learn how build a foundation for reform focused on student achievement results. The second strategy for the Berryessa District was to sponsor those administrators who were ready to bring school leadership teams to the CSLA table and be facilitated in their change efforts at the site. Recognizing the importance of contextual support for schools involved in significant change efforts, the superintendent signed the required form authorizing each team's involvement in the Academy. Teachers were also involved in curricular efforts on specific content areas, such as reading and math. Teachers serving on the performance assessment development teams also earned credits toward salary increases, as did facilitating district grade-level teachers who convened to score performance tests against a rubric.

In the learning community of Berryessa, many professional development opportunities were available, including seminars and professional coaching for new teachers and administrators. The differences between what had happened in the past and what was currently under way were that all participants used data provided by the district as a basis for taking action, and all maintained the integrity of the district's vision focused on student achievement. Although the learning opportunities were as varied as the needs of individual schools requesting support, everyone stayed focused on the vision. District and school administrators were evaluated on their involvement in and support of the board goals, their leadership and management skills in the schools and district, and student success at the location of their responsibilities.

Underlying this thrust at the whole system was a deep-seated belief of the superintendent—and many others in the organization—in systems thinking, a shift from fragments to wholes, as articulated by Peter Senge (1990):

I call systems thinking the fifth discipline because it is the conceptual cornerstone that underlies all of the five learning disciplines of this book [i.e., personal mastery, mental models, building shared vision, team learning, and systems thinking]. All are concerned with a shift of mind from seeing people as helpless reactors to see-

ing them as active participants in shaping their reality, from react-
ing to the present to creating the future. . . . Systems thinking is the
cornerstone of how learning organizations think about their world.
(p. 69)

Design: The Purpose

From the district and school perspective, the purpose of professional development is to further the achievement of students. The purpose, by definition, is in concert with the continuous preparation of teachers, who are
learning to educate in new ways to raise the achievement level of all students. Needing to show results, a district bases its outcomes on academic
needs, with student and teacher learning components. The knowledge
base for the entire educational community includes systems thinking, and
for teachers and principals, it must include the sustainable skills involved
in teaching and learning. According to Linda Darling-Hammond's
research, the content must include

conceptual knowledge of subject matter; knowledge about children's cognitive, social, and personal development; understanding
of learning and motivation; appreciation for the diversity of children's learning experiences and approaches to learning and knowledge of varied teaching strategies to address them; skill in using
collaborative learning techniques, new curriculum tools and technologies, and sophisticated assessments of learning and the capacity to work collectively and reflect on practice with other teachers.
(Darling-Hammond, 1997b, p. 334)

Multiple Perspectives

How do we include diverse participants in the design to bring multiple
perspectives to change efforts? This is a consideration for all professional
development efforts. If only experienced teachers are brought into a planning room, for example, the district will lose the perspectives of teachers
new to the district. When the planning committees pay attention to the
diversity of their members, what they accomplish will be the result of their
collective best thinking about students and about how to improve each student's level of achievement.

Notice the difference in perspective. How many district-generated committees in the past have focused on improving the schools or district but have not affected student learning? In districts determined to raise student achievement, superintendents can ill afford scattered approaches to planning professional development in their schools. Such lack of focus wastes precious resources, fiscal and human. Measuring the value of programs means that districts must have a yardstick, and that yardstick is results.

Time for Learning

Time to invest in this process is directly related to the complexities of the tasks. Just as districts cannot demand profound change in a year, on the balance, neither can they afford to wait. Students cannot delay their education while they wait for schools to change. A year in the life of a student is so critical, it may be the determiner of whether a student stays in school or drops out, whether he or she pursues an education or is indifferent to it. Will the light of academic understanding and excitement be kindled or suffocated? Students can't wait for changes that will connect them to their schools. Neither can teachers wait for the learning that will sustain their efforts to increase academic achievement. State legislators must hear the impassioned pleas of educators to provide for continuous professional learning, and it is the responsibility of districts and boards to help carry the message.

Resource Allocation

For the district, the details of support lie in resource allocations.

> As education results have faltered, the reaction has been to increase bureaucratic controls and specialization, producing a flow of staff and dollars out of classrooms and into side offices and peripheral functions. Schools need policies that reverse that flow, moving both people and funds back into the classroom. (Darling-Hammond, 1997b, p. 335)

Communication Links

As board members are elected and as district office staff members are hired, one criterion that is often underestimated is how well each person communicates. Communication links are very complex in a changing system and are vital to the success of the district's goals (see Figure 6.2, Communication Links, Extensive and Necessary in a Changing System). In forward-looking districts, district offices support every link that the school makes in its restructuring or reforming efforts. In addition, the board of education plays a key role as a vital communication link with the entire community, including the unique communities of individual schools. Once the focus on student achievement has been determined to be the absolute top priority of the district, board members must seize every opportunity to support the schools. When members are interviewed by the media, for example, it is important for them to weave into the conversation support for the change efforts of the schools as well as the focus on student achievement. A board member who is asked about an occurrence of violence in the schools usually responds by describing steps the district is taking to ensure the safety of all students. In the same conversation with media, the second point should always be to recognize steps the district is taking to ensure each student's opportunity for learning, including the continuous preparation of all staff working with students. Taking advantage of such opportunities to support the primary purpose of schooling should be the mental model for each leader in the school community.

When the superintendent or board members are in schools for any reason, it is important that they acknowledge the learning that teachers are engaged in to support student achievement. The symbolic actions of top leadership in support of teaching and learning are very powerful statements about the direction of the district. Through these vital communication links used in continuous support of student achievement, district leadership will align the actions of the district with its purpose.

Where to Be Fluid and Where to Hold Fast: Student Success

It rapidly becomes obvious to readers of educational reform initiatives that districts and schools must hold fast on the improved performance of students and the improved effectiveness of teachers. Failure to organize a district around raising student achievement is to ignore the public's mandate for its schools. High expectations for all students are revealed in the

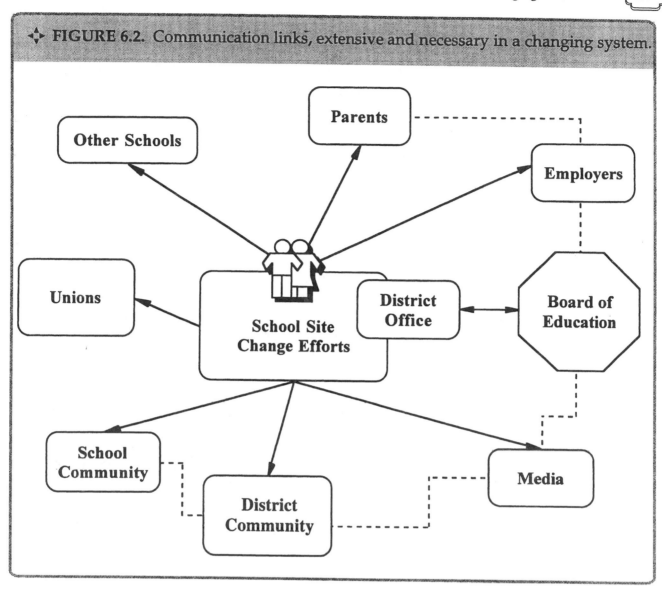

◆ FIGURE 6.2. Communication links, extensive and necessary in a changing system.

district's adopted standards and assessments, which require a demonstration of performance to meet the standards. How do educators teach to the standards? How do they embed standards in the curriculum? What strategies do they learn to expand their capacities to help students meet the standards? How do they report student progress to their unique or collective communities? These are the fluid decisions for individual schools and districts to make.

Virtually everyone at the school concedes that the performance levels of large numbers of students are far below what it will take to reach the standards. . . . To make a performance-based system effective, the school—indeed, the school district, because the policy is in effect district-wide—needs to transform the system to ensure that students succeed. It needs to provide additional help to students who are falling behind. It needs to provide assistance to teachers to enable them to teach students in ways that will ensure that they can meet standards. It needs to reorganize the organization and management of the school so that the principal and the leadership team make decisions based on what students need to reach the standards. It needs to redirect resources so that the resources are concentrated on strategies that enable the school to achieve the desired results. It needs to engage parents and the public to support high standards for all students. (Marsh & Codding, 1999, p. 17)

For lessons we can learn about our changing world, we can turn to recent management books, such as Kevin Kelly's *New Rules for the New Economy* (1998), Harrison Owen's *The Spirit of Leadership: Liberating the Leader in Each of Us* (1999), and Guy Kawasaki's *Rules for Revolutionaries* (1999). Each describes how to respond to the "new world" of demanding, aware, networking clients. From the authors' experiences, educators have yet to tap into this fluid world. A new company or product emerges in this new world because the public is tired of waiting in line, looking in stores that don't sell the product they want, and waiting for people to answer their phones. The public will not be loyal to a product or an organization that no longer serves it well—thus the emergence of e-commerce, a rapidly expanding direct line to improved service. We in education have yet to respond satisfactorily as a profession to the parents and communities who are now expressing their demands through legislation.

If these learnings of the business community are so critical to organizations, how can educators apply the insights to education? We believe the response is in fluidity. It seems that students are tired of waiting until teachers can get around to helping them in a class of 50 or 60. Students are dropping out because they are not connecting to what their instructors are teaching or to how they are facilitating student learning. Districts will be forced to learn how students are processing information and how they are connecting their learning to a foundation of experiences as they struggle to make meaning. If there is a message in books from the business world to educators, it is that instructors must learn to be far more flexible in varying teaching strategies and recognizing the fluidity of how each student learns. If, for example, one strategy isn't working, do teachers have a second, third, or fourth teaching strategy, or do they partner students with mentors who can help them immediately? This is a now generation. For some students, if a few minutes of scanning the materials don't produce an answer, they give up because neither the search nor the outcome is worth the time and effort. In essence, school staffs must continuously increase their effectiveness in teaching students how to learn, how to process information, and what to do when they become frustrated with the complexities.

Teacher effectiveness is the key to a student's success (Darling-Hammond, 1997b); therefore, districts must help teachers continuously expand their knowledge about content, processes, and professional strategies so that they are equipped to teach in this connected world. Teachers can be fluid in how they teach, but districts, in response to the public, will hold fast to the premise that all students will be academically successful and will have the data to prove their results.

Conclusion

At times, districts get caught in a web of political agendas. One member of the school board wants to repave the playgrounds in all the elementary schools. One wants to release a particular administrator. Another has been elected by the teachers' union to represent the financial interests of teachers. And so it goes. One concept is very clear. Unless the district focuses on improved student learning and assesses how every action it takes affects student success, members of the public will become more and more dissatisfied with the schools they support with tax dollars and, as they are already doing, will seek alternatives. Teachers and principals cannot change schools working alone. They must have district support. The time is right for districts to rethink how they have operated in the past and to open themselves to community-wide collaborative actions focused on student success. Teachers and administrators must be prepared to find new ways of connecting with students to enable them to be successful, and at the same time they must commit to continuous improvement of their own skills. Professional growth is part of the question about how educators do "it," and professional development that includes teachers and principals in the planning process is part of the answer. How will schools and districts grow to meet the challenges of the new century? They will grow through collaborative, articulated, comprehensive, and resource-sufficient professional development programs that have the full support of districts and schools.

REALITY CHECK

If districts are focused on standards of student achievement, how can they be assured that professional development designs support the achievement of their goals?

On the Web

The National School Boards Association (NSBA) is responsible for assisting local boards with national issues. For concerns generated by state legislation and department of education actions, state school board associations will assist boards. Both provide key components of policies or actual documents for superintendents and boards to refer to when dealing with current topics. At the NSBA Web site (http://www.nsba.com), boards can find model technology policies on-line that can be very helpful. Access to other information regarding professional development policies in their archives is through e-mail to webmasters or other designated on-line correspondents.

Designing Your
Own Model

In the faculty room of a middle school the planning committee for inservice days met to discuss the possibilities. "I think we ought to contact the regional service center to provide facilitation for the two days," began a fifth-grade teacher.

"Why? What would they do?" her colleague questioned.

"They could do a math or science program. I hear they have a way of presenting math concepts that is really a kick."

The second-grade teacher was thoughtfully sipping her tea. "I don't need that right now. What I need is more information about the reading series we just adopted. It has a very different approach to phonics, one I'm not familiar with. I need help."

The fourth-grade teacher entered the conversation. "I think we need a break from all this stuff about curriculum. Let's have a least one day that we can enjoy. My friend had a speaker from Nordstrom's at her school who did a 'dress for success' presentation that showed a lot of great outfits for the season."

"I don't think they do that any more," another teacher chimed in. "But what about somebody from a science laboratory who can help us get started with our science fair?"

By the end of the meeting the group had narrowed the choices to present to the faculty. They also admitted that because the dates were less than 3 weeks away, the decision about the inservice days was really dependent on which person wasn't already booked for those days.

Unfortunately, the scenario above is not atypical of school conversations. Without a well-thought-out design for professional development in the school and district, faculties often flounder when they plan allocated professional development time. Teachers who plan one segment of professional development without aligning it to the organization's goals and sequencing it with existing standards and assessment are wasting valuable teacher and administrator time and energy. On the other hand, applying the plan to the needs of teachers focused on student success will lead to the payoffs everyone is seeking.

*Pause for a moment to reflect
on this essential question.*

ESSENTIAL QUESTION

How will a school design
professional development opportunities
based on meeting its specific needs?

Introduction

Designing a professional development program is a complex undertaking that includes skill preparation as well as content focus. Becoming more concerned about "what teachers will do" rather than the more speculative "how to prepare them for the work" could determine the success or failure of the efforts. David Thornburg (1994) described two types of professional development—"just in case" and "just in time." Most professional development in the past was "just in case you need this in your teaching." Currently, teachers need specific skills *now* to assist all students in meeting the standards, and they have no time to explore a variety of programs simply because they may be useful at some future time, in some related way. "Just in time" training allows the teacher to determine his or her needs for professional development and conveys the urgency many teachers feel about the new expectations for teaching and learning (Thornburg, 1994).

Because educators and researchers are now designating the school as the locus of professional development, we need more than ever the knowledge and skills to design effective models of professional development. The models emerge from the need to report results—improved student success. This chapter is written to help educational leaders responsible for professional development design their own programs using the "POTENT" method as a guide for long-term and short-term results. We have also highlighted some of the important elements of design to consider when implementing POTENT. When designers address these elements, using systems thinking, for example, as a habit of mind for acquiring strategies to build a learning community, they will create a greater depth to their professional development design. The caution section of this chapter is written as a reminder to planners that even the best advice from researchers has implementation subtleties that must be considered. Designating roles and responsibilities in a seminar planning session, for example, carries with it a caution of avoiding creating the "innies" and the "outies" of a school faculty. This important section examines each recommendation from the experts and helps educators plan effective implementation.

Why Do We Have the Conversation?

It has become increasingly clear that teachers want to play a vital role in the selection and implementation of professional development opportunities; otherwise, teachers may not be interested in professional development. Cathy J. Cook, mathematics educator and professional development specialist, reports her findings: "If teachers feel burdened by their regular classroom preparations, they may believe they cannot spend additional time on personal growth" (Cook & Fine, 1996, p. 6). Teachers may resist opportunities because of their past experiences with irrelevant seminars (Darling-Hammond, 1997b; Sparks & Hirsh, 1997). When they see evidence of the results in student achievement, they will know the power of collaborating to plan their own learning. Results will also give other educators in the school and district a better understanding about the tremendous need for teachers' continued meaningful involvement in the process of professional learning.

Cook and Fine (1996) further note that, according to research by the Coalition of Essential Schools, teachers preferred to make changes that did not require broad consensus and that did not interfere with the school routine. Consider the impact of this research: Teachers don't want to "interfere" in what their colleagues are doing; therefore, implementing changes in the curriculum becomes a delicate renegotiation of boundaries (Cook & Fine, 1996). The need to build a culture of continuous learning is so great that schools that ignore the opportunity will lose the benefits of sustainable change.

POTENT Professional Development

POTENT is an acronym representing a powerful tool created for designers of school or district professional development programs; the acronym stands for Purpose and Preparation; Outcomes; Targets and Tools; Energy, Effectiveness, and Evaluation; Numbers, Names, and Needs; and Timelines. The POTENT planning tool can be used to analyze the current program or to plan for significant events within the scope of a multiyear school plan. Using POTENT as a filter for all professional development proposals will challenge a school and district staff to think about high-quality professional development and its impact on student learning.

Moving from theoretical to the practical, educators know that they must learn new skills in order to teach *all* students. They know now that they can connect to students and their learning styles, their physical environment, their experiences, their communities, and their readiness. They also need to be more strategic and systemic in their thinking about how to become proficient at reaching each student as they align their outcomes with student achievement. Knowledge about teaching and learning is expanding so rapidly, they need opportunities to stay current with research. Educators need help from researchers' findings and from each other to implement innovations and refine practices. They need the space and time to reach mastery as well as leadership opportunities to share their new skills with others. These concerns will be addressed as educators learn to design long-term professional development opportunities at the district and site levels.

The acronym *POTENT* will help to determine the elements of a planning process for high-powered or POTENT professional development opportunities. The concept becomes a fractal, in that planners can use it to analyze the overall program on a larger scale, yet they can also use the frame for significant opportunities within the scope of their plans. Guided by the POTENT frame provided in this chapter, educators will be practicing systems awareness as they define the relationships, information, and vision for professional development in the internal and external systems of their school (see Figure 7.1, How POTENT Is Your Professional Development?). In addition, the writers have included a frame without the significant questions so that designers can write their responses using their own issues and data to complete the plan (Figure 7.2).

After each element of POTENT, the writers have included a list of questions facilitators should ask when planning professional development

❖ FIGURE 7.1. How potent is your professional development?

P	PURPOSE PREPARATION	1. What is the central focus of your work and how does it align with the organization's core purpose? 2. Who cares about this work? 3. How will you clearly define the problem so that the professional development aligns with your needs? 4. Have you prepared staff with information about how change occurs and how groups of people become high performing teams?
O	OUTCOMES	1. Is your outcome worthy of the cost? 2. Is it achievable? 3. Does it involve skill development and mastery? 4. What is the impact on student achievement? 5. Does it promote a learning community - collaboration, working from data, respect, inquiry, dialogue, free of blame?
T	TARGETS TOOLS	1 Who are the target participants? 2. How will you assess their readiness? 3. How will you organize your work? 4. What tools and technology do you need? 5. Will you do presentations, coaching, feedback, action research, follow-up?
E	ENERGY EVALUATION	1. What energy level or passion do you have for pursuing and sustaining the outcomes? 2. How can you restructure the outcomes so that they are worthy of your energy and passion? 3. What processses are in place to evaluate the impact of the work on student achievement?
N	NUMBERS (DATA) NAMES NEEDS	1. What data do you have? 2. What data do you need? 3. Who will be involved? 4. What are their responsibilities? 5. What resources do you need - human, fiscal, material?
T	TIMELINES	1. What can reasonably be expected in 1 month, 1 year, 3 years? 2. What are the short range and long-range goals connected to the timelines? 3. What does success look like?

✦ FIGURE 7.2. How potent is your professional development?

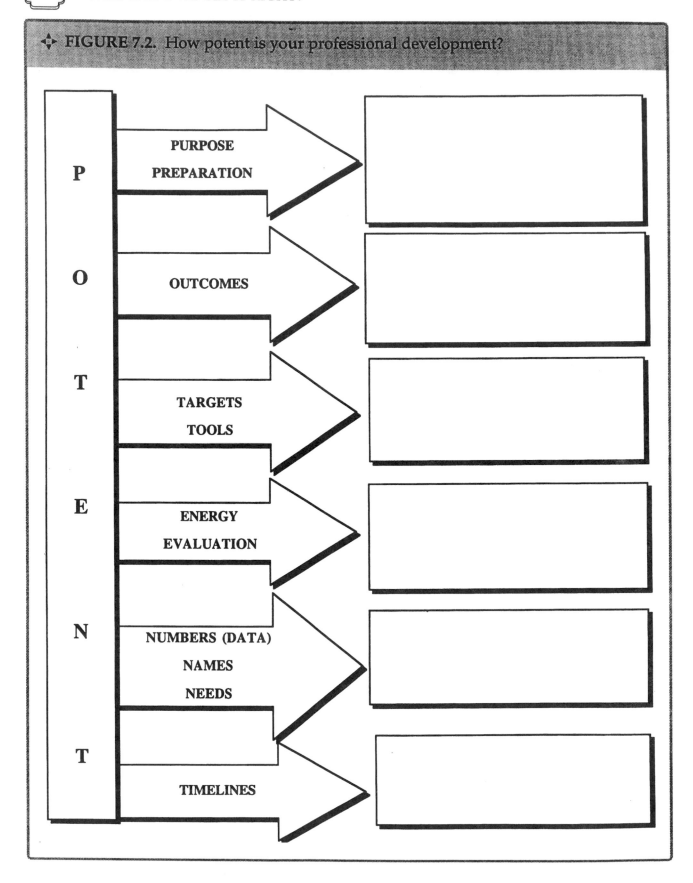

P

PURPOSE

PREPARATION

O

OUTCOMES

T

TARGETS

TOOLS

E

ENERGY

EVALUATION

N

NUMBERS (DATA)

NAMES

NEEDS

T

TIMELINES

opportunities whether they are in grade-level meetings, department meetings, or with an entire staff. The questions are prompts to make certain that designers have covered all the elements. Be aware that two or more elements may be reflected for each letter of POTENT.

P Is a Clear Purpose and Adequate Preparation

Aligning professional development with a single purpose—that is, results in student achievement—ensures that you are pursuing a goal with a single intent over an extended period of time. The purpose must be visionary, with agreement from your district and community that people will care about the results when your purpose is accomplished.

Preparing participants to do the work is often neglected. Teachers, for example, are plunged into profound changes in the way they construct curriculum and assessment without any knowledge of why they are feeling resistant or angry. Learning about change and how it will affect their behaviors is critical to the process. Conversely, ignoring teachers' preparation needlessly delays the change efforts from being implemented in an acceptable length of time, if at all. People must be prepared with high-level communication skills in order to work together as one high-performing team bringing about the necessary changes in all their complexity. In fact, without the ability to communicate effectively on an ongoing formal and informal basis, new information about teaching and learning will stop with a single teacher and never have the systemic impact of shared knowledge on system-wide student success.

PURPOSE AND PREPARATION QUESTIONS TO CONSIDER IN PROFESSIONAL DEVELOPMENT PLANNING

What is the central focus of your work, and how is this focus aligned with the organization's core purpose?

Who cares about this work?

How will you clearly define the purpose so that the professional development aligns with your needs?

How will you prepare staff with information about how change occurs and how groups of people become high-performing teams?

O Is a Worthy Outcome

The outcomes of your professional development activities, seminars, action research, coaching experiences, or team experiences will vary depending on the topic. It is important to determine before approving the expenditures whether or not the outcome is worthy of the cost. The outcomes must be achievable. If the outcomes involve learning a new skill, does your outcome also involve opportunities to progress from awareness to mastery? If the outcome involves teaching and learning, does it detail the student achievement that will result? Professional development outcomes should always build on the attributes of a learning community: collaboration, working from data, reflection, inquiry, dialogue, and blameless discussion.

Having clear outcomes is important to participants, because with outcomes, there are no surprises either about what you are planning or the anticipated results of the experiences.

OUTCOME QUESTIONS TO CONSIDER IN PROFESSIONAL DEVELOPMENT PLANNING

Is your outcome worthy of the cost?

Is it achievable?

Does it involve skill development and mastery?

What is the impact on student achievement?

Does it promote the attributes of a learning community, including collaboration, working from data, reflection, inquiry, dialogue, and blameless discussion?

T Is Target and Tools

When planning, the team needs to establish a target audience as well as a learning target. What level of experience and expertise will the plan target for this work? Experienced teachers become very frustrated if the skill level assumed in the training is out of touch with where they are. Experienced teachers may not need the same depth of involvement in order to implement new strategies. Conversely, beginning teachers need a safe place to say, "I have no idea about how this will work in a classroom, or how to prepare the students." They may not need experienced teachers giving explicit directions. They do need a thoughtful inquiry process that lets them discover and take risks. Professional development planners should take the time to consider these needs. The learning target must be equally specific. Expanding teachers' knowledge of content and their repertoire of teaching and assessment strategies is especially important in teaching to the standards. Teachers using interactive learning to teach specific standards, for example, become proficient in planning not only the learning opportunity, but also the assessment, so that students are learning, doing, and demonstrating proficiency.

What tools will be needed to do the work? Facilitators can explore tools as configurations for activities, such as large-group or small-group facilitation, or tools may be strategies of facilitation, such as using physical movement as a stimulus to evoke deeper thinking. Tools may also be frames, graphics, computer displays, on-line case studies, videos, or use of Web sites to help with researching a topic. Many tools are available to teacher leaders and professional staff developers depending on the format selected: coaching, feedback loop, action research, follow-up. When planning, it is helpful to broaden the selection of strategies by staying current with the tools of the profession through the National Staff Development Council and through the state affiliate (see Chapter 8, Tools for Implementing a Professional Development Design).

TARGET AND TOOLS QUESTIONS TO CONSIDER IN PROFESSIONAL DEVELOPMENT PLANNING

Who are the target participants?

How will you assess their readiness?

How will content and strategies be aligned to purpose and outcomes?

Are the content and strategies aligned with state and district standards and assessments?

What tools do you need?

Will you include facilitated seminars, coaching, feedback loops, action research, and follow-up in your plan?

E Is Energy, Effectiveness, and Evaluation

We earlier addressed the need for high energy by team leaders and facilitators for professional development. If participants don't have some passion for the results of their professional development experience, they need to negotiate with their colleagues about what will increase the overall level of energy. If everyone has low energy for the task, the program may not receive the attention it deserves. Because teachers' needs for high-quality support are so great, a low-energy project may appropriately be put on hold and replaced with one that meets more urgent needs of the staff.

Effectiveness refers to looking at three levels of impact of professional development. First, consider what the impact will be on student achievement. Second, the professional development should affect the teachers' accumulation of effective skills and strategies. Third, the plan should affect other teachers in the system. The professional development plan you are creating should lessen the isolation of teachers and lead to new roles and responsibilities for them within the school organization. One teacher's excellence does not make an effective school, and single schools, although they may be individually effective, do not make an effective district. It is a discipline for individuals to be aware of a school's direction and the impact it will have on the district, but one must regularly assess the bigger picture if education is to serve all students and improve in the eyes of the public.

The evaluation of the design is of critical importance in looking at what works and what does not work. Teachers in the past have tried various strategies to improve performance, but they have not held themselves accountable for the effect of the new strategies by looking for results in student work. A solid evaluation instrument will help determine if the strategy needs to be continued, refined, discarded, or replaced with more effective ways of accomplishing the goal (see also Chapter 9, Evaluating Professional Development).

ENERGY, EFFECTIVENESS, AND EVALUATION QUESTIONS TO CONSIDER IN PROFESSIONAL DEVELOPMENT PLANNING

What energy or passion do you have for pursuing and sustaining the outcomes?

How can you negotiate the outcomes so that they are worthy of your energy and passion?

What processes are in place to evaluate the impact of the work on student achievement?

What processes are in place to evaluate the impact on teachers' repertoires of effective skills and strategies?

Will the professional development plan lead to new roles and responsibilities for teachers within the school and district organization?

N Is Numbers (What Data Do You Need?) and Needs (Human, Financial, and Material)

We suggest that you not embark on professional development activities without data that prove the need. Because teachers are consumed by their daily responsibilities, they should know that what they will do is important and necessary. As you consider their current and projected needs, both should be substantiated by analyzing data. For example, if students need to learn estimation because their performance in this subject area is very low compared with other students of a comparable grade level, you have a valid reason for professional collaboration on new strategies needed to increase student achievement. The need is urgent and must be weighed against a plan for teachers to attend other, less timely training.

Planners should also be clear about the need for resources—human, financial, or material—to build a professional development plan. Frequently, schools will have a need for particular staff members or parents to participate in designated professional development activities because of their roles in the school. Department chairs or lead teachers may be asked to attend district-level seminars so that they can facilitate the key learnings with their colleagues. If participants are expected to relay important information from the sessions, the facilitator should include in the seminar plans who will take responsibility for designing the facilitated informational sessions and when they will occur.

Too often we underestimate the time it takes to implement new strategies and to assess their effectiveness, and planners may forget to budget for coaching and substitute costs or dollars needed for materials. In designing a professional development plan, leaders will undoubtedly be asked to prepare a budget for specific components. Be aware that educators can no longer limit the cost of training new skills or strategies to a few facilitated seminars. They can easily attach dollar figures to these initial costs, but the equation must be reconfigured in order to consider the total investment of human and financial resources in sustained professional skill building. Consider the formula in Figure 7.3, Determining Cost of Human Resources for Professional Growth.

Understanding the dollar figures when initiating professional growth may help planners remember to align the purpose of student achievement with worthy outcomes before investing in a design. This brings up another critical point. Investing in a single professional development strategy without understanding its place in the long-term design is foolish, because doing so will undoubtedly lead to wasted resources.

Materials needed for the design are also important considerations. Hastily duplicated articles or information downloaded from the Internet to a faulty printer may lead to poor-quality materials for use by participants. Team leaders and facilitators show respect for other teachers and the time they are investing to participate by securing the best, most readable materials available. Teachers who are facilitating sessions supported with mate-

❖ **FIGURE 7.3.** Determining the cost of human resources for professional growth.

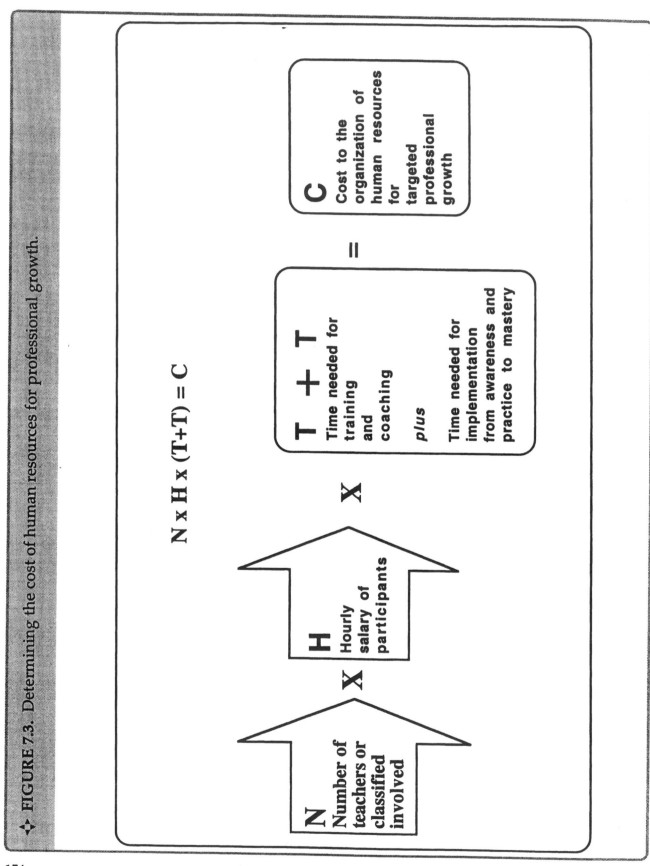

rial budgets will have access to quality printing. The timeliness of materials is another concern in the design. Like outdated textbooks, outdated seminar materials may mislead participants when more recent research could help them with their concerns. The rapid changes so typical of other professional fields are happening in education, too. The need for today's educators to have newer, more effective materials and strategies for working with today's diversified youth cannot be ignored.

As students and teachers become more demanding, schools and districts will be expected to provide more resources for professional development than ever before. When a district invests in its staff and the community by having quality materials for professional learning aligned with the purpose, the rewards will be in student performance.

NUMBERS AND NEEDS
QUESTIONS TO CONSIDER IN
PROFESSIONAL DEVELOPMENT PLANNING

What data do you have to support your design?

What data will you collect on an ongoing basis?

Who will be involved, and
how will they communicate to others?

What are their responsibilities for implementation?

What human, fiscal, and material
resources do you need?

How will you budget for long-term
implementation of skills and strategies?

How will you assure the quality, readability,
and timeliness of materials?

T Is Timelines

When educators create professional development opportunities that span 2 to 3 years, they must also remain flexible. Planning for only 1 year is not recommended unless planners are very much in touch with the direction of the district and that direction has not changed. A reasonable timeline for cohesive efforts is an important consideration in professional development and one that facilitators and teacher leaders should make very clear at the beginning to avoid misguided expectations on the part of both participants and supervisors. At the same time, everyone should understand that other timelines will emerge from doing the work. As each timeline and benchmark is met, everyone should know what success looks like. Without a clear picture of success, efforts can stray from the focus, lacking accountability for results.

TIMELINE QUESTIONS TO CONSIDER IN PROFESSIONAL DEVELOPMENT PLANNING

What results can reasonably be expected in
1 month, 1 year, or 3 years?

What are the short-range and long-range goals
connected to the timelines?

What does success look like?

Participants in the 21st century are far more sophisticated than their counterparts a decade ago. Educators see more involved graphic representations on television. They can view animation on their computer screens. They can order the most up-to-date books and have delivery within 48 hours. Teachers need the most current information a professional development design can offer to help with one of the most difficult jobs in our society, educating today's youth. When planners and facilitators use POTENT as a frame for planning professional development, they are assuring themselves and the people working with them that they are preparing teachers in the best, most effective, professionally executed design they can create.

Design Elements to Consider
When Implementing POTENT

The intensive labor of professional development planning and design is seldom visible to participants. Designers must deal with teaching and learning challenges, adult learning strategies, standards and assessment issues, and teacher work concerns. At the same time, they cannot ignore superintendent directives and board policies. The authors have identified professional development issues that control the design of effective programs. If staff members have experienced programs that seem to be lacking depth, it will be helpful for them to explore the issues in Figure 7.4, Issues That Control the Design of Effective Professional Development Opportunities.

Using Systems Thinking as a Habit of Mind

Peter Senge's research reminds professional developers and other leaders to think of their work in the context of a living system (Senge et al., 1999). We build relationships, facilitate the flow of information, and establish individual vision and identity within a larger context. We live in many systems: organizational, economic, social, political, environmental, and personal. In education, we live within the academic systems of schools, districts, universities, county and regional offices, and departments of education. As members of living systems, we are continually interacting with our environment, generating new knowledge about how to function, and learning how to rebuild our systems.

Knowing about systems is important to leaders who are analyzing their schools and collaborating with their school communities to initiate change. Through systems, leaders learn to look for patterns, processes, and structures that have affected learning in the past and that will affect learning in the future. Without the ability to understand the system, leaders will falter in their attempts to change what is currently happening. They may change one aspect of teaching by adopting a new textbook, for example, but the teaching strategies, curriculum, environment, and culture will stay the same. In leading schools to a standards-based system, leaders begin with the standards and assessment, which then form the basis for all curriculum and, in fact, the basis for all decisions in the school affecting teaching and learning, the school environment, and the culture. Changing whole systems is not a task: It is a commitment to an entirely new way of thinking and acting. When an entire staff decides to change a school to focus on student achievement, information about students and student achievement must permeate the system. The changes they intend to accomplish are

◆◇◆ **FIGURE 7.4.** Issues that control the design of effective professional development opportunities.

PLANNING MEANINGFUL INVOLVEMENT FOCUSED ON STUDENT ACHIEVEMENT

How can a professional development design give decision-making powers to staffs while aligning with the district purpose of student achievement?

CREATING OPPORTUNITIES FOR COLLABORATION

How can a professional development design assure the flow of information to all staff members through continuous opportunities to collaborate?

LEARNING TO IMPACT THE SYSTEM

How can we plan professional development so that feedback from our school community is not an add-on, but an integral part of our learning about how we are impacting the system?

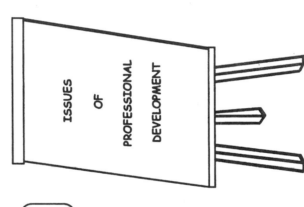

ISSUES

OF

PROFESSIONAL

DEVELOPMENT

CHALLENGING OUR NATURAL CURIOSITY AND DESIRE TO LEARN

What professional development strategies can we design that will stimulate curiosity and a desire to learn?

BUILDING A LEARNING COMMUNITY

What guarantees must be built into our professional development design so that we model learning at all levels?

USING SYSTEMS THINKING AS A HABIT OF THE MIND

Knowing that organizations live within larger systems, how can we develop a systemic professional development design so that we do not become isolated in our thinking or our learning?

based on their data, and each person has a clear vision about the purpose and direction of the school. The staff forms relationships and networks within and outside of the school with the purpose in mind. The interaction of the relationships, information, and self-referencing based on their clear vision will enable them to sustain their focus and accomplish their purpose.

Through professional development, educators are able to gain insights, new perspectives, and creative strategies for affecting the system. They are able to share and create new information and test new strategies and ideas with others they trust who have the same vision. One of the most challenging exercises is to look personally, then collectively, at how the work is affecting, impeding, or propelling student progress at the site. Because schools are parts of larger systems, they cannot be isolated from the larger systems. Every member of the school community has a role in ensuring student success. When individuals acknowledge that they do not live or teach in isolation but that they are vital practitioners within larger systems having continuous interactions affecting students, they are using a very healthy habit of the mind to assess the challenges.

> **Knowing that organizations live within larger systems, how can we develop a systemic professional development design so that we do not become isolated in our thinking or our learning?**

Building a Learning Community

Teachers need to be involved in learning new skills and strategies as models in a learning community. Students can tell us very quickly which teachers and administrators have stopped learning. One principal sends his vice principals to all the professional development seminars "because I already have more ointments in the barn than the cows can use in my lifetime." He said it with tongue in cheek, but in fact, many educators believe that they already know how to manage and teach, if the students would just focus on learning! A futuristic way of looking at teaching and learning

is that we will never know all there is to know about the educational processes. Strategies for learning together, therefore, have to be a part of what
educators, students, parents, and members of a dynamic community do
(Barth, 1990).

> **What guarantees must be built into our professional
> development design so that we model learning at all levels
> as we build our learning community?**

Challenging a Natural Curiosity and
a Desire to Learn

Educators need to be attentive to how the brain functions when planning professional development in the schools. They need to be very aware
of brain research, because although the research continues to produce conflicting reports about our neurons and synapses, conclusions about natural
curiosity and a continuous ability to learn form patterns in the literature.
Rockefeller University's Bruce S. McEwen has observed that "the most
important thing is to realize that the brain is growing and changing all the
time. It feeds on stimulation and it is never too late to feed it" (quoted in
Kotulak, 1996, p. 11). One of the primary assailants on neurons is the sup-
pression of curiosity, of the desire to learn. A failure is that educators work
very hard to stimulate the brains of students and forget that the brains of
adults also need stimulation. Adults need to be challenged to exert their
natural curiosity about teaching and learning.

> **What professional development strategies will stimulate
> curiosity and challenge the desire to learn?**

Planning Meaningful Involvement

Humans want some control over what happens to them in the workplace as a boon to their mental health. Brain researcher Pierce Howard described people who are allowed to take a direct planning and decision-making role in their own lives. In summary, these people live longer, are sick less, are happier, more alert, and have less of the stress hormone cortisol (Howard, 1994, p. 64). Teachers want and need to be part of designing, planning, implementing, reviewing, evaluating, and reconfiguring professional development.

> **How can a professional development design give decision-making powers to staffs while aligning with the district purpose of student achievement?**

Providing Opportunities for Collaboration

Teachers in a learning community experience the power of shared knowledge. To make responsible decisions, workers in any organization must have a steady flow of information about their work (Wheatley, 1994). They need multiple, multilevel opportunities to build their knowledge base. Teachers who examine content standards together and decide how the standards will be assessed have a basis for building shared knowledge as they write new curricula. They decide what skills and strategies will be employed to improve the performance of students and how to collect the results. There is a professional power that comes from having knowledge about how to enable students to be more successful.

> **How can a professional development design ensure the flow of information to all staff members through continuous opportunities to collaborate?**

Learning to Affect the System

Sharing and acting on new knowledge about teaching and learning that results in the success of students will in some way affect the larger system—the district and other schools as well as the local school community. It is from the larger system that teachers need support for their work. Although new knowledge and new strategies don't spread with the same rapidity as bad news or scandal, when educators change their ways of working with colleagues and students, the ripples in the system must become supportive waves. Appropriate planning for professional development is one way of determining what educators will do to affect the system and how they will do it. When they assess their work and communicate their progress to others in the school community, the feedback they receive soon lets them know their impact on the system.

> **How can staffs plan professional development
> so that feedback from their school communities
> is treated not as an add-on but as essential information
> needed to inform their work about how
> they are affecting the system?**

Design Cautions

When Darling-Hammond (1997b) studied successful schools, she identified at least five structures in these schools that supported decentralized information and shared knowledge:

1. Team planning and teaching allow teachers to share knowledge with one another. . . .

2. Cross-group structures are used for planning, communication, and decision making. . . .

3. Professional development is built into the schedule and tied to ongoing homegrown innovations so that teachers learn by doing as they collectively construct new practices. . . .

4. The schools continually share rich information about students, families and classroom work through vehicles like narrative report cards, student and teacher portfolios, class and school newsletters and widely distributed meeting notes. Information about what teachers are doing and how it is working is available everywhere throughout the school. . . .

5. Highly visible shared exhibitions of student work make it clear what each school values and how students are progressing. Aggregated data about student performance are also regularly available and discussed. (Darling-Hammond, 1997b, pp. 167-168)

As educators become increasingly effective in determining priorities for professional development in their design for a high-quality professional development program, they need to be cautious about the subtle implications of implementing some highly recommended strategies. The appropriate test for professional development is "What is the potential impact on student learning and student achievement?" Before a district implements the recommended structures, district leaders need to be aware of what elements will cause the recommended steps to be effective and what potential they have for success. We will analyze eight practices we have adapted from researchers of effective schools to help with planning quality professional development (Darling-Hammond, 1997b; Fullan, 1993; Lieberman, 1996; Schlechty, 1997).

Design Practices for Quality Professional Development

Every teacher is involved in preplanning professional development activities. Teachers have input, for example, into the outcomes, strategies, experts, facilitators, and overall design over an extended period of time. The intent is to involve the staff in assessing its own needs so that students can be successful and to plan professional development around those needs. The caution is that teachers may not have current information about what options are available. The infusion of new information is critical to a staff's high level of performance. The potential impact in this example is long term. Teachers usually know what information they should have on a short-term basis, but they may not be as willing to think about long-term professional development plans until their urgent needs are met. The same is true for principals who are instructional leaders. Teachers and principals who continuously share their learning include each other in the current information loop.

The schedule of professional development activities includes time for clusters of three or four teachers with a common preparation period to share progress on action research. The key to this professional development strategy is "action research." Having teams with a common preparation period meet to plan curriculum may or may not result in a high impact on student achievement if teams have no plans for collecting student data. Are they conducting action research on elements of their curriculum to determine what content and strategies are enabling students to meet the standards? If so, the time devoted to action research preparation, implementation, data collection, and analysis is truly professional development in that it has such a high potential for affecting student learning.

In the weekly schedule, specific professional development time is set aside for teacher sharing across grade levels, district grade levels, and cluster or content areas. The intent in this strategy is that teachers will meet with other teachers to align curriculum, assess performance, and share strategies. Lieberman (1991) summarizes this form of professional development as learning that "recognizes the significance of informal networks as a means for a teacher's intellectual learning and social support" (p. vii). The caution is that the agendas must be planned, not serendipitous. Many teachers do not appreciate spending time with teachers of other grade levels unless they are involved in meaningful work. Some districts, for example, ask teachers at grade levels across the district to meet at least twice a year to review performance assessments and corresponding data about student achievement. Through these examinations, the principals and teachers ensure district-wide consistency in assessing student performance, and they raise their level of awareness about what others are doing to prepare students for the assessment process. Some teachers may not see the immediate impact of these events on their classroom teaching; however, the potential of teachers' sharing their assessments of student work is great for raising the achievement level of entire schools or districts. Administrators, too, must be patient with the process. Assigning days for district-wide grade-level meetings on assessment is an investment. Over time, teachers will become comfortable with giving input and with disagreeing without being disagreeable as they learn to accept the validity of the group's work and to make adjustments in their curricula. The benefits are enormous, but only if the process becomes a part of the continuing high expectations of teachers in the district.

When teachers team-teach, they use their common preparation time to prepare curriculum and discuss strategies. They also schedule professional development time to collaborate with other teams. Teams need to meet with other teams to discuss strategies for making their efforts more effective, as well as for purposes of sharing their standards-based curriculum and assessment strategies. Too often, teams of teachers aren't effective teams. They engage in parallel teaching; that is, each teacher teaches a particular unit while the other teacher assists, and they don't align their content and strategies so that students can enjoy a cohesive learning model. In addition to standards and assessment issues, professional development time should include strategies for teacher groups to become high-performing teacher teams. The potential for student impact by a high-performing team versus a fragmented team would be a project for a researcher. Based on a knowledge of sports teams, industrial teams, and even teams involved in space exploration, the authors assume that high-performing teams in schools will have greater impact on student learning, but they are unaware of specific research that validates this point.

Teachers in working teams schedule ongoing professional development days to discuss student data based on performance testing. They also set aside time to analyze individual students' results and to agree on exemplars. Unless teams are focused on student success, they may get caught up in "This is what I like to teach" or "The students enjoyed the unit, so why shouldn't I teach it?" Working with student exemplars across the school and district is a key issue in this example of a district's good use of professional development time. Using agreed-upon exemplars enables teachers to be consistent in their expectations of student work that meets a standard and work that does not. Performance testing must be accompanied by these professional conversations. Done consistently, the potential for impact on student learning is very high.

Teachers agree not only to use narrative report cards for students, but also to use professional development periods to review narratives and discuss them with teachers from the prior year to learn more about their individual students. The caution is that some teachers object to using professional development time to examine the prior year's student data, and they also do not want to examine these data on their own time. The most common objection to reviewing prior-year data is that the teacher does not want to become biased about a student's abilities. It is unfortunate that educators have thought of data in this way instead of looking at a student's past performance as a way of assessing his or her needs. Deficiencies must be addressed before the student is "passed on" without having the necessary skills to learn at the next level. Reading teachers have become more aware of how to use running records, for example, to identify a student's particular problems. Once the problems are identified, the teacher is able to address the student's deficiency and, in so doing, accelerate his or her overall progress. Prior-year student data are valuable sources of information for informing teachers.

The district updates data each time a round of testing is completed so that the data collection includes the most recent standardized testing, performance assessment, standards data, and specialized testing (e.g., literacy tests). Each time new data are distributed, teachers meet to analyze the data and the potential impact on their teaching. Districts must know that failure to provide teachers with current data inhibits their effectiveness. Educators should exercise caution about supporting the excuses of "too expensive, too labor-intensive, or too great a burden for our old computers." District personnel who are willing to deal with the hardware and software problems can expect teachers to use data-driven decision making to improve student achievement. Teachers investing professional development time in reviewing the downloaded data have a potentially high impact on student learning as teachers change instruction to achieve student success.

Every teacher has an e-mail address and daily access to the Internet, so that when teachers are working with curriculum and need instant feedback from others in the school, district, or nation, they have access to the best and the brightest. Installing and maintaining every teacher's access to the Internet is another district responsibility. The caution is that teachers who are energized by what they discover must have the discipline to bring the new knowledge back to the district's established priorities for teaching and learning. When all members of the school community learn to focus and align efforts with standards and performance assessment, they will be helping all students improve their potential to demonstrate success. Using the Internet to increase teacher effectiveness has a potential of moderate to high impact on student learning.

Participants may be chosen to attend professional development activities because of their particular roles in the school community. The expectation is that the individuals will take the information back to their groups so that everyone is informed. Individuals may or may not relay information to the groups that they represent. Parents, for example, may be asked to attend a school's seminar on the readiness of children for certain curricula. The staff expects that these parents will communicate with other parents and inform them of the school's direction. Unless the professional development design allows for planning who will report to the parents, how it will happen, and when, the expectation that parents will inform others, except at the most informal level, will probably not be met. The same is true for all participants. Although role representatives have a variety of responsibilities and different groups to report to, the facilitator needs to take responsibility for allocating time to design the feedback loop. Closing the feedback loop has the potential of high impact, because everyone in the school community is informed and, ideally, supportive of efforts to improve student achievement.

The board has approved a performance-based system, and the community appears to hold firm on the standards even if large groups of students do not graduate on time. In *The New American High School,* Marsh and Codding (1999) discuss a foundation of changed practices that will be in place in order to transform systems so that students demonstrate performance to graduate. For students who are falling behind, the school should provide additional help. Professional development is an essential component for providing assistance to teachers who are learning to teach to the standards. The organization and management of a systems-based school and district will change so that the principal and school leaders make decisions based on what students need. The school's professional development resources will be focused on strategies that enable the staff to achieve the desired results. In addition, the school will engage parents and the public for their support. If these system-wide changes are not in place, the school will brace itself for the fallout when students fail to graduate on time, "or it can water down the requirements and leave the system essentially as it is, with some students performing well and most doing just enough to get by" (Marsh & Codding, 1999, p. 17).

Conclusion

Educators who thoughtfully design long- and short-term learning experiences know that everyone involved should respect teachers' and administrators' dwindling professional and discretionary time. Furthermore, the research is very clear that to have a major impact on teaching and learning, practitioners must be involved in planning, implementing, analyzing, and reshaping the professional development program. The patterns that emerge in learning about design center on the purpose and the outcomes, how teachers and principals will be involved, where and when it will happen, how frequently, what levels of experience will be considered, and what the alternatives are. Careful planning using a systemic approach helps to ensure that programs will reflect the use of interactive strategies, will ensure a cohesive design, and will align to the system of standards and assessment. Using POTENT as a planning guide will help to ensure high-quality professional development. As designers become familiar with the components of POTENT, they will be compelled to ask critical questions in guiding their learning experiences. When the questions are answered to the leadership team's satisfaction, the program continues, and when there are no satisfactory responses regarding a proposed professional development opportunity, the team may elect not to move in that direction. High-quality professional development that is designed to improve student achievement and that is fully supported and highly valued by schools and districts is of vital importance to educators. Public school educators are running out of time to make significant improvements for the success of all students.

REALITY CHECK

In order to prepare teachers and students
for their roles in the 21st century, what are the
shared agreements about a professional development design
that will address inadequacies of the system
while maintaining a focus on student achievement?

On the Web

Professional development staff members should renew their memberships, if they have not already done so, in two organizations that offer top-quality educational information and resources on their Web sites. The first is the National Staff Development Council (NSDC), and the second is the Association for Supervision and Curriculum Development (ASCD).

Most helpful from the NSDC Web site is "A National Plan for Improving Professional Development" by Dennis Sparks and Stephanie Hirsh. One component of this report, "A New Model—The Learning School," has excellent information about professional development in an emerging learning community.

ASCD now has six different Web sites; go to http://www.ascd.org/services/sites.html for a list of sites and services. The ASCD Web sites are:

♦ The ASCD Web

♦ HireEd.net

♦ PD-Online

♦ The Online Store

♦ ASCD Select

♦ Member Benefits Online

Also a part of ASCD and helpful in planning high-quality professional development around standards and assessment is the Understanding by Design (Wiggins & McTighe, 1998) Web site at http://ubd.ascd.org/index.html. The text is a user-friendly, research-based approach to curricular design developed by Wiggins and McTighe. Particularly engaging are the sections entitled "FAQ (Frequently Asked Questions)" and "Ask the Authors," which offers the opportunity to ask questions directly to Wiggins and McTighe. Other opportunities are Idea Exchange, Unit Data Bases, and Resources and News.

Tools for Implementing a Professional Development Design

Scenario

Members of the assessment team met in the conference room at 1:00 Tuesday afternoon. The whole team had intended to meet once a week during their common preparation period, but that didn't always happen.

Julie started the conversation. "What's the focus for today's meeting? I brought all my assessment data, but who has the agenda?"

"I don't have an agenda," Jorge replied, "but I know what we are supposed to do. We are deciding what forms of assessment we will use for each level of math." He waved to a friend in the hallway. "Yo, Darby! We're at it again. Meet you later." He turned back to the team. "Now, where were we?"

Maria picked up the conversation. "I thought we started making decisions about the lower grades' math assessment at the last meeting." She stared at her calendar. "That must have been at least a month ago. So much has happened since then."

"This team always makes decisions," Jorge responded, "so who knows what they were?"

The silence was very uncomfortable.

"Hmm. We worked really hard." Maria was hesitant. "Didn't anyone take notes?"

"Sure. Lin always takes notes, but she isn't here today," Jorge began. They all looked expectantly at him. "In fact, I think she overcommitted, because now she is chair of a district curriculum committee!" Jorge picked up his leather organizer, still talking as he glanced through it. "Actually, Lin still should have given the notes to one of us, but I'm sure I haven't seen them."

Julie was thoughtful. "Well, I don't think I was at the last meeting! Did we report to the faculty or any other group about what we were doing?"

Maria responded. "No, I remember that we were going to wait until we finished the document before we reported to anyone."

"This is frustrating!" Julie blurted out. "I think we need something really big, like a wall chart. Then we can record our work as we go and post it in the faculty lounge so that teachers can give us feedback before we finalize the project. I mean, are we collaborative in this school or not? If we are collaborative, then we need feedback from our colleagues. If we aren't, we do it all by ourselves and give them the word."

"I like the idea of a wall chart for reporting our progress!" Jorge closed his organizer and looked at the others. "I saw a huge Action Team Planning Chart in the principal's office the other day. I'll ask her where she got it. Something like that—showing our purpose, outcomes, tasks, and progress—would be a great help."

Joe appeared at the door. "Hi, everyone. Sorry I'm late. I was delayed by my sub. She's uncertain about my fifth period class, not that I blame her, of course. They are wild after late lunch." He looked around the room. "Are we just starting or almost finished?"

Jorge looked at the others. "You know, if we had that wall chart in here now, we wouldn't have to start at the beginning. Joe would already know what we had done and where we were heading, so he could pitch right in." He paused, then added, "And I might feel as if we earned the professional development credits we are supposed to get for today's curriculum work."

Joe was quick to catch on. "A chart would help me, for sure."

"Joe isn't the only one who needs a memory," Maria added. "I think a record of the group's memory could be my memory, too."

"Meeting adjourned, everyone!" Julie looked at the clock and checked it against her watch. "Next time, we need a facilitator and a recorder, too, so that we know what we are supposed to do, what we have accomplished, and what we have left to do. I'll do the agenda. Also, we need to bring back all the assessment data we brought today so we can get to the real work without all the delays."

Maria made a few notes in her book. "And I will start by making an official record of our decisions: (a) to get a wall chart; (b) to record our purpose, outcomes, and tasks; (c) to post it in the faculty room; and (d) to figure out how to ask for feedback. It helps when you have a plan." She gathered her papers into a neat pile and put them in a folder. "I just wish we had decided all of this before we got started, but . . . 'mas vale tarde que nunca,' as my Aunt Juanita used to say."

"You got it!" Jorge agreed as he moved toward the door. "See you next Tuesday!"

Should planning from the beginning ever be mas vale tarde que nunca (better late than never)? No, but that's often the way it happens. Faculties that have no criteria for conducting their meetings are seldom efficient. Active participation from all members of a team requires planning and structure on the part of leaders. Educators who express the need for more hours in the day for professional development should look at the time they are already allocated to determine if they are using it effectively. As an integral part of their planning, they should select facilitation tools appropriate for the work to be accomplished.

Pause for a moment to reflect on this essential question.

ESSENTIAL QUESTION

How will a school select the best tools to implement a professional development design focused on optimal teacher learning and resulting in student success?

Introduction

This chapter, "Tools for Implementing a Professional Development Design," is designed to help knowledgeable planners and facilitators to look more intensely at the learning experiences of their colleagues. When educators determine the costs of professional development by computing the daily salaries of the attendees, they are awakened to the need for using techniques and strategies that will make the most of the time teachers and administrators are investing in the learning situations. Using *frames* as organizers of learning, they will choose what will become a group's memory, how they can lead participants to deeper discussions, how they can provide reflective documents to provoke a larger conversation, how they can report new realities to a staff, and how frames can be used in meetings to inform the entire school community.

People *connections* build relationships for deeper shared learning in the community. Just as frames organize our learning and prepare us to move forward, people connections in significant configurations enable school communities to build the relationships essential for work together. Using frames and connections to enhance learning should be as natural to professional development planners as ordering water and juice is in a training to refresh the bodies and brains of participants.

Another tool in the professional toolbox is the *inquiry cycle*. In using this tool, schools and districts prepare participants for action research as the basis for ongoing inquiry into the success and achievement of students. The tools of *reflection* and *dialogue* are of paramount importance in professional development planning. Teaching the skills of dialogue enables participants to learn from their experiences as they prepare future actions. Dialogue and reflection give educators "open space" for thinking about teaching and learning. This chapter is written to introduce tools for implementation that will help educators achieve both long-term and short-term results. Resources in the "On the Web" section will help with other related concepts as the planning progresses.

Implementation of a Professional Development Design

Frames

Frames are visible organizers of our work. They are graphic or written representations of important components to consider when working on a specific topic. Second, they bring specificity about the work, such as the two-column "T" chart, which designates "where we have been" and "where we are going," or a gap analysis using a "T & A" chart, which indicates "current state" and "desired state," followed by articulated "assumptions," as in Figure 8.1, Frames as Visible Organizers of Our Work. Third, frames can ensure that educators view isolated topics from a variety of perspectives, such as using a matrix to summarize data. Fourth, frames can provide a means for participants to narrow attention to ideas or topics or to explore their perspectives by offering a bigger picture illustrating where they are headed. Fifth, frames can be intricate designs with multiple steps that lead participants through an entire planning process or a plan for a single day in a series of events. Sixth, frames enable participants to review what they planned, discussed, analyzed, or decided so that the next time

❖ FIGURE 8.1. Frames as visible organizers of our work.

T Chart

Where We Have Been	Where We Are Going
Without focus	Common purpose
Isolated teaching	Collaboration
Professional development - one size fits all	Prof. dev. differentiated by levels and experience
Learning with experts	Prof. dev. balanced with inside and outside expertise

The Purpose Is to Improve Student Achievement

T & A Chart to Surface Assumptions

The Purpose Is to Improve Student Achievement

Current State	Desired State	Assumptions
Some teachers are using standards in daily work	All teachers are using standards and all students understand the expectations	That a standards-based curriculum gives all students greater access to success
Parents are not aware of standards	Parents understand and support a standards-based curriculum	That students will have greater success if parents are aware of and supportive of standards

the group convenes, the group has a "memory." Using frames helps groups recall what decisions they made and prepares them to move forward.

To understand why educators need frames to do the work, the writers will also explore how frames translate theory to practice, how they focus our energies, and how they individualize specific tasks. The text will reveal how frames provoke a team or group's memory, how they provide reflective time and provoke discussion, how they report new realities to the staff, and how they are used in meetings to inform the entire school community.

Frames translate theory to practice. Brain research indicates that people must interact with content to make it their own, but many group discussions are not focused and are therefore not very useful. Frames enable participants to shift from the theoretical to a focused connection with the topic. In past models of professional training on writing curriculum, for example, teachers heard presentations of new writing strategies and were then left on their own to develop related curriculum. "Here are materials or strategies you could use in your classroom" was the approach. Some teachers tried working with the new information, and some put it aside. In frustration, teachers began to demand "make and take" training so that they could have more immediate application of the concept. Focusing on these short-term innovations, however, did little to improve instruction.

Working collaboratively, teachers use organizers of information as a guide and a means for sharing a process. When teachers write curriculum, for example, they follow guides for discussing the innovations. Because frames reveal the thinking behind the proposed curricular revisions, teachers are able to increase each other's effectiveness. When a teacher sees how colleagues plan to use information, the knowledge base of everyone involved is increased. As one teacher receives feedback on his or her implementation strategies, other teachers are able to learn a variety of strategies using the same content. Frames enable faculty members to have conversations leading to their revised curriculum without seeming to belabor any one point, because the teachers are working collaboratively from the same guides and are able to trace the steps in each other's work.

An elementary staff, for example, requested a seminar on marine biology from a group specializing in life sciences. In theory, the hands-on experience could enable students to become more deeply involved in their learning. The life science group gave the staff a frame for examining how the activities could fit into the bigger picture of revising curriculum to make it more interactive for students. The purpose was for students to attain a higher level of achievement on related standards.

As part of the seminar, the group's facilitators took volunteers to nearby tide pools along the northern coast of the Pacific Ocean to explore the habitat of varieties of animal life. The teachers were both fascinated and energized. When they returned, they were determined to see how they could incorporate what they had just experienced into their science units.

Following their process frame, they first analyzed their grade-level standards and confirmed how the standards would be assessed. Once they came to a consensus on the priorities for learning, they were able to determine if using tide pools would help students achieve the standards. Now that the teachers had affirmed their direction, they could return to the training room for the next steps on writing meaningful curriculum.

The staff was not interested in adopting an entirely different curriculum, so facilitators offered a frame that walked teachers through a process for relating their life science unit to their specific standards and performance assessments. Having already decided how they would assess whether or not their students met the standards, the teachers were ready to revise their units of study with appropriate benchmarks. Although the process took several months, they met on a regular time schedule to share their progress. During the process, they agreed to use another frame for sharing alternative strategies for students who were having difficulty with the learning. As the teachers field tested their units, they prepared to share student work using frames they devised, first, for collecting and analyzing the results, and second, for planning their next steps.

Frames focus energies. When participants are completing team efforts over an extended period of time, they face the need to continuously refocus the energies of the group. With a knowledge of brain research, educators understand that the brain is a parallel processor and that many concerns, pictures, ideas, and floating thoughts occupy one's mental day. The challenge is how to continuously refocus teams to maximize the time they invest in collaboration. Used appropriately, the frame is a discipline, symbolic of "getting to work." When frames as organizers are distributed or posted, the larger group determines the outcomes, and, guided by the frames, the team works through the processes, recording as they go. Teams can sustain their focus for several hours at a time, energized by their very visible progress as recorded on the large frames.

Frames individualize a group's specific work. It is difficult for facilitators to develop a frame that works for every situation or group. One of the group's responsibilities is to look critically at a frame to decide how to tweak it to meet the group's needs while still preserving the integrity of the components. Prior to the training, a representative group may meet to develop the frames for facilitated learning. The more closely the frame reflects the reality of the participants, the more useful it will be. For example, a commercial frame in the form of a large wall chart may use an analysis of specific national or state content standards as a first step. If the district has already adopted content and grade-level standards, facilitators may revise the chart to start with how participants will assess the specific standards.

Frames become a group's memory and lead participants to deeper discussions. Wall-sized charts are frames for group memory. Printed or drawn, they should be from 6 to 8 ft long, with smaller copies in the participant packets. As our society becomes more visually dependent, large and small groups benefit from seeing their progress and the components of their work on a wall chart. See Figure 8.2, Wall Charts Make a Team's Progress Visible. Facilitators are free to move the process along as recorders translate the group's thinking to the chart. Team leaders will know the group is correctly processing frames when a participant says, "That's not exactly what I said" and walks to the chart to correct the record, "Let's rethink that action," or "Let's record what each of us said we would do." The frame is not simply a recording, but a documentation of the group's interactive decision making. When groups individually sign their wall chart, they take ownership from their public declaration for the outcomes.

Frames provide reflective time and provoke a broader conversation. A wall-sized frame is most useful when it chronicles a group's work and is then posted where it can be seen over several days so that participants have an opportunity to reflect on their direction. These frames inform others and provoke conversation outside the teams that created them. As educators develop their system awareness, they will know the importance of getting feedback from others for reshaping the work. Another reason for using 6- to 8-ft charts is that when either a work-in-progress or a completed frame is shared in a school and district, the conversations that took place in other groups are reported accurately.

Frames report new realities to a staff. "No surprises" is the rule in human relations. If a school, for example, is identified by the state as "low-performing," the staff needs to understand first what that means, and second what steps they will take to correct the situation. With several teams working on various aspects of a problem, the information flow can easily be blocked. With the use of frames, the communication lines are opened. The teams can do the work and then post their charts containing their analysis of the problem. The faculty convenes to look at the charts that reflect investigations by the various teams. In data-driven decision-making processes, the data and problem analyses are shared, and action plans are agreed upon as part of a cohesive plan. In comprehensive high schools, large middle schools, or large elementary schools with modular classrooms, it is very important to share these realities in a systematic, highly visible format.

For example, an elementary school was having difficulty with the term *low-performing.* When various teams analyzed the problems of low-performing students using a format of "current problem" and "desired state" along with suggested "next steps," they realized that they did not all

◆ **FIGURE 8.2.** Wall charts make a team's progress visible.

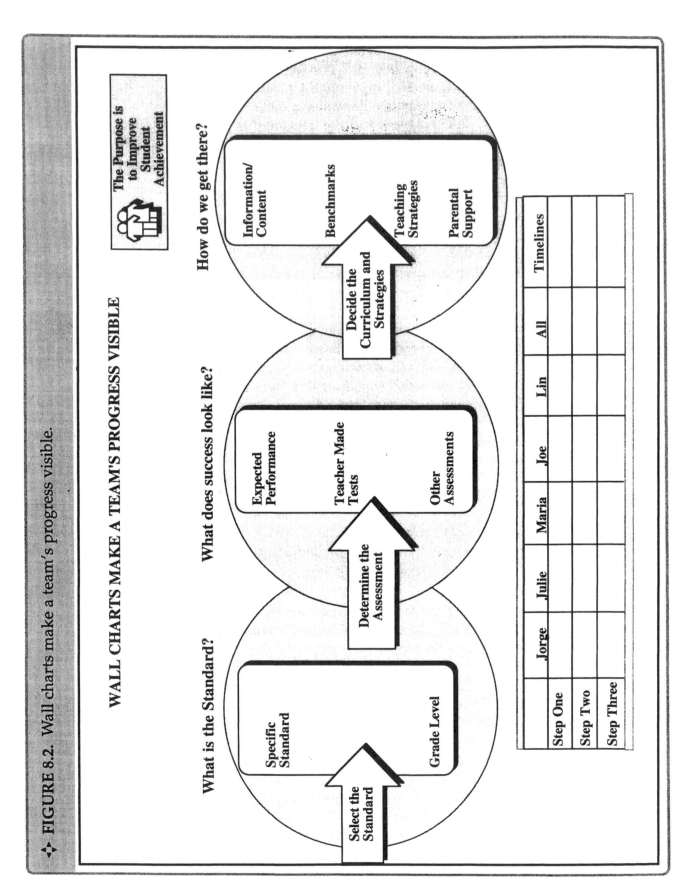

WALL CHARTS MAKE A TEAM'S PROGRESS VISIBLE

The Purpose is to Improve Student Achievement

What is the Standard?

- Specific Standard
- Grade Level

Select the Standard

What does success look like?

- Expected Performance
- Teacher Made Tests
- Other Assessments

Determine the Assessment

How do we get there?

- Information/Content
- Benchmarks
- Teaching Strategies
- Parental Support

Decide the Curriculum and Strategies

	Jorge	Julie	Maria	Joe	Lin	All	Timelines
Step One							
Step Two							
Step Three							

agree on what the problems were, nor did they agree on what was a desired state for all students. Retracing the problem to their values, beliefs, and assumptions about their students' abilities made arriving at conclusions about how to turn the school around more complicated. Easy answers—including blaming others—that were suggested at the beginning of the meeting were replaced by more thoughtful ways to approach the problem of low performance and by possible steps they could take that would have lasting impact.

Frames inform the entire school community. Frequently, wall-sized frames are taken to the community to form a backdrop while the principal or other key leaders explain the direction of the school. A faculty may ask a leadership team, for example, to research how class schedules influence student learning. The result may be a major decision to revise class schedules that has implications for the entire school community. Frames can show how the leadership team's work included community involvement. When a community has been asked for feedback, it is important for that community to see how the feedback was used. Bringing proposed actions back to a group using a graphic format is a way of closing the communication loop: from being informed and giving feedback to seeing what happened as a result. It is a reasonable way to inform the school community in that it also publicly honors the time people invested in providing feedback. Because the district values community involvement, community members will be more willing to participate in the future. Figure 8.3, Using a Feedback Loop Within the School Community, explains to community members how their feedback is integrated into the planning process.

People Connections in Professional Settings

Connections are the way we link people engaged in their own professional learning. How to connect people involved in various professional development constructs should be a part of the overall plan. First, think about the level of experience. In grade-level teams, experienced teachers should be linked with new teachers. Because they may be more familiar with recent research through their classes at the university, beginning teachers provide a fresh perspective to established ways of thinking. More experienced teachers provide the reality of years of working with students. Forming these connections helps teachers to view units of study from different perspectives. These various perspectives are essential for understanding and changing a system.

Second, schools are becoming more aware of how connections within and among a diverse faculty provide a distinctive richness to the curriculum. In preparing a unit on ancient cultures, for example, teachers discov-

❖ FIGURE 8.3. Using a feedback loop within the school community.

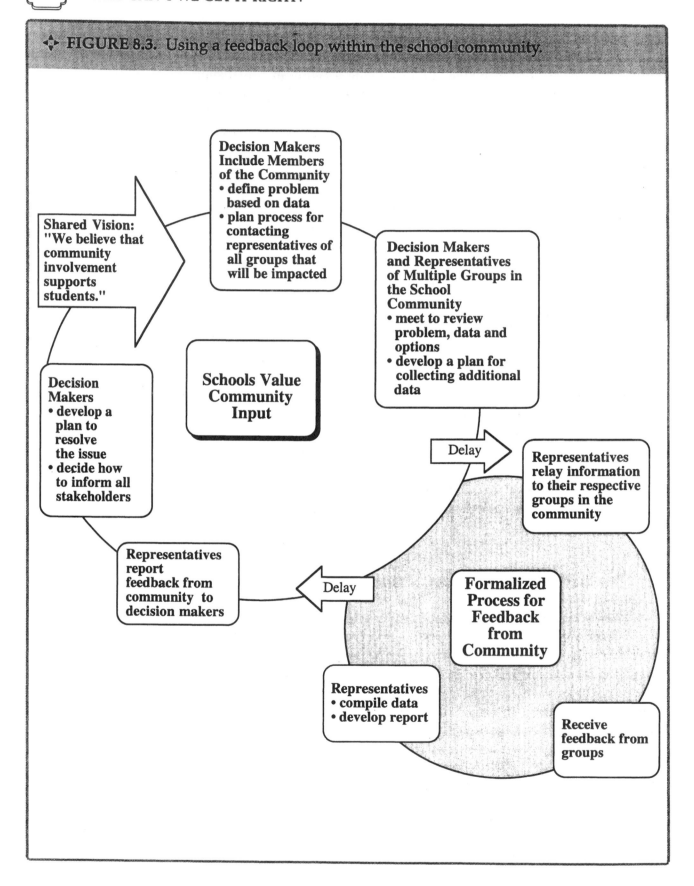

ered that one faculty member had been raised with traditions that were thousands of years old. Her father was a Buddhist monk in Japan. Her personal knowledge greatly enriched students' ability to contrast cultures, which was embedded in the history standard. Without the collaboration, only the teacher's own class would have benefited from her vast knowledge and collection of artifacts. Because the faculty was working in cross-grade-level teams, teachers were able to deepen their own knowledge of the curriculum and make it richer for students.

Third, ensuring that faculty members make connections with other teachers they don't normally talk with is a way of developing professional relationships that will perpetuate a school's culture of openness to ideas. When an entire district is focused on student achievement, district-wide teacher-led discussions of student performance and curricular strategies become a necessary part of the strategic plan.

A matrix is a helpful tool for principals who want to see their faculty's involvement at a glance, as in Table 8.1, Matrix of Teacher Involvement. Across the top, the principal lists the many teams and committees in the school and district. Down the left side of the paper is a list of faculty members. The principal assesses each teacher's investment of time by moving across the table of possible involvement, recording yes or no for each activity. As the principal reads across the matrix, it is easy to see which committees each teacher has chosen or was assigned to. Principals who take the time to keep the list current quickly see which faculty members are involved and which ones haven't made any connections. Although new teachers especially need to be protected while they are learning their skills, experienced teachers need to be system-wise. Teachers who experience networking and learning with teachers from other schools can reduce their feelings of anxiety and competition when test scores are published. The negative feelings are replaced by the knowledge that schools are helping each other. Teachers feel supported when they are involved in meaningful, collaborative activities on a larger scale.

Traditional ways of connecting people (large and small groups within a particular setting or training, grade-level teams, content-area teams, cross-grade-level teams, action research teams, school-wide teams focused on a particular task, assessment teams, and committees for various purposes) are amounting to greater investments of time by staff and administration. When teachers complain about their time being consumed by meetings unrelated to student performance, principals need to listen carefully and collaboratively establish priorities for commitments of time and energy. Some schools have distinguished what is creditable professional development by looking at the impact on the learning of all students. If the impact is high, as in performance assessment teams, the time is counted as credit for professional development units on the salary schedule. Weekly meetings of the grade levels to conduct business—establish schedules, distribute memos, give feedback, assign space, and so forth—are not considered

TABLE 8.1   Matrix of Teacher Involvement

Teacher Name	Grade Taught	District Curriculum Committee	District Assessment Committee	Faculty Senate	Mentor Teacher	School Improvement	Articulation
Amonte	1		X	X			
Barker	5			X		X	
Benet	5	X					
Chan	3				X	X	
D'Mar	1						
Effen	2	X					
Franks	2	X				X	X
Gillan	3			X			
Horillo	K						
Janrette	1			X			
Jensen	K						
Kirby	4						
Lang	4						
Lema	K						
Moreno	3			X			
Nava	5						
Ogden	2						
Ono	2		X	X			
Phong	1		X	X			
Rameriz	K						
Ramos	3			X			X
Solario	4						X
Tupa	5				X		
Wilson	4	X					

professional development. Meetings to analyze disaggregated student performance data or to examine multiple forms of student assessments certainly will affect teaching and learning and are indeed professional development.

A caution in working with the tool of connections is that people are generally more comfortable with people they have worked with over time. They will routinely sit in the same seats with the same people for the same function, as in a faculty meeting, for example. Many new teachers have been reproached for sitting in a seat that is "reserved" for a veteran faculty member. In faculty seminars in which teachers are experiencing new strategies, staying with the same comfortable group is sometimes a block to teachers' learning, because they may be reluctant to make mistakes in front of their close associates as they try something new. Experienced facilitators recognize the importance of varying the connections. Discussing ways of grouping faculty members is a good topic for your leadership team to grapple with, especially when planning to introduce new concepts to colleagues.

Variety is the spice of a professional's life. According to brain researchers, adults crave novelty, creativity, and a variety of choices. As educators collaboratively design a professional development plan for their school or district, they must consider the needs of the adult learner. In providing opportunities for teachers to make new connections, they also address the systemic need of a healthy organization by infusing it with multiple perspectives.

The Team's Cycle of Inquiry

As new forms of professional development emerge, including writing curriculum, collaboratively examining student work, analyzing data, prioritizing and implementing standards, constructing performance assessments, and peer coaching, the expectation is that because people teach in the same building or on the same campus, they know how to be with each other. But do they really know the skills of inquiry, dialogue, and discussion and under what circumstances they should be used? Learning to identify when advocacy is interfering with an open exchange or exploration of an idea is a most useful skill. Knowledgeable teachers, however, seldom remind their colleagues that there is a difference between advocacy and dialogue. Instead of investing their time with colleagues to learn the skills of communication, teachers prefer to accomplish tasks associated with teaching in isolation. As principals and teachers experience new forms of professional development, however, they will understand the realities of needing communication skills to work with colleagues in developing curriculum and applying new teaching strategies.

Why is inquiry mentioned so frequently as a tool of school site facilitators? Could it be that no one has all the answers? When teachers have been in the profession for 9 or 10 years, does anyone really believe that they have no ideas regarding school improvement? Where is the dissonance that will cause them to go deeper? With the rapid communications of today, people often fall into mental traps. Sometimes they stop thinking about how to improve, and they appear to rely on others to come up with answers or innovations. Educators may be tempted to ignore the need to think deeply and come to personal conclusions about teaching and learning, but they must not be encouraged to evade their professional responsibilities. As one teacher commented, "We can figure this out. We just need the time and the resources to continue our investigations."

Educators cannot fall into the mental trap of "someone else will do it." For example, a school is labeled a low-performing one by a state accrediting committee, and the information is reported in the newspaper. The data is conclusive. Test scores are very, very low. Teachers are annoyed. They see the data, but they don't believe the data show just how hard they have been working. They assign to their teacher leaders the need to discuss their dissatisfaction with the district for making them look bad, so that they can get back to teaching without disruption. The teacher leaders call the union representatives. The union representatives tell them that few schools have figured out exactly what to do about low test scores in inner-city schools. Someone mentions Texas and their results with inner-city students, but the teachers claim that students in Texas are different from their populations. The union representative tells them he or she is in contact with the district and will let them know if further action is needed.

The truth is that teachers need to think deeply about the testing summary and the disaggregated data so that they can use their professional development time and resources to investigate possible root causes, no matter how painful such investigation is. Together teachers must analyze, reflect, and formulate hunches about why test scores are so bad and what is happening in their school to allow so many students to fall through the system's cracks. They can't begin to set goals of student achievement until as a school they face the reality that what they are doing may not be effective with the students they are teaching. In essence, they cannot assign responsibilities for speaking about students to someone else. They must shoulder the responsibility by using their professional knowledge and skills to think more deeply about the challenge of low-performing students. This is the essence of professional development—to think more deeply about how to change old patterns, structures, and processes of teaching and learning to help more students be successful.

In the public schools, educators can't afford to believe that another school or district has the formula for achieving widespread student success. Anyone can go to the Internet; engage a powerful search engine such as Google, Yahoo, or Ask Jeeves; and check on many schools in the country. Their Web pages indicate how successful they are, so some teachers assume that these other schools must have the problem of student achievement figured out. Then critical thinking begins to have a voice: No, the Web page could be public relations. Public relations experts know how to do the Emily Dickinson perspective of "Tell the truth, but tell it slant." Educators want the real story, so they read books and articles by researchers and practitioners. Some attend conferences to hear knowledgeable people discuss issues, and they visit "successful schools" to uncover how they did "it." Others listen to talk shows so that they can get a flavor for public opinion of the challenges. Teachers in the 21st century search the Web for position papers from universities and professional associations. Although knowledgeable people have opinions about the issues, educators should not be relieved of the need to think deeply for themselves.

Members of a learning community understand that they don't need the virus brought on by "public think," because they really can figure it out, given time, resources, and district commitment, added to their passion for students and learning. Using professional development opportunities to think through the issues, they can learn more about the causes, examine student data, share their knowledge of students, and balance their learning with their experiences. They can look at students with fresh eyes as they figure out how to accomplish this enormous task the public has given them: to educate the youth of America. Professional development planners, too, must not be seduced by easy answers or lecturing experts. They must design programs collaboratively so that teachers and principals have time to reflect, examine, analyze, collaborate, and take risks by trying again and again to discover how to educate all students.

Figure 8.4, The Team's Cycle of Inquiry, illustrates why inquiry into a specific concern is an effective professional development tool. For a school focused on student success, the first level is to propose a broad plan for raising student achievement as a result of looking at data. For example, a school noted that reading scores in the seventh grade dipped dramatically. Once the team of seventh-grade teachers identified gaps in student learning, the team members developed achievement goals, such as "the seventh-grade reading scores in identification of key vocabulary words and reading comprehension will increase by 15% over the next year." Using inquiry, teachers explored multiple strategies for reaching the goals, narrowed the strategies during the ensuing discussion, and decided the appropriate action research design. They considered the issue of alignment so that the goals and strategies reflected the standards and assessment of the standards. Implementation concerns caused the planners to look at timelines attached to their data collection plan. Next, they took action and reflected on the results. Using student data, they determined what caused the students to improve or not and whether further changes were needed in their practices. Another continuous point of inquiry was how they would share their results with the larger community as they acknowledged the need for breadth as well as depth in their school. The term *cycle of inquiry* is a reminder that the process is never completed.

The cycle becomes a systems loop when facilitators either acknowledge what has caused greater learning in a particular phase or recognize what has given the cycle a flat tire. Let us say, for example, that strategies to improve reading scores became the basis for inservice training. After the

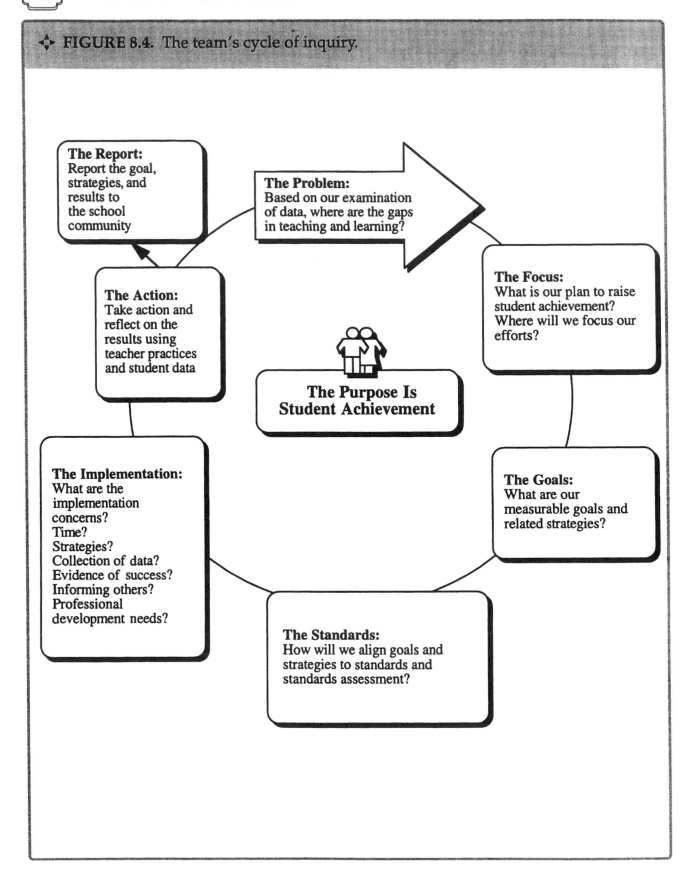

✦ **FIGURE 8.4.** The team's cycle of inquiry.

training, several teachers applied for coaching as they implemented the strategies, but the district office did not approve the coaching segment. Without support, staff members lost interest. A few teachers tried the strategies and were able to show student improvement, but not to the extent they were expecting. When the results were in, the conclusion by staff was that this was an ineffective approach to reading. In this situation, when teachers learned the strategies but had no support for follow-up or coaching, chaotic implementation resulted. The interruption of the cycle became "A Causal Loop With Poor Results" (Figure 8.5). The new approach that produced no gain for students shows what can happen when teachers have no support for new, complex learning.

School improvement is such an enormous task that unless teachers are able to follow targeted improvement cycles on teaching and learning in their classrooms with appropriate support, they may waste their energies on activities that are not aligned or focused on long-term or short-term goals.

Reflection and Dialogue

How do educators clarify their understandings and make meaning from education and experience? Schon's (1983) work suggests that a way to personal growth and development is through reflection. Mulling over what we have experienced is not what we are describing. Rather, *reflection* is a purposeful strategy for reshaping or adapting our behavior based on new understandings that result from gaining new perspectives of the problem. Repeated use of reflection as a habit of mind enables us to frame our future actions based on learnings from our experiences. Because modern life seems to become more frantic each day, reflection is not something we normally insert into our work schedule. In fact, it is a learned behavior that, for some participants, may have its beginnings in professional development seminars. When facilitators ask participants to reflect on what they have just learned, they are able to have deeper conversations with their colleagues, because the initial sorting of ideas has already taken place. Schon's (1983) studies demonstrate that this self-reflection leads to continued growth over time.

Few facilitators would accept the title of professional developer without having Bohm's (1996) text on conducting dialogues in their personal toolboxes. Sometimes faculties get into a learning situation where hidden or exposed feelings of hurt and frustration turn into explosive exchanges. The group may insist on putting everything out on the table. A free-for-all has no positive gain, only negative, perpetuated losses. The facilitator may want to open a dialogue after setting ground rules and demonstrating the

❖❖ FIGURE 8.5. A causal loop with poor results.

- Staff loses interest
- Funding for coaching and follow-up not approved
- Unintended consequences from chaotic implementation
- Implement the strategies
- Delay
- Delay
- Student test scores indicate no gain
- The Purpose is to Improve Student Achievement
- Learn new strategies based on teacher needs
- Decision to try something different

differences between inquiry, dialogue, and advocacy. The purpose of the dialogue is not to get one's way but to learn of other realities. It is a place to test assumptions and a safety zone for questioning how one has previously thought about a given topic.

Bohm (1996) suggests that we don't need an extensive knowledge of personal history to have trust and openness in a group. We can use a dialogue where we give open space for others to talk while we listen and then ask thoughtful questions. Such dialogue is aimed at deepening our understanding while exploring problems or issues. Participants come to the seminar knowing they will learn a new skill for use with colleagues or with students. Of particular value is dialogue around related concepts, such as a reading about what students bring to the classroom in cognitive readiness. Another opportunity is learning about a person's experience in a new culture. Teachers are able to use their deeper understanding from dialogue to help new students. The dialogue can be extended as time and interest permit or conducted within a limited amount of time. Occasionally, an opportunity for ad hoc dialogue arises out of a need to solve a problem or discuss an issue. When the need becomes obvious in a meeting, it is helpful for the facilitator to announce a break and get permission from the group to move into dialogue. They rearrange the chairs so that everyone can see the faces of everyone else in the room. The facilitator reviews the elements of a dialogue and moves from an escalating polarization of participants to a thoughtful exploration of the issues.

Conclusion

No one wants to do complicated work without the proper tools for the job. It is too frustrating and time consuming to work with outdated or inadequate tools. When educators invest in learning about new tools to aid in the professional growth of their colleagues, they communicate the value of the work. Using appropriate visual tools for implementing professional development opportunities, for example, can make a big difference in how teachers perceive their work, because such tools allow them to see both their processes and their results. Understanding the increased reliance of all people on visual interpretations will better prepare teacher leaders, principals, and other facilitators for working with large or small groups. Attending to an array of conditions that may hinder growth is the work of leaders, who will find it necessary to equip themselves with communication tools and to explore multiple opportunities to connect with others in order to strengthen their community. Educators who are willing to examine themselves to discover how to be more effective with students and colleagues and who are willing to expand their capacities by trying new processes and approaches are indeed building a learning community.

REALITY CHECK

In order to prepare teachers and students
for their roles in the 21st century, what are the tools
that teachers will use in a professional development design
to address the needs of participants in a learning community
to be focused on student achievement?

On the Web

The National Staff Development Council can be found at http://www.nsdc.org for access to articles and journals about professional development. For excellent graphic guides, wall charts, and presentation aids, consider Grove Consultants International at http://www.grove.com and visit the Grove Store on-line.

Evaluating Professional Development

A standing committee for professional development planning met in the high school library conference room. Two members were new to the committee, two had served for 2 years, and the chair was in his 3rd year. Thien, the chair, was eager to leave for his next meeting with the other coaches.

"In the agenda I sent I asked you to think of professional development activities we have had in the past three years," Thien began. "What worked for you and your departments and what would you label as 'never-do-it-again'?"

The four other members of the committee read through the seminar list and rated the seminars.

"The program everyone really appreciated was the last diversity series, because it focused on how we were helping or hindering student learning," Marcus commented.

"Well, some teachers didn't like the first part, where they got into stories about exclusion."

"I thought that was the best!" exclaimed Isaac. "Before we looked at ourselves objectively, we couldn't understand what others were concerned about."

"Wait a minute," Thien broke in. "This meeting isn't about the diversity workshop. It's about getting our act together and presenting a professional development plan at tomorrow's faculty senate meeting."

Manny looked very pensive. "You know, Thien, we really need to look at an evaluation design so that we have some credibility with our colleagues. Right now, I don't have any data to help us with this planning. I don't have a clue how people felt about our activities, how the program helped them with their teaching, or what impact it had on student learning."

Thien was thoughtful. "You're right, Manny, but evaluations are too expensive. We spent a lot of money on a design for our grant last year. I don't think we have the funds to do a big evaluation design."

At last Berta spoke up. "I have to agree with Manny. I'm not willing to face the other members of the math department with suggestions about this year until I have a proposal that includes an evaluation design." She looked at the others. "Does anyone here have an evaluation background?"

"No," said Thien. "Tell you what. I'm in a rush today, but I'll contact the district office and ask Marla from Evaluation in the district office to sit in on our next meeting. Maybe she can help us figure this thing out."

The meeting was adjourned until the following Tuesday at 4:00 p.m.

Pause for a moment to reflect on this essential question.

ESSENTIAL QUESTION

How will a school or district evaluate its professional development programs?

Why Do We Have the Conversation?

Historically, many professional developers have considered evaluation a costly, time-consuming process that diverts attention from important planning, implementation, and follow-up activities. Others believe they simply lack the skill and expertise to become involved in rigorous evaluations. As a consequence, they either neglect evaluation issues, or leave them to "evaluation experts" who are called in at the end and asked to determine if what was done made any difference. The results of such a process are seldom very useful. (Guskey, 1998a, p. 36)

School and district leaders who are committed to professional development need to demonstrate whether their professional development activities and processes have made any difference for their school or district. Generally, educators plan and implement, but they fail to evaluate whether what they are doing makes a difference for the individuals and the system involved in professional development. It is important for a school and district to stop and analyze the progress they have made by evaluating the outcomes of their efforts. The question "How far have we come in relation to the goals and desired outcomes we have set to achieve with our professional development plan?" is important to answer. Asking this question allows the school and district to evaluate the achievements made possible by the professional development processes. Bull and Buechler (1996) summarize some key evaluation questions educators should be asking about professional development:

> All the rhetoric about professional development and school improvement, all the theories about program design and peer coaching, all the action research and collaboration in the world ultimately give way to a single question: Is professional development working? To be more specific: Is professional development reinvigorating teachers? Is it expanding their repertoire and improving their ability to teach? Is it leading to new roles and responsibilities for teachers within the school organization? Is it contributing to a richer, more positive school culture? *Most importantly, is professional development leading to improved student performance?* (Bull & Buechler, 1996, p. 27)

In other words, is the outcome of the professional development initiative worth the human and fiscal resources that have been invested? Systematic evaluation of professional development that is purposeful and driven by results is needed if it is to be supported by the school board, administrators, teachers, parents, and the community. What has your district or school done to support effective evaluation of professional development?

Research and Best Practices

Most districts and schools do not have a formalized, consistent process for evaluating professional development designs, programs, activities, or events (Guskey, 2000; Sparks, 1998). The common practice is to plan a professional development program and begin implementation without an agreed-upon set of expectations of what "full" implementation and success look like. The rigor of evaluating such a program is almost nonexistent. The traditional questionnaire survey of participants after an inservice as to whether or not they found the speaker interesting, visual aids helpful, and other parts of the activities interesting does not get to the heart of whether the professional development brought about change in teacher behavior and increased success for students (Loucks-Horsely, Hewson, Love, & Stiles, 1998).

Sparks and Hirsh (1997) emphasize the importance of the shift in evaluating professional development from teachers' perception regarding their needs to a focus on student learning:

> Ultimately, systemic change efforts must be judged by their contribution to student learning. It is no longer sufficient to determine the value of staff development efforts by assessing participants' perceived satisfaction with those efforts. While participants' satisfaction is a desirable goal, assessment efforts must also provide information about changes in on-the-job behavior, organizational changes, and the improved learning of all students. (Sparks & Hirsh, 1997, p. 41)

Multifaceted, long-term evaluation that examines professional development in some depth and tries to determine its effect on teachers and students is needed (Bull & Buechler, 1996). Evaluation designs need to be started in the early part of the professional development planning process and to continue after the particular professional development activity is completed (Guskey, 1998a, 2000). Evaluation should provide information about the implementation process and should document effects, especially effects on student achievement. Evaluation reports not only provide information to teachers and administrators, but are an important tool to inform parents and the community on the progress being made in the school or district. When parents and school board members see the hard evidence and results of professional development, there is less skepticism about future release time or about noninstructional time's being devoted to professional development activities.

The need for concrete evidence that professional development is making a difference is important for maintaining credibility with teachers, administrators, and the community. A formal evaluation process demonstrates that the school or district is interested not only in teacher growth, but also in the growth of students. Professional development needs an ongoing evaluation process to ensure that goals are being achieved, that needs are being met, and that resources are being used wisely (Zepeda, 1999). Without systematic evaluation of efforts based on hard data, it is almost impossible to determine if the changes are sustainable and, more important, if the professional development activities improved teachers' abilities to increase student achievement.

Components of Effective Professional Development Evaluation

Components of an evaluation process for professional development will include the following questions:

QUESTIONS FOR PROFESSIONAL DEVELOPMENT EVALUATION

What are the desired outcomes?

What are the professional development activities for reaching the outcomes?

Who will be responsible for the evaluation?

How will the evaluation be conducted?

What types of data will be collected?

How and when will the data be analyzed?

Who is responsible for reporting and distributing the results?

How can this evaluation contribute to the continuous improvement process for teachers and increase student achievement?

Table 9.1, Professional Development Evaluation Planning Guide, provides a systematic way of planning the evaluation process. The components and questions regarding professional development and its evaluation can be organized and clarified by using the guide. The guide is intended to help professional development planners, principals, and teachers focus on the desired outcomes first and then develop the activities that

TABLE 9.1   Professional Development Evaluation Planning Guide

Directions: Use the questions and the planning chart to set a Professional Development Evaluation Plan.
Questions for Professional Development Evaluation:

1. What are the desired outcomes?
2. What are the professional development activities for reaching the outcomes?
3. Who will be responsible for the evaluation?
4. How will the evaluation be conducted?
5. What types of data will be collected?
6. How and when will the data be analyzed?
7. Who is responsible for reporting and distributing the results?
8. How can this evaluation contribute to the continuous improvement process for teachers and increase student achievement?

Desired Outcomes	Professional Activities	Individual(s) Responsible	Evaluation Methods	Data Required	Analyze Data	Reporting Data	Continuous Improvement Outcomes

will meet those outcomes, rather than planning the activity and hoping for the outcome, which is usually the case. Evaluation planning helps focus on the outcomes rather than the activities (Guskey, 2000).

What are the desired outcomes? What are the professional development activities for reaching the outcomes? Professional development plans typically have a wide range of goals, but they are often not articulated as outcomes. How would you describe your successes with professional development activities and plans? What changes have occurred? By whom? Generally, professional development results are reported as activities completed (conducted series of workshops or summer institute) rather than as accomplishments (teachers using inquiry-based strategies in their classrooms have higher student achievement rates in problem solving). Outcomes for professional development can be described as new abilities (knowledge, skills, strategies, and attitudes) by a variety of individuals (teachers, students, administrators); organizations (departments, teams, schools, and districts); and areas (teaching, leadership, change management). "Being clear about desired outcomes, articulating what they would look like if they were present, not only lays important groundwork for evaluation but also causes the program to be more focused and purposeful" (Loucks-Horsely et al., 1998, p. 221).

WHAT ARE THE DESIRED OUTCOMES?

Knowledge level?
Skills level?
Strategies available?
Attitude changes?

Who will be responsible for the evaluation? Establishing who is responsible for the evaluation process helps in clearly defining the roles individuals play in making sure the evaluation process occurs. When various role participants take ownership of the evaluation process, they provide perspectives on the professional development opportunities, which in turn provide insights to the evaluator. Teachers and administrators who share responsibilities for the evaluation process commit to a representative process focused on outcomes. When responsibility is shared, there is an understanding of how the evaluation outcomes were developed. Participants who are informed throughout the process understand when adjustments are needed to better serve both the participants and the outcomes they establish.

How will the evaluation be conducted? What types of data will be collected? The evaluation process needs to be accomplished in a variety of ways to provide information on the progress of the participants and to define whether the outcomes have been met. To help understand the impact of the professional development plan and activities, a wide range of evidence is needed. Evidence from participants in the form of surveys, interviews, observations, lesson analysis, performance tasks, student work, and focus groups can provide data that contribute to the evaluation process. The type of data collected will depend on the outcomes to be measured as a result of the professional development. Clearly stated outcomes for professional development help frame the short- and long-term data collection process. If, for example, the outcome is to improve students' reading scores, it would be important to gather data substantiating teacher strategies that develop students' abilities to read (i.e., Has the use of a teaching strategy increased student capacity in reading? How would we know? What evidence do we have?).

Evaluation baseline data on students (i.e., achievement scores, grades, attendance rates, discipline rates); teachers (i.e., assessment of current knowledge, teaching skills, and attitudes); and the school (i.e., related procedures, policies, roles, and the extent of teacher collaboration) are needed in the initial stages of planning to provide beginning data to compare with the results of the professional development work. Also, these initial data give a clearer picture of the status, abilities, and needs of the students, teachers, and school and should be reviewed as the plan is developed. Developing a plan without understanding student achievement and teacher and school levels of need does not address the specific professional growth requirements for expected outcomes. Understanding the abilities and needs of participants in professional development is critical and can easily be identified through the collection of baseline data. Failure to assess the current status and level of professional development of participants condemns the process to one-size-fits-all professional development. Further, it builds resentment among participants, because their individual abilities and knowledge are not recognized and valued.

During the implementation process, participants should document their involvement, including types of training, follow-up coaching, and feedback. Leaders already have many sources to help with this in-depth evaluation, such as questionnaires, peer observations, school records and reports, student portfolios, student performance, and achievement tests.

How and when will the data be analyzed? Choosing the means by which data are analyzed in the evaluation process continues to clarify the outcomes. Data must be subaggregated and reviewed for their significance. Do the data show evidence of the impact the professional development activity is having on the participants? The process by which the analysis of data takes place is important. Involving participants in looking at results becomes part of the professional development plan as it reinforces ownership in the success of the process and anticipated outcomes. When individuals are engaged in analyzing the data, they inform their own practice and understanding (Lieberman & Miller, 1999; Sagor, 1992; Schmoker, 1996).

Who is responsible for reporting and distributing the results? Evaluation information often goes unreported in the rush to the next professional development activity by leaders. Reporting and distributing the results of the professional development plan as it unfolds helps clarify whether the goals are being met, what outcomes are having success, and what the next steps should be. School site and district leaders, including administrators and teacher leaders, must be prepared to report and distribute results to a variety of audiences. This crucial step in the evaluation process of reporting the results to the key stakeholders should include the following elements:

- Goals for the program
- Activities implemented to meet the goals
- Individuals involved and their roles
- Resources used
- Participants' reactions
- Data to support impact on participants, students, specific programs, and the school
- Recommendations for changes in the program

Evaluation results will provide information on outcomes and on the gaps that need to be filled in order to continue to progress. Educators who are able to communicate the results of professional development contribute to an understanding of what was learned and of how the learning was interpreted through the information-gathering process. Periodic reporting of results by a variety of leaders at the school and district level keeps faculties, school boards, parents, and the community informed about the purpose and progress of professional development to improve student achievement.

How can this evaluation contribute to the continuous improvement of students? The evaluation process provides informed results of the professional development initiative. It does not allow the typical responses of

"We think it is working" or "We feel good about it." Evaluating the progress made by teachers and students and reporting it helps inform the school's continuous improvement cycle. It clearly focuses the school and teachers on the needed next steps. Evaluation provides for informed decision making about which learning needs of teachers should be addressed in the professional development plan to improve student achievement.

The evaluation process must include feedback for teachers, the use of data to show evidence, and data about student progress or lack of it. Evaluation serves as a means to observe, reflect, and analyze the work. Administrators and teachers need to focus on the evaluation processes and results as soon as they begin to plan for professional development. Unfortunately, educators too often buy into reform initiatives because of the hype around the program. The first question should be, "Is the objective to improve student achievement, and how will that be demonstrated?"

The evaluation data that are collected will help inform decision making using both formative and summative data. Common formative assessment tools include informal and formal classroom observations by colleagues and administrators, construction of teaching portfolios and student portfolios, and student achievement on standardized tests.

The evaluation will inform future work as each assessment event in itself provokes new learning, leading to enhanced teaching practice as a natural outcome of engaging in the assessment (Guskey, 1998b; Sparks, 1998).

Continuous improvement in schools must involve an ongoing cycle of inquiry that looks at data and the professional development program to determine if progress is being made. Inquiry into what is working or not working in the professional development program encourages a process of ongoing feedback. Adjustments can be made to meet the needs of the teachers as they learn new skills and practice them in the classroom. Through the evaluation process, teachers learn to examine their teaching, reflect on practice, try new practices, and evaluate their results based on student achievement. This ongoing reflection must be seen as a part of the professional development process and must be nurtured.

Effective evaluation programs should have both long-term and short-term objectives (Rutherford, 1989). Short-term objectives usually target changes in teacher behaviors, in the school, or in the curriculum, whereas long-term objectives focus on improvements in student achievement or behavior. Professional development can be justified only if its ultimate goal is to improve education for students. Monitoring results has proven to be a major factor for achieving success in schools and districts. Results-oriented professional development planning requires that the theory and research presented, modeled, and practiced in workshops or inservice settings be supported with on-the-job coaching to promote transfer to the workplace and to facilitate change in teacher behavior that will affect student achievement.

The professional development evaluation process has implications for principals as they provide leadership for their schools' continuous improvement. Principals must help create a sense of ownership and risk taking by teachers as professional development initiatives are designed and implemented. For example, teacher-driven action research involves teachers who identify teaching-learning issues of importance, try out new methods, and determine their effect on student learning without fear of a negative evaluation of their efforts by the principal (Sagor, 1992). The results of their research often lead to a further cycle of inquiry, which deepens the teacher's knowledge and understanding. It is a self-renewing process that models taking action on new learnings and examining results. Monitoring continuous improvement of teachers' learning through effective evaluation procedures also reinforces results and accountability. We can no longer afford professional development activities that do not have measurable results. Although each person may be willing to be personally involved, the administrative and teacher leadership is responsible for school-wide and district-wide accountability and results.

Conclusion

Professional development opportunities are designed for a wide variety of reasons, and it is the role of evaluation to determine whether and in what ways these activities were successful. Fulfilling that evaluation role, however, is rarely easy. It is important to get professional developers and participants to use evaluation processes to better understand results and challenges for continuous improvement. Being clear about desired outcomes for professional development and articulating them lay an important foundation for focused and purposeful evaluation. Ultimately, the evaluation process must answer the question, "Is the professional development plan improving student learning?"

REALITY CHECK

What procedures does your school or district have in place for evaluating professional development and reporting the results?

On the Web

Resources for evaluation of professional development can be found on the Web through a variety of professional, governmental, and search engine Web sites. Before searching the Web for evaluation research, be sure to narrow your search parameters to key outcomes you hope to achieve with your professional development plan.

Professional and Governmental Resources

- American Educational Research Association: http://www.aera.net

- Association for Supervision and Curriculum Development: http://www.ascd.org

- National Staff Development Council: http://www.nsdc.org

- American Association of School Administrators: http://www.aasa.org

- The National Association of Elementary School Principals: http://www.naesp.org

- National Association of Secondary School Principals: http://www.nassp.org

- National Middle School Association: http://www.nmsa.org

- National School Board Association: http://www.nsba.org

- U.S. Department of Education: http://www.ed.gov

- National Center for Educational Statistics: http://nces.ed.gov

- Educational Resource Information Center: http://ericir.syr.edu (known as "ask eric")

- RAND Education: http://www.rand.org

Regional Educational Lab Network

The Regional Educational Lab Network (http://www.relnetwork.org) provides links to 10 U.S. Regional Educational Labs:

- Appalachian Educational Laboratory (specialty: rural education): http://www.ael.org

- North Central Regional Educational Laboratory (specialty: technology): http://www.ncrel.org

- Northwest Regional Educational Laboratory (specialty: school change process): http://www.nwrel.org

- Western Regional Educational Laboratory (specialty: assessment and accountability): http://www.wested.org

- Mid-Continent Regional Educational Laboratory (specialty: curriculum, learning, and instruction): http://www.mcrel.org

- Pacific Region Educational Laboratory (specialty: language and cultural diversity): http://www.prel.org

- Northeast and Islands Laboratory at Brown University (specialty: language and cultural diversity): http://www.lab.brown.edu

- Mid-Atlantic Laboratory for Student Success (specialty: urban education): http://www.temple.edu/departments/LSS

- SouthEastern Regional Vision for Education (specialty: early childhood education): http://www.serve.org

- Southwest Education Development Laboratory (specialty: language and cultural diversity): http://www.sedl.org

Search Engines

- Google: http://www.google.com

- Infoseek: http://www.infoseek.com

- Dogpile: http://www.dogpile.com

- MetaCrawler: http://www.metacrawler.com

- Education World: http://db.education-world.com/perl/browse

- Northernlight: http://www.northernlight.com

- Inference Find: http://inferencefind.com

Revisiting Past Perspectives to Underscore the Need for Change

The professional development room at the district office was filled to capacity. One chart showed the agenda for the day. A second held outcomes highlighted in red. Each small group of eight or nine participants used a wall-sized chart to frame the direction group members planned to take when they returned to their sites. The energy in the room was contagious as voices rose and fell with the intensity of the topic. "Well," commented the superintendent, approaching her assistant as he completed a cell phone call outside the training room. "Everyone appears to be involved with this inservice. We'll see what they do when they return to their classrooms."

The assistant superintendent of instruction shook his head. "That's the hard part. We bring the best presenters we can afford with up-to-the-minute strategies for working with our kids. Teachers give the seminars top ratings, but when I look at how many students are not meeting standards, it's really discouraging."

"And?" the superintendent questioned. "What's the next step? Our teachers are as bright and talented as any in the state. Why aren't our test scores going up? Why aren't all students meeting the standards? The board needs answers. I need answers!"

"I was just checking the arrangements. We are convening an advisory group of teachers and principals this afternoon. I distributed some articles about successful professional development and asked them to be prepared to discuss how the key concepts apply to our district. If we really want to make a difference, we will 'transform' professional development in this district."

"Now we are talking dollars, right?" asked the superintendent.

"Teachers can't make profound changes in how they teach unless they are supported by the district. In addition to learning new information, support means time for planning, time for the work, time to evaluate, time to make changes, and the will to start all over again. Yes, it's dollars, but it's a whole lot more. We are talking mind-set. How we think about professional development in our district will have to change."

The superintendent looked at the wall clock. "I'm off to have lunch with the board president. It will be a hot one. The community wants new playgrounds at all the elementary schools in the north side. I can't fault their reasoning. I just don't know where we will get the financing. Keep me informed. I don't mind dealing with playgrounds if I know our students are being successful." She paused at the door. "Let me know how the meeting goes this afternoon. I don't know how we'll do it, but if the group can come up with short- and long-term strategies to improve our achievement and can prove to me that others have made it work, we'll find a way to support the efforts."

"Of course," the assistant superintendent thought to himself as he turned toward the seminar. "Just prove it. Now there's a challenge for a lifetime."

**Pause for a moment to reflect
on this essential question.**

ESSENTIAL QUESTION

What have we learned from historical perspectives and current research that will affect our professional development practices and designs?

The current-effort to reform the nation's schools seeks to develop not only new (or reframed) conceptions of teaching, learning, and schooling, but also a wide variety of practices that support teacher learning. These practices run counter to some deeply held notions about staff development and inservice education that have long influenced educators' and the public's views of teachers.

—Lieberman, 1995a, p. 591

Introduction

Systemic school change efforts must be sustained through transformed professional development practices so that schools become professional learning communities. Ongoing professional development must be a continuous thread through the daily life of the school. No longer can schools, principals, teachers, and staff be involved in professional development activities that are episodic, decontextualized, or unfocused on the long-term goals (University School Support for School Reform, 1997, p. 14). Educational reform requires educators (both administrators and teachers) to rethink their own practices and to construct new strategies to increase everyone's ability to improve student achievement. Professional development must be viewed very differently from the way it has historically been practiced in our schools.

Linda Darling-Hammond and Milbrey W. McLaughlin (1995) emphasize this disparity between what we know the nation's reform agenda is asking of educators and the professional development policies and practices that exist in today's schools:

> The vision of practice that underlies the nation's reform agenda requires most teachers to rethink their own practice, to construct new classroom roles and expectations about student outcomes, and to teach in ways they have never taught before—and probably never experienced as students. The success of this agenda ultimately turns on teachers' success in accomplishing the serious and difficult task of learning the skills and perspectives assumed by new visions of practice and unlearning the practices and beliefs about students and instruction that have dominated their professional lives to date. Yet few occasions and little support for such professional development exist in teachers' environments. (Darling-Hammond & McLaughlin, 1995, p. 597)

Why is the historical perspective on professional development important for educators to understand? How can understanding past practices help educators reconceptualize professional development in the future to meet teachers' learning needs and to support their continuous growth? What have we learned from these perspectives and current research that will affect school and district professional development practices and designs?

Historical Perspective on Professional Development

To transform professional development using new concepts of professional learning, educators need a better understanding of past practices and processes. Historical insights will inform the rethinking of current and future professional development practices, with the goal of enabling educators to provide students with expanded and enriched learning.

Historically, educators received their professional development through university teacher training programs that developed their content knowledge and teaching strategies. Generally, after a brief year of exposure to understanding curriculum and learning instructional and assessment strategies, teachers were certified to teach for life. Upon graduation from teacher training institutions and state certification programs, teachers were left to orchestrate their own professional learning. Each individual teacher had the prerogative of finding and attending workshops, continuing advanced university study, or reading educational journals about new concepts and practices in teaching. From the turn of the century until about the 1950s, teachers, according to their initiative and personal preferences, were really left to pursue professional learning whenever and wherever they could. Schools and districts were not concerned with the development of their teachers as long as teachers fulfilled the requirements of a teaching position.

1950s–1960s

Not until the Soviets launched Sputnik in 1957 and the space race began did Americans realize that it was critical for them to support education and the development of educators, especially in science and math. It was equally important for teachers to be professionally current. The National Defense Education Act, funded during the 1960s, created opportunities for teachers in a new kind of professional learning, with curriculum development and instructional strategies that helped them improve their work. Because the goals to improve science and math programs were very clear, districts were more focused and organized in providing professional development opportunities. The previous practice—individuals seeking isolated professional development activities for themselves—was no longer appropriate. Major curriculum projects, such as the Biological Science Curriculum Study and the Physical Science Curriculum Study, started using summer training institutes to inform teachers of current research. Teachers also learned new curriculum and a variety of teaching practices. University professors and teachers worked together on these projects to create curricular materials that were "teacher-proof." The packaged curricula, supposedly easy for any teacher to use, included key concepts that teachers and students needed to understand to master the subject matter. Publishing companies created teacher texts that guided each instructor step by step in the implementation of the textbook-driven curriculum. Most teachers were ill prepared to deal with the conceptual basis and the strategies to increase student learning that these new programs intended to bring to the classroom. The few teachers who attended the intensive summer training returned to classrooms and schools where they had little support for implementation. They had limited resources and materials for developing new curriculum and practicing instructional strategies. Because administrators and parents did not understand the power of the new approach to teaching and learning, it was difficult for the individual teacher to sustain the changes.

Administrators, parents, and community members believed that the successful program consisted of the "proven" curriculum and instruction that teachers had used before making changes; they feared that because the new methods were still being tested, no proof existed that using the new curriculum and instructional strategies would increase student learning. No wonder classroom teachers closed their doors and turned inward to work with students in isolation. Professional development was disconnected and sporadic, unrelated to their daily lives in the classroom. Educational reformers and observers learned that nationally created curriculum projects were not the answer for teacher growth and continued learning.

1970s

The 1970s saw the increased use of individual, episodic professional development activities for teachers by schools and districts. These included attendance at conferences, keynote speakers, workshops, seminars, and "make it and take it" sessions over a wide range of curriculum and instructional areas. The one-day, episodic professional development events were generally required of all teachers, mandated by a district or school. Teachers were not consulted about their depth of understanding about the topic or their needs for learning. Many of these districts mandated conferences, meetings, and workshops that were at the awareness level of learning. No ongoing professional development or discussions followed the events. Many teachers saw these professional development activities as "flash and dash" or "dog and pony shows" that some principal or district office person had seen at a conference and decided would be good to share with teachers back in the district.

Professional development at this level had very little meaning for teachers, except to instill in their minds a feeling that as professionals, they could not determine their own professional development. Someone else, who presumably had more knowledge of what teachers needed than teachers themselves did, directed their professional development. Teachers did, however, like attending workshops with a "make it and take it" or "implement it Monday morning" approach to professional development. Unfortunately, the practice remains today. This paternalistic view of professionally developing or inservicing a teacher has deep roots in the teaching profession. Some critics of the educational system would say that these conditions exist because teaching is not a profession and because teachers have not taken charge of their own professional learning in a systematic and professional manner. The issue of whether professional development is done "to" or "for" teachers is a critical one raised in the last 20 years.

Sparks and Hirsh (1997) describe this type of professional development as

> teachers . . . sitting passively while an "expert" exposes them to new ideas or "trains" them in new practices, and the success of the effort is judged by a "happiness quotient" that measures participants' satisfaction with the experience in addition to their off-the-cuff assessments regarding its usefulness. (p. 1)

1980s

By the 1980s, to determine under what circumstances teachers continued to grow and improve student learning, educators began to look at research on the relationship between teacher learning and aspects of coaching (Joyce & Showers, 1983). Through the research and practices of the 1980s, educators gained insights about how teachers learn and apply their new knowledge in the classroom. Professional development began to evolve from episodic events into a series of workshops or seminars focused on content knowledge and teaching strategies. These workshops included the critical elements of demonstration and practice. Most important, they included follow-up with coaching and feedback while the teacher was practicing the new learning in the classroom. It is interesting to note that professional development was still seen as training or inservicing for teachers. A clear belief statement is communicated to teachers when statements about their professional development include such terms as *training* and *inservicing* to describe their professional learning.

The development of a coaching model to enhance and reinforce the training of teachers while establishing an ongoing learning process was a critical breakthrough. Coaching by a professional coach or by a trained peer coach developed teachers' ability to reflect on their implementation of the newly learned strategies and to hone their skills as professionals. A coaching process broke down the "inspection model" of evaluating teachers and initiated important professional development concepts such as collegial support, reflection, and continuous improvement through collaboration and sharing.

During the 1980s the use of the term *professional* development rather than *staff* development began to emerge. Again, the use of *staff* versus *professional* clearly defines how a teacher is perceived. During the 1980s, the teachers' unions began to redefine professional development for their members. American Federation of Teachers (AFT) President Albert Shanker made a very revealing statement when he said that teachers were no longer blue-collar workers but professionals, and that they needed to act as professionals or the union would not represent them. The emergence of teachers taking charge of their own profession and wanting to determine their own professional growth could be considered a breakthrough for the profession. Unions were no longer focused solely on "bread and butter" issues of wages, benefits, and hours, but on how they could support their teachers as professionals improving their skills. The AFT models in Rochester, New York, and Toledo, Ohio, demonstrated the union's commitment to professional development with increased ownership of the plans and activities, including the development of peer coaching, mentoring, and peer evaluation programs (Shanker, 1990).

1990s

Since the release of *A Nation at Risk* (National Commission on Excellence in Education, 1983), hundreds of commission reports have been issued and thousands of pieces of legislation have been passed to try to redesign schools so they can prepare a more diverse group of future citizens to learn at much higher levels, cope with complexity, use new technologies, and work cooperatively to frame and solve problems. In just over a decade we have experienced a "first wave" of reforms that sought to raise achievement through courses and testing mandates. A "second wave" argued for improvements in teaching and teacher education (Holmes Group, 1986; Carnegie Forum on Education and the Economy, 1986; National Governors' Association, 1986). A "third wave" focused on defining more challenging standards for learning while restructuring schools to produce dramatically better outcomes (Schlechty, 1990; Sizer, 1992; Smith & O'day, 1990).

Increasingly, the redesign task is defined as one of transforming the education system rather than merely getting schools to do better what they have always done. If the challenge of the twentieth century was creating a system of schools that could provide minimal education and basic socialization for the masses of previously uneducated citizens, the challenge of the twenty-first century is creating schools that ensure—for all students in all communities—a genuine right to learn. Meeting this new challenge is not an incremental undertaking. It requires a fundamentally different enterprise. (Darling-Hammond, 1997b, p. 5)

Given the mandate to transform schools, educators in the 1990s school reform movement clearly recognized the need to emphasize the central role of professional development interwoven with the organizational development of schools. Having started in the 1980s, educators had a clearer understanding that improvements in individual teacher performance alone were insufficient to produce the desired results for students and schools. Greater recognition, based on organizational development work by experts such as Deming (1986), showed that an organization's structure and processes were the barriers to improvement, not the performance of individuals. Professional development had to play a key role in school reform efforts, both at the organizational and individual level, if reform efforts were to succeed and be sustained. The continued reports from government bodies, state legislatures, business groups, and various commissions provided a greater recognition and impetus at the local, state, and national level to sustain high-quality, ongoing professional development. Doing so was essential if all students were to achieve high standards. Unless individual learning and organizational changes were emphasized simultaneously, supporting one another, the reform efforts could not work, and more problems would be created.

In the 1990s, the importance of systems thinking and of the interrelationships of individuals to the whole organization, and vice versa, began to be seen. Fragmented approaches to change, based on fads and onetime, piecemeal approaches, had to be replaced by a systematic, coherent plan for professional development and organizational change (Fullan, 1991; Sarason, 1991). A comprehensive approach to reform makes certain that the various parts of the system work together with clear outcomes for the efforts. The focus on district office professional development was moved to a school-based focus to have the greatest impact. A wide range of professional development activities was embedded in the daily work of the school and teachers. District office professional development departments began changing their approach to assisting schools with ongoing support, site-level coaching of individuals and teams, and facilitation of new knowledge and programs. The emergence of 3- to 5-year school plans designed and implemented by school faculties with district office input and technical support illustrates the changing nature of professional development.

With the standards movement, student needs and learning outcomes emerged as the key focus, rather than adult needs. Determining what teachers need to know and be able to do to ensure that students meet the standards enables educators to place professional development in a larger context. Evaluation of professional development began to be measured based on increased student learning rather than on whether the teacher participants were satisfied with the professional development activities (Guskey, 2000). Although comprehensive training programs using coaching continued to be the preferred method for developing teachers' skills, increased use of on-site, job-embedded professional development allowed for diverse professional learning, such as action research, teacher study groups, problem-solving groups, peer observation, journal writing, and other school improvement processes. The emphasis was on standards and content-specific skills to raise student achievement and performance levels. Educators are directing professional development to everyone who affects student learning, not just teachers, in order that all individuals working with students upgrade their skills. Professional development is seen no longer as a frill, but as a necessary process that is continually upgraded and expanded to improve student achievement. The standards movements and increased expectations of results demand no less of the educational system than to have well-prepared and professionally competent educators to work with students.

Professional development consultants are emerging into support providers with more than just training. They must have multilevel consultation, coaching, planning, and facilitation services that will carry a school's improvement efforts over a period of years. Professional development is beginning to be seen as the responsibility of all educators (principals, teacher leaders, classroom teachers, and support staff). As professional colleagues, the development of one another's skills is an important responsibility (i.e., mentor teaching, peer coaching, reflecting on practice, and strategy specific coaching).

Historic Paradigm Shifts for Professional Development

In *A New Vision for Staff Development* (1997), Sparks and Hirsh provide a summary that outlines the major paradigm shifts in professional development that have taken place over the last 30 years in education.

TABLE 10.1 Professional Development Paradigm Shifts: 1960s to 1990s

From	To
Individual development	Balanced individual and organizational
Fragmented and piecemeal	Clear, coherent, systemic plan
District focused	School focused
Adult needs and satisfaction	Student needs and learning outcomes; changes in on-the-job behavior
Training apart from job	Multiple forms of job-embedded learning
Transmission of knowledge by experts	Study by teachers of teaching and learning process
Generic instructional skills	Combination of generic and content-specific skills
Professional developers as trainers	Professional developer as consultant, planner, facilitator, trainer
Function of professional development department	Multiple role responsibilities by administrators and teachers
Directed at teachers	Directed at everyone who affects student learning
Financial frill	Indispensable process for growth
Measures individual outcomes	Measures student achievement

Developed by Speck; adapted from Sparks and Hirsh (1997).

Although the following "shifts" represent a change in focus in the nature of staff development, the use of newer processes does not necessarily exclude the application of more traditional approaches. In essence, the shifts describe a change in practice in which certain processes are used more and others less. What is critical is the match between learning processes and the goals of the staff development effort. (Sparks & Hirsh, 1997, pp. 12)

These paradigm shifts are presented in Table 10.1 for readers to use as a planning tool for reviewing professional development plans, designs, and procedures within their school or district.

A professional development design with desired goals and outcomes must use learning processes that reflect these paradigm shifts and that are substantiated by current research and exemplary practices. The change in focus for professional development is on "long-term" career development, with teachers using the cycle of inquiry and reflection to inform their work.

When teachers, principals, support staff, and students in a school are all learners and teachers are engaged in continuous professional renewal, they exemplify the learning community. No longer will educators need to be "professionally developed." Instead, they will be engaged in an ongoing process of development that is embedded in their professional lives.

Current Research

Professional development of school employees and significant changes in the organizations in which they work are both required if schools are to adequately prepare students for life in a world that is becoming increasingly complex. Staff development is at the center of all education reform strategies—without it, such strategies are merely good ideas that cannot find expression. (Sparks & Hirsh, 1997, p. 96)

Continued research and best practices have taught us that widespread, sustained implementation of new practices in classrooms, principals' offices, and district offices requires new forms of professional development that are evolving out of significant school reform work. Not only must professional development affect the knowledge, skills, attitudes, and behaviors of individual teachers, administrators, and other school professionals, but it also must alter the organizational cultures and structures of schools and districts in which they work. Lessons from failed school reform efforts have shown that fragmentation, multiple initiatives, lack of focus, overload, and incoherence with other change efforts have led to few changes in teaching practices, the organization of schools, or success rates for students.

Recent research, however, has shown the linkage between quality professional development practices and successful school organizational change. Ann Lieberman, Lynn Miller, Linda Darling-Hammond, Milbrey McLaughlin, Carl Glickman, Dennis Sparks, and Stephanie Hirsh, among other leading school reformers, have helped define the evolution of what professional development means for teachers and school change efforts. Educators have new understandings as they examine best practices of teachers and administrators engaged in school reform. The key current forces affecting professional development are the standards and accountability movement, systems thinking, constructivism, and understanding brain-based learning. A summary of these key forces in current research will be shared as an overview for the reader to provide a broader understanding of the direction professional development is taking to more effectively support sustained school change and success for students (see Figure 10.1).

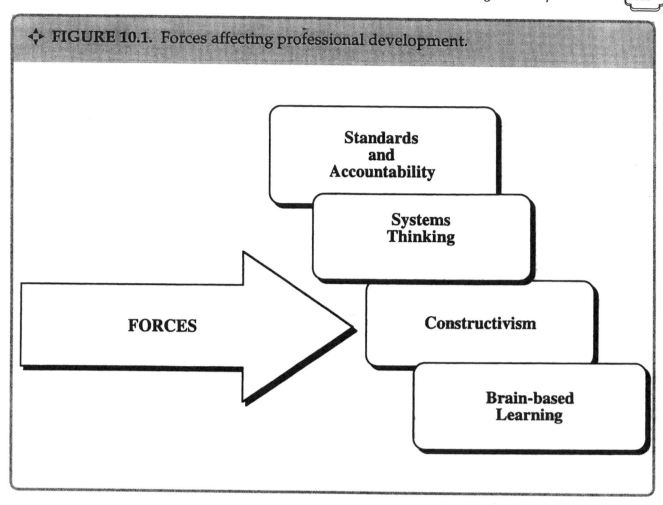

✦ FIGURE 10.1. Forces affecting professional development.

Forces Affecting Professional Development

Standards and Accountability

The standards and accountability movement has established clear measures for student achievement and expected results. Teachers are given direct feedback on what their students know and are able to do related to established standards. The National Standards, the National Council for Accreditation of Teacher Education, and the California Standards for the Teaching Profession have established content standards for subject areas as well as national and state standards for the teaching profession. These standards describe the practices and expectations for teachers. The accountability for reaching the standards is measured by the results demonstrated. The assessment is based on what knowledge, skills, and understanding students were expected to acquire as a result of their educational experiences. Standards and accountability have provided a dramatic change in how educators think about the purpose of schooling and what is expected of students.

Standards-driven education, with clear accountability, requires that professional development practice be driven by results. The tradition of mandating "seat time," offering hourly credits for workshops and courses, and computing satisfaction ratings of participants are no longer acceptable strategies for proving the importance of professional development. Professional development must show what has changed in the behavior of a teacher in the classroom and how the new work has improved student learning. The value of professional development is centered on results in altering the behavior of the educator and benefiting student learning. The perceived value for participants or records of participants' attendance are not the indicators of success when defined standards and improved performance are the goals (Guskey, 2000). Sparks and Hirsh (1997) summarize the essence of accountability-driven professional development in the following statement:

> Staff development's success will be judged not by how many teachers and administrators participate in staff development programs or how they perceive its value, but by whether it alters instructional behavior in a way that benefits students. The goal is improved performance—by students, staff, and the organization. (Sparks & Hirsh, 1997, p. 5)

The National Staff Development Council has developed *Standards for Staff Development* (1995) that are intended to be used by schools and districts to improve the quality of their professional development efforts so that student learning will be increased. The standards are organized into three categories (context, process, and content), which guide the development, implementation, and evaluation of professional development plans for individuals as well as the organization. The context element of the standards addresses the organization, system, or culture in which the new learnings will be implemented. The process element refers to the "how" of professional development. It describes a means for acquisition of new knowledge and skills. The content element refers to the actual skills and knowledge that effective educators need to refine or acquire through professional development. These standards set clear expectations for what professional development should be for individuals as well as for the organization. Results can be judged by measuring each student's progress in reaching the standards against a professional development program. This accountability is key in professional development and will make a difference in student achievement.

Systems Thinking

Systems thinking provides professional development planners with the perspective of viewing the whole system and the interrelationships of the parts while assuring planners that change is continuous. School reformers have traditionally not used systems thinking but have instead approached school reform in a piecemeal fashion. They tinker with the parts and fail to consider how certain changes affect the system. Systems thinking can help educators understand how organizations change and can help them to make sense of the chaos. Educators who begin to think in terms of systems will have tools for dealing with the complexity of schools and the need to sustain systematic change. To be effective, educators must view professional development practices in the context of the larger system with the interconnectedness of all parts and the continuous flow of change.

In *The Fifth Discipline: The Art and Practice of the Learning Organization*, Senge (1990) helps define system thinking:

> System thinking is a discipline of seeing wholes. It is a conceptual framework for seeing interrelationships rather than things, for seeing patterns of change rather than static "snapshots."
>
> It is a discipline for seeing the "structures" that underlie complex situations, and for discerning high from low leverage change. (Senge, 1990, pp. 68-69)

Systems thinkers believe that educators can provide a way to confront the disconnectedness of reform efforts by identifying professional development structures, processes, and activities and recognizing the high-leverage points in a system that will produce significant, enduring improvements (Senge, 1990, p. 64). Using systems thinking, educators, upon determining the critical leverage points for change, will provide the proper means through professional development to sustain school reform efforts.

Our nonsystemic ways of thinking do not allow us to see the whole picture, so we tend to focus on low-leverage changes or symptoms of problems (Senge, 1990). Professional development planners must understand and apply systems thinking to each school's structures, patterns, and processes in order to strengthen the change process with new knowledge that will promote learning and sustain change in the school organization. Because professional development plays a central role in systemic change efforts, educators interested in school reform must change their mental models about schools and use the lens of systems thinking to see what has to be done and how to do it. Understanding and thinking systematically can help educators (leaders and teachers) plan, implement, and evaluate in a holistic way for sustained school reform with a greater impact on student achievement.

Constructivism

The constructivist viewpoint allows educators to move from the current dominant mode of training-focused professional development with "direct teaching" to the constructivist community of learners approach of "learning in and out of school" (Sparks & Hirsh, 1997, p. 2). Constructivism emphasizes that learners create their own knowledge structures rather than merely receiving them from others. Constructivists believe that knowledge is not simply transmitted from teacher to student but instead is constructed in the mind of the learner (Brooks & Brooks, 1993). Darling-Hammond and McLaughlin (1995) believe that professional development must support a learner-centered view of teaching and a career-long perspective of teachers' learning.

Using the constructivist philosophy, teachers have the serious and difficult tasks of learning the skills and perspectives assumed by new visions of practice and unlearning the practices and beliefs about students and instruction that have dominated their professional lives to date (Darling-Hammond & McLaughlin, 1995). Professional development planners must honor teachers as learners who construct their knowledge, and they must model processes that guide rather than tell and direct.

Teachers must have opportunities to discuss, think about, try out, and hone new practices by taking on new roles (teacher researchers, peer coaches); creating new structures (action research teams, problem-solving groups); working on new tasks (standards and assessments); and creating a culture of inquiry (Lieberman, 1995a). New forms of professional development are not limited to events, but become part of district-wide expectations for teachers, and the related practices are integrated into the culture of the schools. From a deep sense of changing practices based on new knowledge and skills, inquiry and reflection, coaching, and working on important tasks, teachers will construct meanings that will affect schools in significant ways over time. "Professional development today also means providing occasions for teachers to reflect critically on their practice and to fashion new knowledge and beliefs about content, pedagogy, and learners" (Darling-Hammond & McLaughlin, 1995, p. 597).

The "transmittal" view of learning, wherein teachers receive information through lectures, readings, and direct instruction, is outmoded. Professional development must honor a teacher's abilities; autonomy; initiative; and capacity to inquire, dialogue, interact, seek out experts, and process and learn new concepts and strategies in a constructivist manner. Professional development that models constructivist practices for teachers is critical if teachers are expected to make sense of the teaching-learning process in their own contexts.

Rather than receiving "knowledge" from "experts" in training sessions, teachers and administrators will collaborate with peers, researchers, and their own students to make sense of learning process in their own contexts. Staff development from a constructivist perspective will include activities such as action research, conversations with peers about the beliefs and assumptions that guide their instruction, and reflective practices such as journal keeping—activities that many educators may not even view as professional development. (Sparks & Hirsh, 1997, p. 11)

Teachers need multiple strategies and opportunities to learn in constructivist settings so that they construct for themselves educational practices to reflect on. Otherwise, professional development instructional programs will be trivialized into "cookbook" approaches to learning (Brooks & Brooks, 1993, pp. 121-122).

Brain-Based Learning

The ability to understand and apply the ideas of brain-based learning in the design and implementation of professional development is critically important, based on recent research about how we learn. From brain research, we know that people learn best through active involvement, reflection, and articulation about what they have learned (Jensen, 1998). Processes, practices, and policies built on brain-based learning are at the heart of an expanded definition of teacher development that encourages teachers to involve themselves as learners. Brain-based learning research has informed classroom practices of teachers and should therefore inform how professional development activities and plans are designed. A brain-based learning model supports an interactive, constructivist model. The learners engage in learning and guide their own instruction (Bruer, 1999). Professional development must have meaning and understanding for participants based on how the brain processes new information. Traditional professional development assumes that learners need to be informed and that when they need the new content, they will know how to apply it. Brain-based learning focuses on the real world of the teacher and classroom and immerses the learner in processing, analyzing, and examining this complex experience for meaning and understanding. The brain resists having meaninglessness—isolated pieces of information unrelated to what makes sense to a learner—imposed on it. Learners need to formulate their own patterns of understanding so that the brain can recognize them. New learnings take place in natural, complex, and "messy" experiences in which the learner interacts dynamically with information, seeking patterns that make sense rather than absorbing information (Caine & Caine, 1997). The challenge for professional development using brain-based learning is to fit the skills and content to the learner rather than to mold the learner to the content.

Currently, there is an ironic shortcoming in the traditional approach to professional development, which is eloquently pointed out by Lieberman (1995a):

> What everyone appears to want for students—a wide array of learning opportunities that engage students in experiencing, creating, and solving real problems, using their own experiences, and working with others—is for some reason denied to teachers when they are learners. (p. 591)

Brain-based professional development design requires that educators incorporate Gardner's (1985, 1993) concept of multiple intelligences and learning styles to better meet a learner's needs. As professional developers begin to employ multiple paths to understanding and structure learning to meet the adult need for choice, they also must provide the learner time to process, establish meaning in a personal context, and apply the new learning to professional practice. Allowing time to process and practice new learning is a part of knowing how the brain functions and what learners need to succeed in adopting new practices. Although individuals find meaning in experience, they do not automatically extract all the potential meaning that is implicit in the content or move beyond their current meanings without being challenged. Using brain-based learning, participants actively process learning through thinking critically, asking probing questions, exploring alternative perspectives and points of view, solving problems, recognizing details, and searching for big ideas and broad implications. It is this active processing with their peers that leads to true understanding and mastery of content.

Further, brain-based learning has provided the understanding that complex learning is enhanced by challenge and inhibited by threat. Teachers need to be challenged to improve their practices to support increased student achievement, but they shouldn't feel threatened if they take risks. The presence of threat can cause an individual to downshift, which is the psychophysiological response to perceived threat, accompanied by a sense of helplessness, fatigue, or both. The presence of threat and downshifting are important concepts for educators to understand when they are designing professional development activities. When individuals downshift, they revert to more primitive, instinctual responses or to early programmed behaviors. A downshifted brain is less able to engage in a complex intellectual task requiring creativity, and the ability to engage in open-ended thinking and questioning is decreased (Caine & Caine, 1994). Thus, a downshifted individual is not open to new learning. The brain learns optimally and makes maximum connections when appropriately challenged in an environment that encourages taking risks. Professional development activities must create and maintain an atmosphere of relaxed alertness, involving low threat and high challenge. In this brain-compatible professional development environment, individuals can learn new skills, content, and behaviors.

Conclusion

Are we going to be condemned to the past, or will we use historical perspectives and current research on professional development to inform our practices? This brief historical perspective of professional development provides a background for understanding the evolution of practices. It raises questions about the key current forces influencing professional development: standards and accountability, systems thinking, constructivist practices, and brain-based learning. The challenge is to understand and design professional development opportunities that honor the learner as an individual and that provide in-depth understanding over a sustained period of time for true changes to take place in practice. Challenged learners can then integrate the new learnings into personal experiences as they refine their abilities to teach, improve their students' learning, and help school-wide reform. The challenges and rewards of increased student achievement are too great to be condemned to past practices in professional development. Multiple opportunities for learning and knowing await professional educators.

REALITY CHECK

If professional development for educators
should reflect the best practices known to our profession,
how will you align your current professional development
practices with the most recent research about learning
and quality professional development?

On the Web

The Web sites provided here offer a variety of sources for accessing current professional development practices and the most recent research.

Associations, Government, and Private Educational Resources

- American Educational Research Association: http://www.aera.net

- Association for Supervision and Curriculum Development: http://www.ascd.org

- National Staff Development Council: http://www.nsdc.org

- Phi Delta Kappan: http://www.pdkintl.org

- American Federation of Teachers: http://www.aft.org

- National Education Association: http://www.nea.org

- National Board for Professional Teaching Standards: http://www.nbpts.org

- American Association of School Administrators: http://www.aasa.org

- The National Association of Elementary School Principals: http://www.naesp.org

- National Association of Secondary School Principals: http://www.nassp.org

- National Middle School Association: http://www.nmsa.org

- National School Board Association: http://www.nsba.org

- Council of Chief State School Officers: http://www.ccsso.org

- Education Commission for the States: http://www.ecs.org

- U.S. Department of Education: http://www.ed.gov

- National Center for Educational Statistics: http://nces.ed.gov

- Educational Resource Information Center: http://ericir.syr.edu (known as "ask eric")

- RAND Education: http://www.rand.org

◆ Regional Educational Lab Network (links to 10 U.S. Regional Educational Labs): http://www.relnetwork.org

Educational Information

◆ Education Week: http://www.edweek.com

◆ School Services: http://www.ssc.com

◆ EdSource: http://www.edsource.org

◆ Education Trust: http://www.edtrust.org

◆ New Teacher Center: http://www.newteachercenter.org

◆ Harvard Education Letter: http://www.edletter.org

National Reports

◆ Professional Development: Learning From the Best—A Toolkit for Schools and Districts Based on the National Awards Program for Model Professional Development: http://www.ncrel.org/pd

◆ A National Plan for Improving Professional Development—National Staff Development Council: http://www.nsdc.org

◆ Prisoners of Time: http://www.emich.edu/public/emu-origrams/tlc/Better3.html

◆ What Matters Most: http://www.tc.columbia.edu/~teachcomm/Conference-99Quality

◆ Third International Math and Science Study: http://www.timss.org/ and http://www.ed.gov/nces/timss

Search Engines

◆ Google: http://www.google.com

◆ Infoseek: http://www.infoseek.com

◆ Dogpile: http://www.dogpile.com

◆ MetaCrawler: http://www.metacrawler.com

◆ Education World: http://db.education-world.com/perl/browse

◆ Northernlight: http://www.northernlight.com

◆ Inference Find: http://inferencefind.com

Facing the Emerging Issues and Challenges of Professional Learning

Scenario

"Hey Bob, why aren't you at the University? I thought you needed credits for your credential."

"Wait until I log on, I'll be at the University."

"A virtual classroom?"

"Right. I'm in a virtual classroom through the Net. I can drop in and drop out twenty-four hours a day!"

"Who's the dean? Every school has a dean."

"Not this one. It has a student adviser, though."

"Does it have teachers or professors?"

"Of course. They design the curriculum."

"Do you get grades?"

"Sure, if I want them. Sometimes I just like to learn stuff."

"Do you have to be there every day?"

"Only if I want the credits. I actually complete the coursework at my own pace within the semester or sometimes by the end of the year."

"What if you want to talk with someone about the class?"

"The professors set up chat rooms that are monitored by student advisers who respond to us. Sometimes the professor comes on-line, too."

"What about meeting with the professor?"

"It's by e-mail, of course. You e-mail the professor directly when you need help, and either the professor or the student adviser responds."

"Can't you just drop by his office?"

"I wouldn't want to. She lives on the East Coast; I live in California."

"Do you ever work in teams with classmates?"

"Sure. We opened our own session under the chat room where I work with my regular team. Some professors won't have it any other way. It's forming relationships the technological way, and actually, it's great using collaborative inquiry when you can focus on what's being said, not who is saying it."

"What don't you like about your virtual classroom?"

"Hmmm. That's a tough one. Oh yes, here it is. If I fall asleep on-line, it runs up my phone bill."

As many educators know, this conversation is not about the future; it is about now. Universities from Harvard to Stanford are offering on-line classes, and many community colleges are wondering what took them so long. With so much information at the foot of a mouse, why do we think professional development will be the same as it has always been?

Pause for a moment to reflect on this essential question.

ESSENTIAL QUESTION

How will future trends and indicators be used to rethink professional development opportunities in schools?

Why Do We Have the Conversation?

How difficult is it to think about the future without including technology? Beginning several years ago, prominent authorities commented that if teachers weren't personally using technology, they couldn't have any idea about the future needs of their students. One social psychologist suggested that computer-illiterate teachers should not cross the threshold of a school. For most educators who try to imagine the world of high school graduates 18 years from today, it is a tremendous challenge. What in their experience has prepared them to predict how future generations will live, what they will see, or how they will communicate?

For professional growth, is it possible that the collaborative actions of teachers will increase in proportion to the amount of knowledge they access electronically? As greater numbers of computer-literate students and teachers come through the system, they will build upon these resources with far greater speed and skill. As people change and organizations reshape their operations, will educators seek new ways for students and staffs to share their ideas? Will principals and teachers use technology for data-driven learning, measurements, information access, data collection, and analyses in their daily lives? Will they use input data, environmental data, and performance data to drive improvements? Electronic access seems to empower the receivers to be masters of their learning. Will educators take advantage of professional development opportunities from all over the world to increase their knowledge, expertise, and mastery of strategies for working with all students? Will students find in the public schools both models and motivation for their own successes in cyberspace? Educators may not know the answers, but they should at least know enough about today's technology to keep up with the questions. Table 11.1 introduces many of the transformational changes we can expect to see in professional development as well as the implications of these shifts for teachers and students.

Research and Best Practices

Effective relationships and human interactions will become increasingly important in the future. The use of communications technology has the potential to bring people closer than ever before. They will form relationships, and that capacity will be, according to Margaret Wheatley (1994), "the power of the organization" (p. 39). As educators become more connected and learn to trust each other's expertise, they will be less dependent on colleagues for answers and more familiar with discovery through collaborative inquiry. Their relationships through networks and collaboration with colleagues will empower them to improve, to be more effective, and to enjoy their work. Educators who have experienced the power of professional collaboration will also accept more responsibility for thinking deeply about how to help students improve their collaborative relationships. Students who are connected to school and to other learners in the

TABLE 11.1 Transforming for the Future of Teaching and Learning

From	To	Implications
Communications technology is useful, mostly for e-mail.	Continuous access on-line for personal and professional growth.	Professional learning opportunities on-line will expand educators' repertoires.
Relationships are comfortable with a few selected people.	Networks and collaboration are the power of an organization.	Relationships are at the foundation of all professional development.
Decisions about professional growth are made according to what looks or feels good.	The school will synchronize its resources to reach the goal.	Professional learning will have only one purpose—to affect student achievement.
Physical presence of all teachers and administrators at professional development seminars is mandated.	Schools mandate results but leave the pathways to get to the results open.	Professional development will be viewed as opportunities to exercise professional judgment about how to improve student achievement.
Professional learning resources are in a single location, available according to date and location of training.	There are multiple opportunities for teacher learning, including collaboration with peers working from standards.	Choices for professional growth will no longer be limited by location, time, and date.
Educators learn new content, skills, and strategies while they are in credentialing programs.	Educators demand an ongoing variety of options to support them in their classrooms and schools.	Everyone needs a rich, diverse, and current portfolio of skills to be an educator in the public schools.
Teachers may or may not have a sense of community with their students and colleagues.	All teachers understand that belonging is a basic human need and that their success with students and colleagues may be contingent upon the integrity of the relationships they build within a learning community.	Professional development plans incorporate a conscious effort to model and practice skills for creating a sense of community with students, staff, parents, and community members.
Only colleges and universities are authorized to provide credentialing classes for experienced educators.	Educators have choices at many levels to develop mastery in their profession.	On-demand professional learning uses Information Age technology, and multiple suppliers are available for educators to access.
Educators demonstrate loyalty to a school or district.	Educators move to where the best offers are made for their talents.	Districts recognize the need to attract and retain good staff and are flexible in what they can offer educators.
The need for help is urgent as demands for educators' time and attention increase.	The district recognizes the demands on the time and energy of staff to do the work and supports them by focusing only on what is most important, teaching and learning.	Professional development plans honor educators' needs for time and space to reach higher levels of skills and competence so that they can become the coaches and leaders of their peers.

school already have the potential to achieve at higher levels (Brendtro, Brokenleg, & Van Brockern, 1990; Krovetz, 1999). The same is true for adults. Those who are connected to other learners and leaders at the school already have the potential to achieve higher organizational, as well as individual, success.

Decision Making in the Context of Student Success

When adults in the public schools have similar values focused on student success, they have a foundation for decision making to improve student learning. We have listened to young teachers frustrated by experienced teachers who refuse to change their curriculum to help more students succeed. In the eyes of beginning teachers, the veterans appear to cling to strategies that no longer work for all students, and the context of student success appears to have been replaced by what is comfortable for adults. The adults in this setting have not accepted the concept of a learning community in which each person in the school community is learner, teacher, leader, and collaborator, sometimes simultaneously and at other times in a spontaneous, voluntary exchange of roles. In fact, experienced teachers could learn a great deal about how to connect with students from conversations with beginning teachers, who are usually closer in age and experience to the students. In the future, as all people become more connected through values, networking, lifestyles, and economic and political necessity, isolation will become a conspicuous burden to a staff and will not be tolerated. Continuous learning will be the substance of these professional connections. Margaret Wheatley (1994) explains in scientific terms that when we become synchronized within a small system, we will have an impact (p. 42). Synchronization can occur in public schools. When the goal of every student's success is clear, when commitment to the goal is universal, and when learning permeates the school community, the result will be student achievement.

Professional development will be the impetus for these professional interactions. The authors interviewed the principal of an elementary school after he had participated for 3 days in "Beyond Diversity" professional development seminars, studying strategies to help students improve their performance. He was in a very deep and troubled reflection about his practice. The facilitator had asked, "How will it be different for students?" and now this mature principal was rethinking what he had done for many years. He reflected,

I used to think that moving students around when they had blown a relationship with a certain teacher was the wrong thing to do. Now I am thinking that the most important thing we do is help a student learn and if he is having trouble with one instructor, then maybe we need to move him into a different situation as soon as possible so that he can focus on learning. I know this isn't a simple solution. But I also know that what I was doing may not have been fair to students or their instructors.

After 3 days of internalizing information and processing with colleagues, the principal mentioned above was already into a deeper level of professional learning. He absorbed the new knowledge and reflected on his personal practice. He thought about a student's performance and hypothesized what did or did not work based on his examination of evidence. After sharing his insights with colleagues, he was ready to plan for his future actions concerning the teacher-student relationship. His justification was student success. By necessity, more and more teachers and principals will rely on their professional judgment to make decisions about how to help students improve their academic achievement. In Sparks (2000), Schmoker refers to such decisions as shaping the environment to get results. As professional development becomes more learner centered, individuals will feel compelled to take actions that extend beyond a series of formal learning experiences.

Flexibility

For the future, it appears that flexibility is a personal attribute educators must develop for joining today's workforce or teaching young people. Changes are coming too rapidly for people to be rigid and unaccepting. With flexibility comes the challenge to think about homework, classes, grades, schools, postsecondary institutions, and professional development in new ways. Teachers know how hard they work to make classes interesting and challenging for students raised on video games with flashing lights, thundering crashes, and in-your-face visuals shrieking across the screen every 30 seconds. Many teachers have taken the challenge to provide interactive learning opportunities for their students to help focus their energies as well as their intellectual awareness. Schools are seeking partnerships with higher institutions of learning, with businesses, and with service organizations, as educators reach outside their walls for educational experiences for students.

Flexibility also means that educators committed to professional development will look at information, relationships, and processes in new, and perhaps unusual, ways. The next few years may find schools moving away from mandating educators' physical presence at professional development seminars to mandating that teams of teachers and administrators learn new content and strategies to improve student achievement, while leaving the "how" up to them. For students, access to the same kind of flexibility for learning is in their future as well. In the meantime, educators will use their flexibility to learn more about nontraditional approaches to teaching and learning to increase their personal capacity as well as to increase the potential of their students for learning.

On-Demand Resources

From sitting through sessions to discover what professional development seminars are about to accessing a review on the Internet written by people who attended the same seminar, educators will increasingly turn to technology for professional information. In the past, educators have made decisions with little or no available data as to whether or not a seminar series would help them improve student achievement and whether or not they should attend. Now they will be able to make informed decisions by accessing everything from previews of seminars to evaluations of outcomes and facilitators by other educators.

On-demand resources will make a difference for teachers, just as on-demand products have made a difference for consumers. We used to wait several weeks for a new pair of glasses. Now we can have an eye exam and a new pair of contacts or glasses in a day. From waiting 6 weeks to 3 years for a new text and accurate maps for world geography students, teachers now download new maps and related information from the Internet. To teach students about weather systems in various parts of the world, teachers access expeditions via the Internet for first-hand information available to students and teachers at the same time. Educators are able to teach complex content, including new products and innovations, from doing a Web search. As extensions of their own learning, they may request further conversations with researchers, or they may ask to observe someone in the area who claims expertise in using a particular strategy so that they have instant access to information and help with processing it. At the same time, decision making may include distance learning and "Internetworking" to provide key information in support of improvement strategies, including data by cohorts, longitudinal information on results of using specific strategies, comparative data, and expansion of resources. With the student as a focus for decision making, teachers' demands for the tools of technology can greatly expand their ability to center their actions on student success.

Teachers' lives are changing. From long meetings about organizational issues to ad hoc team meetings in school or in cyberspace, educators collaborate on planning strategies for students and professional development for themselves. From asking what a theory really means and looking through the library shelves for related subjects, teachers can "Ask Jeeves," "Google," or other search engines to sift through millions of books for related topics. Teachers gather insights from authors and experienced practitioners available to them no matter how often the need arises. On-demand resources are a necessary part of a professional's future as time for connections and research dwindles and demands for knowledge and expertise increase.

Teachers also need to access local resources when they need them. Districts should have current videos available to download, for example, on discipline, classroom management, strategies for teaching to the standards, curriculum content, teaching tools, or local history. These should be available to teachers at home or to teams at school. Lead teachers can provide access via live video to their classrooms so that other teachers have opportunities to see master teachers working in specific content areas. (Some classrooms are already accessible by cable at certain times of the day so that parents can see what their children are learning and doing.) Researchers have not thoroughly explored what on-demand resources could mean for professional development. On-demand professional development offers new opportunities for teacher learning that will only be expanded in the future.

Trickle Learning

The use of time will dictate many changes in the future, just as it has in the past. When educators begin to feel fragmented, their learning diminishes as personal time, professional time, and learning time get more frantic. Educators can turn to other professionals to see how they manage something that gets more precious every day, the big T: time. On the Public Broadcasting Service Web site, David Thornburg (2000) published an article entitled "Trickle Learning and Technology," in which he observed,

> While I might only have ten minutes in one place and five in another, over the course of a week, my total wait time probably runs to several hours. My supply of reading materials turns this otherwise wasted time into learning time for me.
>
> Unlike traditional classrooms, these learning periods are short, unpredictable in length, and virtually impossible to plan ahead of time. Even so, trickle learning is quite powerful, since it gives me

(over the span of a year) many productive hours of information gathering.

Thornburg (2000) continues with how to use the tools of technology to help with our learning. Trickle learning is just one example of the creative approaches to living we will see in the future as students, teachers, principals, parents, and others involved in education struggle to make it a priority in their lives. Professional reading and learning are important activities in a community that prides itself on building relationships and facilitating the flow of information as important components of the educational system.

Why Must Professional Development Change?

Vocal Teachers Demand Choices

Just as parents are becoming more vocal about choices for their children, asking questions, making demands, and sometimes choosing alternatives to local schools, teachers will become more vocal about the kind of support they need to do the job in the public schools. In order to be credentialed to teach or administer the schools, educators take classes and schedule professional growth activities. By necessity, in the future they will seek an increasing variety of options to help them be more effective in their roles. The increasing diversity of cultures, languages, social backgrounds, and learning styles all make demands on a teacher's effectiveness. Because students may have backgrounds unfamiliar to their teachers, and students may have learning and language needs different from those the school has served in the past, educators are openly searching for connections and help. Professional development through technology can help to resolve teachers' demands for assistance and options when they need them most. In teaching, we call the acute need for learning "teaching to the moment" or "optimal learning time." Educators' demand for professional knowledge is justified when the results include increased achievement of students. Effective teachers need current content, the latest in carefully researched strategies, and multiple opportunities to hone their skills. In essence, educators have a right to demand the tools to do the work. Professional development must operate on the premise that every educator needs a rich, diverse portfolio of skills to be successful in the public schools.

How will "what's out there" beyond the
gates of the school affect a child's ability to learn
and a teacher's ability to teach?

How will teachers identify the help they need
if their students' situations with poverty, hunger, and personal
safety are beyond their own knowledge and experiences?
How will they learn when they don't know what
they need to know in order to teach their students?

How will schools and districts assist teachers and principals
in finding the help they need to be more effective
in classrooms and schools?

Multiple Providers for Teacher Learning

Districts, regional providers, state agencies, and universities will lose their influence as sole providers for teacher learning. New technologies enable teachers to reach out to connect with other teachers, in other states, in other nations. With international access to experts, teachers can search for their own professional growth support. However, even for the most adept user, searching can absorb huge amounts of time. The term *facilitator of learning* may take on an entirely new definition. A content expert facilitator could access specific sites and prepare summaries of what may be found there. The facilitator could prepare learning organizers with button information about how to move from one source to a related screen for different perspectives on the same issue. A facilitator could convene a subgroup of staff and make the arrangements to interact with researchers or other practitioners in a different city so that the teachers could take the new knowledge to their colleagues.

How many educators consciously limit their ability to know more about what they are teaching or how they are teaching it? The fascinating extension for the service agencies mentioned above is that segmented learning is possible, but it is not the way most people want to be informed about a topic. With technology, educators are able to cross subject boundaries as they access information about the economy, politics, geography, demographics, and culture from a single Web site. At the same time, they can look at curriculum, instruction, brain research, systems thinking, and content updates as they relate to the previous topics using other sources. With this knowledge available to all teachers, why would they even consider formal limitations on their learning to credits at a regional center or university? "Networks for teachers challenge the spatial conventions of professional development as either school based or university based, and raise status issues about who controls such development by being able to define and distribute where it takes place" (Hargreaves, 1997, p. 5).

> How will educators determine their personal growth needs?
>
> How will schools and universities meet the challenge of control issues, such as teacher and administrator credentialing, professional development units on the salary schedule, or teacher workday concerns?
>
> What agencies will support teacher networks?

Future Educators Will Not Have the Loyalties of Yesterday's Faculty

Technology businesses may well be offering a glimpse of what employers can expect to see in the future workforce, for example, employees who are more loyal to themselves than to the organization. They demand greater respect and rewards for their talents, targeted benefits for their age group's needs, and opportunities to advance in their careers. Districts will have to rethink their traditional approaches, which rely on financial incentives in connection with seniority in a district, if they expect to attract and retain talented new and experienced educators. Some communities are already taking steps to provide housing for new teachers who are unable to afford to live in the area. Others offer incentives for teachers who become nationally certified or whose students all meet the standards. Still others have upgraded their professional development incentives and have institutionalized inviting teachers and principals to collaborate in structuring the opportunities. As districts invest more dollars in updating the skills and increasing the effectiveness of their employees, they will also explore new avenues for retaining their highly skilled and talented workforce.

How will districts determine financial incentives and rewards
for teachers and administrators who continue
to demonstrate superior skills and talents?

Will student achievement be a factor in the
conversation about skills and rewards?

Will access to excellent, diverse professional
growth opportunities be offered as an incentive?

What other avenues can districts explore to attract
and maintain excellent staff?

Urgent Need of Collaboration for Sense of Community

As self-help classes, support groups, car clubs, athletic clubs, day care parent groups, college and university alumni chapters, and virtual communities become a way of life, we are increasingly aware of each person's need for community. Schools are no different. Teachers' informal comments tell you about the vitality of community within the school:

- ◆ "I love where I work. It feels like family."

- ◆ "I used to enjoy being with our staff. With the new leadership, every staff meeting feels like a cold business event."

- ◆ "I just go to work and come home when I can legally leave. There is nothing at that school for me."

- ◆ "I keep asking myself, do I belong yet? How long will it take for a new teacher's ideas just to be heard?"

- ◆ "You would enjoy meeting the people I work with. They are a tremendous group of professionals. I'm lucky to be with them."

- ◆ "We work so hard! When we have a few moments, we really try to enjoy each other's company."

- ◆ "I never have to ask for help. It seems that it's always offered before I even realize I have been asking the questions. It's a great place to work, and it always has been since my first day on the job."

Educators struggle with the concepts of collaboration and community in schools because they are not certain how to develop the relationships, create the common purpose, and foster a sense of attachment among people to something greater than themselves (Sergiovanni, 1994). They often try to create a common purpose superficially, through strategic planning or visioning activities, but it takes an internal commitment on the part of everyone involved to form a true collaborative community in a school. Even neighborhood schools, which would seem to be natural places for projecting a sense of community, often have teachers and administrators who commute daily, sometimes from long distances. They may resist forming a community with the entire neighborhood, yet it is becoming more obvious that educators need the school community. The more difficult the job, the more educators need others to stand by them and the more they need to stand by students and their parents. One way to build community in a school is to start with professional development activities that focus on student work and then move to collaborative professional meetings about how to work with each child. Teachers who get to know their students and families—those who can build trust with them and their colleagues, connect with parents, continually focus on what's good for students, and develop collaborative efforts within the community—are beginning to invest in a greater concept of worth and respect for all.

Teachers in the future will have more recognition of their talents by the community. As needs for professionally competent knowledge workers increase, teachers, who are involved in daily communications with large groups of people, are obvious resources. If the community encourages contributions by teachers as knowledge workers, creative problem solvers, and multimedia experts in the construction of knowledge, then professional development delivery strategies must include opportunities to model and to practice all of the above.

How can schools build a sense of community that makes all adults and students feel a part of something greater than themselves?

How can professional development build community?

How should the community recognize and support the talents of teachers as professional knowledge workers?

Educators Need a Lot More Help

More and more social work and paperwork is getting in the way of classroom work with children. Scarcely a week goes by without schools being confronted by more imposition of endless change. My earlier research . . . has shown how working more closely with colleagues can reduce duplication, share the burden, provide moral support, and give teachers the collective strength to set priorities among all the demands placed upon them. But this is no longer enough. (Hargreaves, 1997, p. 7)

If the roles of public school teacher and administrator are to reflect the highest quality of educator effectiveness, is the system supportive of making their goals achievable? What will it take? Researchers have a myriad of suggestions about how to connect, reflect, partner, nurture, network, lead, and grow in the profession. As teachers look at the needs of their students, they are asking, "How and when do I concentrate on my teaching?"

Perhaps that is the greatest challenge for leaders. How do they help teachers concentrate on their teaching? How do leaders place such a high value on teachers' time that whatever else they are asked to do becomes less important if not related to teaching and learning? Strategies such as using teaching assistants, teacher aides, parent volunteers, and student teachers are intended to help a teacher, but there is no doubt that these innovations also take teacher time to coordinate, train, and monitor. Teacher collaboration is another commitment of time. The flip side of the collaboration coin, however, is doing everything alone, and that is fast becoming impossible. Somehow districts must find a way for teachers and administrators to reach higher levels of skills and competence through professional development while redefining their positions so that they and their students can be effective and successful.

> If teachers need more help than ever before,
> how do schools work collaboratively with them
> to structure their time to support the work?
>
> If teachers need to reach higher levels of skills
> and competence than ever before, how do schools, districts,
> and universities collaboratively work with them
> so that they are able to achieve mastery and
> become coaches and leaders?

Conclusion

Every time educators attend conferences, scan the latest technology magazine, read the latest issue of a professional magazine, pick up a newspaper, browse through a new catalogue, or surf the Web, they are aware of what it means to be current in this rapidly changing world. By maintaining their awareness of changes in communication structures and strategies, for example, teachers can refocus on how to bring these tools into the classroom to help students achieve. Professional development for teachers must address these current needs. Policies and practices that include requirements for electronic communications about individual, grade-level, school, and district progress toward the goal of student achievement will help to institutionalize the new practices. Technology isn't the only challenge educators are facing, but to separate technology from students and their learning or from teachers and their professional development is to be blind to the outside world. Figure 11.1, Future Issues Affecting Professional Development, provides an overview of the issues educators are facing as they prepare for the future of teaching and learning.

The future for educators is as bright as it has ever been. Although frustrated at the public's obsession with achievement and test scores, educators have nevertheless chosen to ignore how teachers are connecting with students and parents. Now they are encouraged to make these connections as support for students so that success is achievable. Teachers have been exasperated by the need to look at data without having the technology in place to manipulate data. Now systems are in place for compiling, disaggregating, and reporting data at multiple levels. Better use of technology for collegial sharing, collaboration, and problem solving must be part of each educator's renewed commitment to student success. Ideally, the technical possibility of multiple learning opportunities available whenever needed for teachers will translate to multiple learning opportunities available for students. Through technology and a willingness to take on the challenges so that students can be successful, educators will make our public school system one that can respond with pride and a sense of accomplishment to public pressures for accountability.

REALITY CHECK

What is your school or district doing to adequately prepare teachers and students for a resource-demanding, rapidly changing, technology-based future?

♦ **FIGURE 11.1.** Future issues affecting professional development.

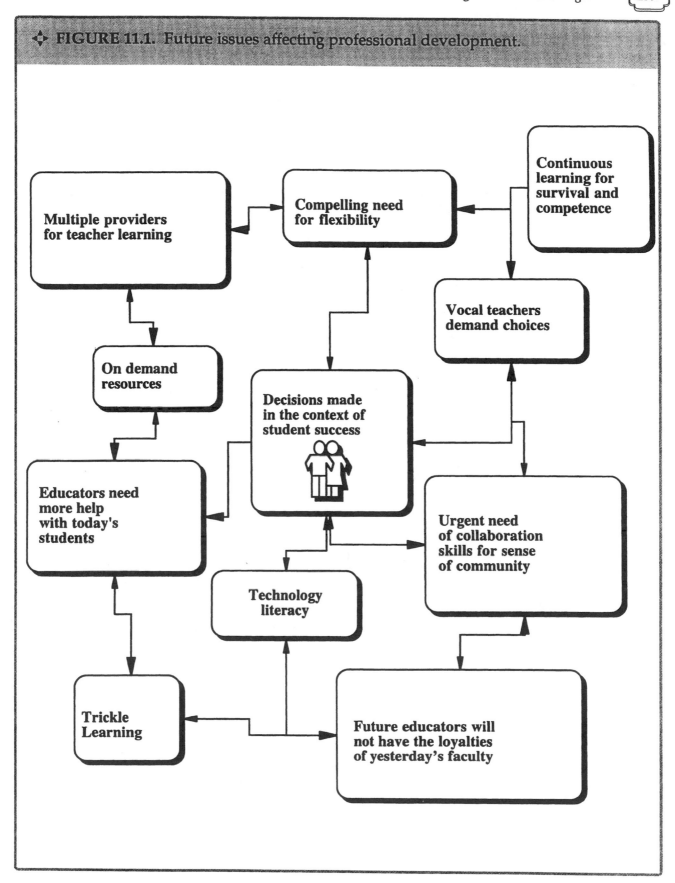

On the Web

For more information about what is happening in teaching and learning, visit TeacherSource and find more articles by David Thornburg at http://www.pbs.org/teachersource. For information about the future of all organizations, visit the Chaordic Alliance at http://www.chaordic.org. The founder of Visa, Dee Hock, is a regular contributor to this site. Peter Senge, who with his colleagues authored *The Dance of Change* (1999), introduced the Chaordic Alliance to many educators in his yearly conversations about the future sponsored by Pegasus Communications. Others sites associated with systems thinking are Pegasus Communications at http://www.pegasuscom.com and Systems Dynamics in Education at http://sysdyn.mit.edu.

References

Barth, R. (1990). *Improving schools from within.* San Francisco: Jossey-Bass.

Bohm, D. (1996). *On dialogue.* London: Routledge.

Brendtro, L., Brokenleg, M., & Van Brockern, S. (1990). *Reclaiming youth at risk: Our hope for the future.* Bloomington, IN: National Educational Service.

Brooks, J., & Brooks, M. (1993). *The case for constructivist classroom.* Alexandria, VA: Association for Supervision and Curriculum Development.

Brooks, M., & Brooks, J. G. (1999). Courage to be constructivist. *Educational Leadership, 57*(3), 18-24.

Bruer, J. (1999). In search of . . . brain-based education. *Phi Delta Kappan, 80,* 649-657.

Bull, B., & Buechler B. (1996). *Learning together: Professional development for better schools.* Bloomington: Indiana Education Policy Center.

Burden, P. (1982, June). *Developmental supervision: Reducing teacher stress at different career stages.* Paper presented at the Association of Teacher Educators National Conference, Phoenix, AZ.

Burke, P. J., Christensen, J. C., & Fessler, R. (1984). *Teacher career stages: Implications for staff development* (Whole No. 214). Bloomington, IN: Phi Delta Kappan Educational Foundation.

Caine, R. N., & Caine, G. (1994). *Making connections: Teaching and the human brain* (Rev. ed.). Menlo Park, CA: Addison-Wesley.

Caine, R. N., & Caine, G. (1997). *Education on the edge of possibility.* Alexandria, VA: Association for Supervision and Curriculum Development.

California Commission on the Teaching Profession. (1997). *California standards for the teaching profession.* Sacramento: Author.

Carnegie Forum on Education and the Economy. (1986). *A nation prepared: Teachers for the 21st century.* New York: Carnegie Corporation of New York.

Christensen, J., Burke, P., Fessler, R., & Hagstrom, D. (1983). *Stages of teachers' careers: Implications for professional development.* Washington, DC: National Institute of Education. (ERIC Document Reproduction Service No. ED 227 054)

Cohen, D. K., & Hill, H. C. (1998). *Instructional policy and classroom performance: The mathematics reform in California.* Philadelphia: Consortium for Policy Research in Education.

Collins, D. 1998. *Achieving your vision of professional development.* Tallahassee, FL: SouthEastern Regional Vision for Education.

Cook, C., & Fine, C. (1996). *Critical issue: Realizing new learning for all students through professional development, NCREL Pathways* [On-line]. Available: http://www.ncrel.org/sdrs/pathwayg.htm

Cooper, H., Nye, B., Charlton, K., Lindsay, J., & Greathouse, S. (1996). The effects of summer vacation on achievement test scores: A narrative and meta-analytic review. *Review of Educational Research, 66,* 227-268.

Corcoran, T. (1995). *Helping teachers teach well: Transforming professional development* (Research Brief No. 16-6/95). Philadelphia: Consortium for Policy Research in Education.

Darling-Hammond, L. (1997a). *The future for democratic education* [On-line]. Available: http://www.ncrel.org/cscd/pubs/lead41/41future.htm

Darling-Hammond, L. (1997b). *The right to learn: A blueprint for creating schools that work.* San Francisco: Jossey-Bass.

Darling-Hammond, L., Ancess, J., & Falk, B. (1995). *Authentic assessment in action: Case studies.* New York: Teachers College Press.

Darling-Hammond, L., & Ball, D. L. (1998). *Teaching for high standards: What policymakers need to know and be able to do.* New York: National Commission on Teaching and America's Future and Consortium for Policy Research in Education.

Darling-Hammond, L., & McLaughlin, M. W. (1995). Policies that support professional development in an era of reform. *Phi Delta Kappan, 76,* 507-604.

Deal, T., & Peterson, K. (1993). *The principal's role in change: Technical and symbolic aspects of school improvement* [On-line]. Available: http://www.ncrel.org/sdrs/areas/sdrsdb/00175.htm

Deming, W. E. (1986). *Out of crisis.* Cambridge: Massachusetts Institute of Technology Center for Advanced Engineering Study.

Drucker, P. (1973). *Management: Tasks—Responsibilities—Practices.* New York: Harper & Row.

Elmore, R. (1996). *Staff development and instructional improvement: Community District 2, New York City.* New York: National Commission on Teaching and America's Future.

Feiman, S., & Floden, R. (1980). *What's all this tale about teacher development.* East Lansing, MI: Institute for Research on Teaching. (ERIC Document Reproduction Service No. ED 189 088)

Fullan, M. (1991). *The new meaning of educational change.* New York: Teachers College Press.

Fullan, M. (1993). *Change forces: Probing the depths of educational change.* New York: Falmer.

Gardner, H. (1985). *Frames of mind: The theory of multiple intelligences.* New York: Basic Books.

Gardner, H. (1993). *Multiple intelligences: The theory in practice.* New York: Basic Books.

Gardner, H. (1999). *Intelligence reframed: Multiple intelligences for the 21st century.* New York: Basic Books.

Guskey, T. (1998a). The age of our accountability. *Journal of Staff Development, 19*(4), 36-43.

Guskey, T. (1998b). Follow-up is key, but it's often forgotten. *Journal of Staff Development, 19*(2), 7-8.

Guskey, T. (1999). Apply time with wisdom. *Journal of Staff Development, 20*(2), 10-14.

Guskey, T. (2000). *Evaluating professional development.* Thousand Oaks, CA: Corwin Press.

Hargreaves, A. (Ed.). (1997). *1997 ASCD yearbook: Rethinking educational change with heart and mind.* Alexandria, VA: Association for Supervision and Curriculum Development.

Hargreaves, A., & Dawe, R. (1990). Paths of professional development: Contrived collegiality, collaborative culture, and the case of peer coaching. *Teaching and Teacher Education, 6,* 227-241.

Hassel, E. (1999). *Professional development: Learning from the best—A toolkit for schools and districts based on the national awards program for model professional development.* Oak Brook, IL: North Central Regional Educational Laboratory.

Haycock, K. (1999). Good teaching matters . . . a lot. In J. Richardson (Ed.), *Results* (Vol. 3, pp. 1, 6). Oxford, OH: National Staff Development Council.

Holmes Group. (1986). *Tomorrow's teachers: A report of the Holmes Group.* East Lansing, MI: Author.

Howard, Pierce J. (1994). *The owner's manual for the brain: Everyday applications from mind-research.* Austin, TX: Leornian Press.

Jensen, E. (1998). *Teaching with the brain in mind.* Alexandria, VA: Association for Supervision and Curriculum Development.

Joyce, B., Murphy, C., Showers, B., & Murphy, J. (1989). School renewal as cultural change. *Educational Leadership, 47*(3), 70-78.

Joyce, B., & Showers, B. (1995). *Student achievement through staff development.* White Plains, NY: Longman.

Joyce, B., & Showers, B. (1996). The evolution of peer coaching. *Educational Leadership, 53*(6), 12-16.

Katzenmeyer, M., & Moller, G. (1996). *Awakening the sleeping giant: Leadership development for teachers.* Thousand Oaks, CA: Corwin Press.

Kawasaki, G. (with Moreno, M.) (1999). *Rules for revolutionaries: The capitalist manifesto for creating and marketing new services.* New York: Harper Business/HarperCollins.

Kelly, K. (1998). *New rules for the new economy: 10 radical strategies for a connected world.* New York: Viking/Penguin-Putnam.

Kotulak, R. (1996). *Inside the brain: Revolutionary discoveries of how the mind works.* Kansas City, MO: Andrews and McMeel, Universal Press Syndicate Company.

Krovetz, M. (1999). *Fostering resiliency: Expecting all students to use their minds and hearts well.* Thousand Oaks, CA: Corwin Press.

Kruse, S. D. (1999). Collaborate. *Journal of Staff Development, 20*(3), 14-16.

Lambert, L. (1998). *Building leadership capacity in schools.* Alexandria, VA: Association for Supervision and Curriculum Development.

Lambert, L., Walker, D., Zimmerman, D., Cooper, J., Lambert, M. D., Gardner, M. E., & Ford-Slack, P. J. (1995). *The constructivist leader.* New York: Teachers College Press.

Lieberman, A. (1995a). Practices that support teacher development: Transforming conceptions of professional learning. *Phi Delta Kappan, 76,* 591-596.

Lieberman, A. (Ed.). (1995b). *The work of restructuring schools: Building from the ground up.* New York: Teachers College Press.

Lieberman, A. (1996). Creating intentional learning communities. *Educational Leadership, 54*(3), 51-55.

Lieberman, A., & Miller, L. (Eds.). (1991). New demands, new realities, new perspectives. *Staff development for education in the 90's.* New York: Teachers College Press.

Lieberman, A., & Miller, L. (1999). *Teachers—Transforming their world and their work.* New York: Teachers College Press.

Lipton, L., & Greenblatt, R. (1992). Supporting the learning organization: A model for congruent system-wide renewal. *Journal of Staff Development, 13*(3), 20-25.

Little, J. W. (1993a, June). *Excellence in professional development and professional community.* Paper presented at a planning meeting of the U.S. Department of Education Blue Ribbon Schools Program, Washington, DC.

Little, J. W. (1993b). Teacher professional development in a climate of educational reform. *Educational Evaluation and Policy Analysis, 15,* 129-151.

Loucks-Horsely, S., Harding, S. K., Arbuckle, M. A., Murray, L. B., Dubea, C., & Williams, M. K. (1987). *Continuing to learn: A guidebook for teacher development.* Andover, MA: Regional Laboratory for Educational Improvement of the Northeast and Islands.

Loucks-Horsely, S., Hewson, P., Love, N., & Stiles, K. (1998). *Designing professional development for teachers of science and mathematics.* Thousand Oaks, CA: Corwin Press.

Marsh, D., & Codding, J. (1999). *The new American high school.* Thousand Oaks, CA: Corwin Press.

McLaughlin, M. (1994). Strategic sites for teachers' professional development. In P. Gimmet & J. Neufeld (Eds.), *Teachers' development and the struggle for authenticity: Professional growth and restructuring in the context of change* (pp. 31-51). New York: Teachers College Press.

National Commission on Excellence in Education. (1983). *A nation at risk.* Washington, DC: U.S. Government Printing Office.

National Commission on Time and Learning. (1994). *Prisoners of time.* Washington, DC: U.S. Government Printing Office.

National Governors' Association. (1986). *Time for results: The governors' report on education.* Washington, DC: Author.

National Staff Development Council. (1995). *Standards for staff development—High school edition.* Oxford, OH: Author.

NCREL (North Central Regional Educational Laboratory) Pathways. (1999). *Critical issue: Realizing new learning for all students through professional development* [On-line]. Available: http://www.ncrel.org/pathways.htm

Newman, K., Dornburg, B., Dubois, D., & Kranz, E. (1980). *Stress to teachers' midcareer transitions: A role for teacher education.* (ERIC Document Reproduction Service No. ED 196 868)

Owen, H. (1999). *The spirit of leadership: Liberating the leaders in each of us.* San Francisco: Berrett-Koehler.

Peterson, K. (1994). *Building collaborative cultures: Seeking ways to reshape urban schools* (Urban Education Monographs) [On-line]. Available: http://www.ncrel.org/sdrs/areas/issues/educatrs/leadrshp/le0pet.htm

Ponticell, J. A., & Zepeda, S. (1996). Making sense of teaching and learning: A case study of mentor and beginning teacher problem solving. In D. McIntyre & D. Byrd (Eds.), *Preparing tomorrow's teachers: The field experience* (pp. 115-130). Thousand Oaks, CA: Corwin Press.

Purnell, S., & Hill, P. (1992). *In time for reform.* Santa Monica, CA: RAND.

Rutherford, W. (1989). How to establish effective staff development programs. *Tips for principals* (pp. 1-3). (Available from the National Association of Secondary School Principals, 1904 Association Drive, Reston, VA 20191-1532)

Sagor, R. (1992). *How to conduct collaborative action research.* Alexandria, VA: Association for Supervision and Curriculum Development.

Saphier, J., & King, M. (1985). Good seeds grow in strong cultures. *Educational Leadership, 42*(8), 67-74.

Sarason, S. (1991). *The predictable failure of school reform.* San Francisco: Jossey-Bass.

Schlechty, P. (1990). *Schools for the 21st century: Leadership imperatives for educational reform.* San Francisco: Jossey-Bass.

Schlechty, P. (1997). *Inventing better schools.* San Francisco: Jossey-Bass.

Schmoker, M. (1996). *Results: The key to continuous school improvement.* Alexandria, VA: Association for Supervision and Curriculum Development.

Schon, D. (1983). *The reflective practitioner.* New York: Basic Books.

Senge, P. (1990). *The fifth discipline: The art and practice of the learning organization.* New York: Doubleday.

Senge, P., Kleiner, A., Roberts, C., Ross, R., Roth, G., & Smith, B. (1999). *The dance of change: The challenges to sustaining momentum in learning organizations.* New York: Doubleday.

Sergiovanni, T. (1992). *Moral leadership: Getting to the heart of school improvement.* San Francisco: Jossey-Bass.

Sergiovanni, T. (1994). *Building community in schools.* San Francisco: Jossey-Bass.

Shanker, A. (1990). Staff development and the restructured school. In B. Joyce (Ed.), *Changing school culture through staff development* (pp. 91-103). Alexandria, VA: Association for Supervision and Curriculum Development.

Sizer, T. R. (1992). *Horace's school: Redesigning the American high school.* Boston: Houghton Mifflin.

Smith, M., & O'Day, J. (1990). Systemic school reform. In S. H. Furman & B. Malen (Eds.), *The politics of curriculum and testing: 1990 yearbook of Politics of Education Association* (pp. 233-267). London: Taylor and Francis.

Sparks, D. (1998). Making assessment part of teacher learning: Interview at issue with Bruce Joyce. *Journal of Staff Development, 19*(4), 33-35.

Sparks, D. (2000). Interview with Mike Schmoker: Results are the reason. *Journal of Staff Development, 21*(1), 51-53.

Sparks, D., & Hirsh, S. (1997). *A new vision for staff development.* Alexandria, VA: Association for Supervision and Curriculum Development.

Sparks, D., & Hirsh, S. (1999). *A national plan for improving professional development* [On-line]. Oxford, OH: National Staff Development Council. Available: http://www.nsdc.org

Sparks, G. M. (1986). The effectiveness of alternative training activities in changing teacher practices. *American Educational Research Journal, 23,* 217-225.

Speck, M. (1996). Best practice in professional development for sustained educational change. *ERS Spectrum—Journal of School Research and Information, 4*(2), 33–41.

Thornburg, D. (2000). *Trickle learning and technology* [On-line]. Available: http://shop2.pbs.org

Thornburg, D. D. (1994). *Education in the communication age.* San Carlos, CA: Thornburg and Starsong.

Tracy, S., & Schuttenberg, E. (1990). Promoting teacher growth and school improvement through self-directed learning. *Journal of Staff Development, 11*(2), 52–57.

University School Support for Educational Reform. (1997). *Essential questions and practices in professional development* (Professional Development Task Force Report). San Francisco: Author.

Wheatley, M. (1994). *Leadership and the new science.* San Francisco: Berrett-Koehler.

Wiggins, G., & McTighe, J. (1998). *Understanding by design.* Alexandria, VA: Association for Supervision and Curriculum Development.

Wood, F. H., & Thompson, S. R. (1993). Assumptions about staff development based on research and best practices. *Journal of Staff Development, 14*(4), 52–56.

Zepeda, S. (1999). *Staff development: Practices that promote leadership in learning communities.* Larchmont, NY: Eye on Education.

Bibliography

Achieve. (1999). *1999 National Education Summit briefing book*. Palisades, NY: Author.

Alexander, D., Heaviside, D., Farris, E., & Burns, S. (1998). *Fast Response Survey System: Status of education reform in public elementary and secondary schools: Teachers' perspectives* (NCES 1999-045). Washington, DC: U.S. Department of Education, National Center for Education Statistics.

Armour-Thomas, E., Clay, C., Domanico, R., Bruno, K., & Allen, B. (1989). *An outlier study of elementary and middle schools in New York City: Final report*. New York: New York City Board of Education.

Behling, H. E. (1981). *What recent research says about effective schools and effective classrooms*. Chelonsford, MD: Update Northeastern Region Exchange.

Berman, P., & McLaughlin, M. (1978). *Federal programs supporting educational change: Vol. 8. Implementing and sustaining innovation*. Santa Monica, CA: RAND.

Berman, P., & Pauley, E. W. (1975). *Federal programs supporting educational changes: Vol. 2. Factors affecting change agent projects*. Santa Monica, CA: RAND.

Bertani, A. A., & Tafel, L. S. (1989). Theory, research, and practice: Foundations of staff development. In S. D. Caldwell (Ed.), *Staff development: A handbook of effective practices* (pp. 140-154). Oxford, OH: National Staff Development Council.

Bridges, W. (1991). *Managing transitions: Making the most of change*. Reading, MA: Addison-Wesley.

Caldwell, S. D. (Ed.). (1989). *Staff development: A handbook of effective practices*. Oxford, OH: National Staff Development Council.

Calhoun, E. F. (1994). *How to use action research in the self-renewing school*. Alexandria, VA: Association for Supervision and Curriculum Development.

Choy, S. P., Chen, X., & Ross, M. (1998). *Toward better teaching: Professional development in 1993-94* (NCES 98-230). Washington, DC: U.S. Department of Education, National Center for Education Statistics.

Crandall, D. (1983). The teacher's role in school improvement. *Educational Leadership, 41*(3), 6-9.

Darling-Hammond, L. (with Sclan, E.). (1992). Policy in supervision. In C. D. Glickman (Ed.), *Supervision in transition* (pp. 7-29). Alexandria, VA: Association for Supervision and Curriculum Development.

Darling-Hammond, L. (Ed.). (1994). *Professional development schools*. New York: Teachers College Press.

Darling-Hammond, L. (1999). Target time toward teachers. *Journal of Staff Development, 20*(2), 31-36.

Deal, T. E., & Kennedy, A. A. (1982). *Corporate cultures: The rites and rituals of corporate life*. Reading, MA: Addison-Wesley.

Edmonds, R. (1979). Effective schools for the urban poor. *Educational Leadership, 37*(12), 15-24.

Ellis, S. (1989). Putting it all together: An integrated staff development program. In S. D. Caldwell (Ed.), *Staff development: A handbook of effective practices* (pp. 58-69). Oxford, OH: National Staff Development Council.

Elmore, R., & Burney, D. (1997). *Investing in teacher learning: Staff development and instructional improvement in community school district #2, New York City*. New York: National Commission on Teaching and America's Future and Consortium for Policy Research in Education.

Erickson, F. (1987). Transformation and school success: The politics and culture of educational achievement. *Anthropology & Education Quarterly, 18*, 335-356.

Ferguson, R. (1991). Paying for public education: New evidence on how and why money matters. *Harvard Journal of Legislation, 28*, 465-498.

Fullan, M. (1988). *What's worth fighting for in the principalship*. Andover, MA: Regional Laboratory for Educational Improvement.

Fullan, M., & Hargreaves, A. (1996). *What's worth fighting for in your school*. Toronto, Canada: Public Schools Teacher Federation.

Glickman, C. (1991). Pretending not to know what we know. *Educational Leadership, 48*(8), 4-10.

Glickman, C. (1993). *Renewing America's schools: A guide for school-based action*. San Francisco: Jossey-Bass.

Goodlad, J. I. (1984). *A place called school*. New York: McGraw-Hill.

Greenwald, R., Hedges, L. V., & Laine, R. D. (1996). The effect of school resources on student achievement. *Review of Educational Research, 66*, 361-396.

Grimmett, P., & Neufeld, J. (Eds.). (1994). *Teachers' development and the struggle for authenticity*. New York: Teachers College Press.

Hart, L. B. (1992). Faultless facilitation: A resource guide for group or team leaders. Amherst, MA: Human Resource Development Press.

Henderson, E., & Perry, G. (1981). *Change and development in schools*. London: McGraw-Hill.

Johnson, D., & Johnson, R. (1980). The key to effective inservice: Building teacher-teacher collaboration. In D. Sparks (Ed.), *The developer* (pp. 1-3). Oxford, OH: National Staff Development Council.

Joyce, B., & Beck, L. (1977). *Inservice teacher education project report: II. Interviews*. Syracuse, NY: Syracuse University.

Joyce, B., & Showers, B. (1980). Improving inservice training: The messages of research. *Educational Leadership, 37*(4), 379-385.

Joyce, B., & Showers, B. (1982). The coaching of teaching. *Educational Leadership, 40*(1), 4-10.

Klein, S., Medrich, E., & Perez-Ferreiro, V. (1996). *Fitting the pieces: Education reform that works*. Washington, DC: U.S. Department of Education, Office of Educational Research and Improvement.

Koppich, J. (1999). *You can't teach what you don't know: Rethinking the federal role in teacher professional development.* Unpublished manuscript.

Kotter, J. P. (1996). *Leading change.* Boston: Harvard Business School Press.

Krupp, J. A. (1989). Staff development and the individual. In S. D. Caldwell (Ed.), *Staff development: A handbook of effective practices* (pp. 44-56). Oxford, OH: National Staff Development Council.

Lewis, L., Parsad, B., Carey, N., Barfai, N., Farris, E., Smerdon, B., & Greene, B. (1999). *Teacher quality: A report on the preparation and qualifications of public school teachers* (NCES 1999-080). Washington, DC: U.S. Department of Education, National Center for Education Statistics.

Lieberman, A. (1986). Collaborative research: Working with, not working on. *Educational Leadership, 43*(5), 28-32.

Lieberman, A., Falk, B., & Alexander, L. (1994). *A culture in the making: Leadership in learner-centered schools.* New York: National Center for Restructuring Education, Schools, and Teaching, Teachers College, Columbia University.

Lieberman, A., & McLaughlin, M. (1992). Networks for educational change: Powerful and problematic. *Phi Delta Kappan, 73,* 673-677.

Lieberman, A., & Miller, L. (1984). *Teachers: Their world and their work.* New York: Teachers College Press.

Lieberman, A., & Miller, L. (1992). The professional development of teachers. In M. Atkin (Ed.), *The encyclopedia of educational research* (6th ed., pp. 1045-1053). New York: Macmillan.

Little, J. W. (1981). *School success in staff development: The role of staff development in urban desegregated schools.* Boulder, CO: Center for Action Research.

Little, J. W. (1982). Norms of collegiality and experimentation: Workplace conditions of school success. *American Educational Research Journal, 19,* 325-340.

Little, J. W., Gerritz, W., Stern, D., Guthrie, J., Kirst, M., & Marsh, D. (1988). *Staff development in California.* San Francisco: Far West Laboratory for Educational Research and Development.

Little, J. W., & McLaughlin, M. (1991). *Urban math collaboratives: As the teachers tell it.* Palo Alto, CA: Center for Research on the Context of Secondary School Teaching, Stanford University.

Little, J. W., & McLaughlin, M. (Eds.). (1993). *Teachers' work: Individuals, colleagues, and contexts.* New York: Teachers College Press.

Lortie, D. (1975). *Schoolteacher: A sociological study.* Chicago: University of Chicago Press.

Marsh, D. (Ed.). (1999). *The 1999 yearbook: Preparing our schools for the 21st century.* Alexandria, VA: Association for Supervision and Curriculum Development.

Marzano, R. (1992). *A different kind of classroom: Teaching with dimensions of learning.* Alexandria, VA: Association for Supervision and Curriculum Development.

McGreal, T., & Wood, F. H. (1988). Clarifying relationship and connections: Supervision, teacher evaluation, and staff development. *Wingspan, 4*(2), 13-15.

McLaughlin, M. (1992). How district communities do and do not foster teacher pride. *Educational Leadership, 50*(1), 33-35.

McLaughlin, M., & Talbert, J. (1993). *Contexts that matter for teaching and learning.* Palo Alto, CA: Center for Research on Secondary School Teaching, Stanford University.

McQuarrie, F. O., & Wood, F. H. (1991). Supervision, staff development and evaluation connections. *Theory and Practice, 30*(2), 91-96.

Metzdorf, J. (1989). District-level staff development. In S. D. Caldwell (Ed.), *Staff development: A handbook of effective practices* (pp. 14-25). Oxford, OH: National Staff Development Council.

Miller, L., & O'Shea, C. (1996). School-university partnership: Getting deeper, getting broader. In M. McLaughlin & I. Oberman (Eds.), *Teachers learning: New politics, new practices* (pp. 161-184). New York: Teachers College Press.

National Commission on Teaching and America's Future. (1996). *What matters most: Teaching and America's future.* New York: Author.

National Commission on Teaching and America's Future. (1997). *Doing what matters most: Investing in quality teaching.* New York: Author.

National School Boards Foundation. (1999). *Leadership matters: Transforming urban school boards.* Alexandria, VA: National School Boards Foundation.

National Staff Development Council. (1995a). *Standards for staff development— Elementary school edition.* Oxford, OH: Author.

National Staff Development Council. (1995b). *Standards for staff development— Middle school edition.* Oxford, OH: Author.

O'Neil, J. (1995). On schools as learning organizations: A conversation with Peter Senge. *Educational Leadership, 52*(7), 20-23.

Recruiting New Teachers. (1998). *The essential profession: A national survey of public attitudes toward teaching, educational opportunity and school reform.* Boston: Author.

Rubin, L. J. (1971). *Inservice education of teachers: Trends, processes, and prescriptions.* Boston: Allyn & Bacon.

Sagor, R. (1996). Building resiliency in students. *Educational Leadership, 54*(1), 38-43.

Senge, P., Kleiner, A., Roberts, C., Ross, R., & Smith, B. (1994). *The fifth discipline fieldbook: Strategies and tools for building a learning organization.* New York: Doubleday.

Sizer, T. R. (1984). *Horace's compromise: The dilemma of the American high school.* Boston: Houghton Mifflin.

Sizer, T. R. (1996). *Horace's hope: What works for the American high school.* Boston: Houghton Mifflin.

Sparks, D., & Loucks-Horsely, S. (1989). Five models of teacher development. *Journal of Staff Development, 10*(4), 40-57.

Sparks, G. M. (1983). Synthesis of research on staff development for effective teaching. *Educational Leadership, 41*(3), 65-72.

Speck, M. (1999). *The principalship: Building a learning community.* Upper Saddle River, NJ: Prentice Hall.

Stigler, J. W., Gonzales, P., Kawanaka, T., Knoll, S., & Serrano, A. (1999). *The TIMSS videotape classroom study: Methods and findings from an exploratory research project on eighth-grade mathematics instruction in Germany, Japan, and the United States* (NCES 99-074). Washington, DC: U.S. Department of Education, National Center for Education Statistics.

Stigler, J. W., & Hiebert, J. (1999). *The teaching gap: Best ideas from the world's teachers for improving education in the classroom.* New York: Free Press.

Stout, R. T. (1996). Staff development policy: Fuzzy choices in an imperfect market. *Education Policy Analysis Archives* [On-line serial], 4(2), 1-12. Available: http://olam.ed.asu.edu/epaa/v4n2.html

Thompson, S. R., & Wood, F. H. (1982). Staff development guidelines reaffirmed: A response to Fonzi. *Educational Leadership, 40*(1), 43-45.

Wiggins, G. (1993). *Standards, not standardization.* Geneseo, NY: Greater Insights Productions.

Withall, J., & Wood, F. H. (1979). Taking the threat out of classroom observation and feedback. *Journal of Teacher Education, 30*(1), 55-58.

Wood, F. H. (1984). Mining good staff development ideas in business. *Journal of Staff Development, 5*(1), 69-80.

Wood, F. H. (1989). Organizing and managing school-based staff development. In S. D. Caldwell (Ed.), *Staff development: A handbook of effective practices* (pp. 26-43). Oxford, OH: National Staff Development Council.

Wood, F. H., Caldwell, S., & Thompson, S. R. (1987). Practical realities for school-based staff development. *Journal of Staff Development, 7*(1), 52-66.

Wood, F. H., & Kleine, P. F. (1988). Rural staff development research: A small step forward. *Journal of Staff Development, 9*(4), 2-7.

Wood, F. H., & Kleine, P. F. (1989). Staff development research and rural schools: A critical appraisal. *Research in Rural Education, 6*(1), 13-18.

Wood, F. H., & Lease, S. A. (1987). An integrated approach to staff development, supervision, and teacher-evaluation. *Journal of Staff Development, 8*(1), 52-55.

Wood, F. H., McQuarrie F. O., & Thompson, S. R. (1982). Practitioners and professors agree on effective staff development practices. *Educational Leadership, 40*(1), 28-31.

Wood, F. H., & Thompson, S. R. (1980). Guidelines for better staff development. *Educational Leadership, 37*(5), 374-378.

Wood, F. H., Thompson, S. R., & Russell, F. (1981). Designing effective staff development programs. In B. Dillion-Peterson (Ed.), *Staff development/Organizational development* (pp. 59-91). Alexandria, VA: Association for Supervision and Curriculum Development.

Index